THE ESCHATON:
A COMMUNITY OF LOVE

THE ESCHATON:

A

COMMUNITY OF LOVE

Edited by

Joseph Papin

The Villanova University Press

BT
823
.E8

Volume V
Library of Congress Catalog Number 76-189-872
Complete Series SBN—87723-007-2
Volume V—SBN 87723-012-9

Printed in the United States of America by
Abbey Press
Saint Meinrad, Indiana 47577

First printing: 1000 copies

Dedicated to James J. Cleary whose efforts made the publication of the Villanova University Series possible.

Joseph Papin

Contents

When my spirit is faint within me, you know my path. I have lost all means of escape; there is no one who cares for my life. Ps 141:4-5
Man is . . . like a passing shadow. Ps 143:4

All that is of earth returns to earth, and what is from above returns above . . . there is joy when a child first lifts his hands, yet all too soon comes his final end. Sir 40:1, 11-13

O death! how bitter the thought of you . . . O death! how welcome your sentence to the weak men of failing strength . . . Fear not death's decree, . . . Thus God has appointed for all flesh. Sir 41:1-4

. . . Isaias, who saw the truth in visions. Sir 48:23

A great anxiety has God alloted . . . ; from the day one leaves his mother's womb . . . till the day he dies. Sir 40:1-3

On those who live in the darkness of death the light will shine. Matt 4:16

If we have died with Christ we believe that we will also live with him. Rom 6:8

O death, where is thy victory? O death, where is thy sting? I Cor 15:55

The community of believers was one in mind and heart. Ac 4:32
. . . add goodness to your faith; and to your goodness add knowledge . . . and to your brotherly love add love; 2 Pet 1:5-7

> GOD IS LOVE 1 Jn 4:16
> Amor vincit omnia
> Ex umbris et imaginibus in veritatem Newman

Maranatha—Our Lord, Come! I Cor 16:22

Our message is that Christ has been raised from death . . .
. . . if the dead are not raised, neither has Christ been raised. And if Christ has not been raised, then your faith is a delusion . . . If our hope in Christ is good for this life only . . . then we deserve more pity than anyone else in all the world. But the truth is that Christ has been raised from death, as a guarantee that those who sleep in death will also be raised. I Cor 15:21

. . . as though we were dead, but, as you can see, we are alive.
II Cor 6:9

Who, then can separate us from the love of Christ? Rom 8:85

It is not the dead who praise the Lord, not those who go down in silence; but we bless the Lord, both now and forever. Ps 113:17

Whoever does not love is still in death. I Jn 3:15

For just as all men die . . . in the same way all will be raised to life because of their union to Christ I Cor 15:21

It is love, then, that you should strive for. Set your heart on spiritual gifts. I Cor 14:1

x

Like the cover of an old book
Its contents torn out and stripped of its lettering
and gilding lies here food for worms.
Yet the work itself shall not be lost,
For it will, as he believed, appear once
more in a new and more elegant edition
revised and corrected by the Author.
                    Epitaph of Benjamin Franklin.

Eschaton in the Vision of the Russian Newman (Soloviev)

Joseph Papin

I

ESCHATOLOGY as theological science constitutes only a small part among other well developed treatises and is usually placed at the end of the entire dogmatic theology. This is not in harmony with speculative, systematic theology as the eschaton stands in the center of the economy of salvation. Parousia (1 Thess 4:15f) cannot be separated from the kerygma and must not be robbed of its eschatological reality in man's ultimate destiny. The entire history of Christianity rests on the Parousia expectation. Man's past and present are eschatologically oriented. Modern man is increasingly aware of the future eschatological event. Theology therefore must provide a solid ground for the eschatological search of today's man.

The term eschatology does not appear in England before the nineteenth century. In the Old Testament, eschatology is closely associated with the coming Messiah and is confined mostly to the later books, especially Daniel. But the prophets Isaiah, Ezekiel and Zechariah play an important role in the eschatological preaching of judgement and salvation.

Many Catholic theologians have made an attempt to place eschatology in its proper theological focus. Among these especially R. Guardini, M. Schmaus, H. U. von Balthasar, Jean Danielou and Karl Rahner must be mentioned.

In Protestant theology A. Schweitzer attempted to give a new meaning to eschatology, interpreting Christ's teaching on a chiliastic assumption that Jesus expected the end of the world in the immediate future. According to Schweitzer, primitive Christianity was exclusively preoccupied with the immediate consummation of the end of the world. Eschatological considerations are also dominant in Karl Barth's theology.

C. H. Dodd and O. Cullmann made new attempts to elucidate the
conception of 'realized eschatology.'

The theology of the Orthodox Church stressed eschatology. N.
Berdiaev and S. N. Bulgakov were deeply involved in the problem
of eschatology. But V. Soloviev, more than any thinker at the turn
of the twentieth century, turned his eyes towards eschatology. Therefore
I dedicate this study to Soloviev's thought on eschaton to further eschatological studies in our times. Eschaton is *"magna [est] veritas et
praevalet."*

Vladimir Sergeevich Soloviev,[1] leading Russian philosopher, theologian, poet, journalist, ecumenist, mystic (also known as Solovyev,
Solovjoff, Solov'ev, Solowjew), was born in Moscow on January 16
(28),[2] 1853, and died in Uzkoe, near Moscow, on July 31 (August
13),[3] 1900. Although reared in a devout Russian Orthodox home,
Soloviev became an atheist while in secondary school after reading the
lives of Christ written by David Friedrich Strauss (1808-74) and
Joseph Ernest Renan (1823-92). He also embraced the materialism of
Ludwig Büchner (1824-99) and the nihilism of Dimitri Ivanovich
Pisarev (1840-68). During his university years in Moscow (1869-74)
he experienced another religious crisis: he gained from Baruch Spinoza
(1632-77) a living sense of God's reality and a clear experience of the
total spiritual unity of the world. Other influences on the development
of his religious thought were Arthur Schopenhauer (1788-1860),
Eduard von Hartmann (1842-1906), Friedrich Wilhelm Schelling
(1775-1854) and Georg Wilhelm F. Hegel (1770-1831). He attended
the Theological Faculty of Moscow (1873-74) and published his widely
acclaimed dissertation against Auguste I.M.F. Comte (1798-1857) and
positivism, *Crisis of Western Philosophy* (1874). After lecturing at
the university, Soloviev studied mysticism and theosophy in London
(1875). He then went to Egypt where he claimed to have had a vision
of Sophia,[4] Wisdom (1875-76). In 1876 he resumed teaching but
soon departed Moscow University because of a dispute concerning
slavophilism. In St. Petersburg he served on the Scholarly Committee
of the Educational Ministry and delivered *Twelve Lectures on Godmanhood*[5] (1877). He thought the essence of Christianity consisted in the
union of God and man in the Incarnate Word, but that Eastern Orthodoxy neglected man while Western Christianity tended to forget God.
These lectures attracted much attention. The audience included[6] Fëdor
Michailovich Dostoevsky (1821-81) and Leo Nikolayevich Tolstoy
(1828-1910). The former had been a friend of the lecturer since 1873,
and seemingly fashioned the character Alyosha in *The Brothers Karamazov* after V. S. Soloviev. However Leo N. Tolstoy's denial of
Christ's resurrection caused Soloviev to be wary of him. *A Critique of
Abstract Principles* (1880), Soloviev's doctoral dissertation, met wide
acclaim, but its author was compelled to retire from teaching in 1881
because he had publicly sought clemency for Alexander II's assassins.

This proved a turning point in Soloviev's life. Thereafter he devoted himself entirely to writing and to the ecumenical movement. He described himself as an eternally wandering, homeless pilgrim seeking the Heavenly Jerusalem.[7] Friends were never lacking, however, to provide him with hospitality. Some of his writings at this time concerned contemporary problems, but his most significant works were published abroad because of his growing sympathy with the Roman Church. These tendencies occasioned a break with his slavophile friends, especially the 'senior Slavophiles' headed by Aleksei Stepanovich Khomiakov (1804-60) and Ivan Vasilyevich Kireyevsky (1806-56). In his *Great Dispute and Christian Policy* (1883) he defended the papal primacy. His *History and Future of Theocracy* (1884) indicated that he had been little influenced by Peter Yakolevich Chaadayev's (1794-1856) slavophile views about the Kingdom of God.[8] During Soloviev's travels in Croatia (1886-88), his association with Bishop Joseph G. Strossmayer[9] strengthened his desire for reunion with Rome. In 1887 he lectured in Paris on the Russian Church, and in 1889 published *La Russie et L'eglise Universelle*,[10] which met a very hostile reception in Russia. The Holy Synod forbade him to write further on religious topics.

In 1896 he made a profession of faith,[11] confessed to a Catholic priest, N. Tolstoy, and received Holy Communion. He hoped to see all men united religiously in Christianity (which would be in practice a theocracy under the Pope, and politically under the Czar). His thought became more and more eschatological in *Three Conversations* (1889-90) as he became increasingly pessimistic and concerned with the problem of evil and of Antichrist.[12] On his deathbed Soloviev received the Last Rites from a Russian Orthodox priest. Since he believed that Roman Catholicism and the Orthodox Churches remained mystically united despite their outward separation, he definitely considered intercommunion justifiable because the separation of the two churches was only *de facto* and not *de iure*. His action, therefore, was apparently not based on disregard for Canon Law.[13] One is tempted to see in Soloviev's action an anticipation of the present revision of Canon Law regarding the Orthodox Church. So broad was his erudition that Soloviev has been called the Russian Newman.[14] Several of his works have been translated into English.

Soloviev as a student at the age of eighteen abandoned the study of sciences and, in a practical Russian impulse to be of service to others, immersed all his talents in the study of philosophy, especially Plato (427?-327), Origen (185?-254? A.D.), Seneca (4 B.C.-65 A.D.), Augustine (354-430 AD.), Francis Bacon (1561-1626), John Stuart Mill (1806-1873), René Descartes (1596-1650), Louis-Gabriel-Ambroise Vicomte de Boland (1798-1827), Immanuel Kant (1724-1804), Arthur Schopenhauer (1788-1860), Georg W. F. Hegel (1770-1831) and Friedrich W. J. Schelling (1775-1854). At the age of nineteen,

Soloviev was on the way towards an adequate insight into the aspect of the inner life and the secrets of the universe. His understanding of the relationship of love between the sexes became a source of his mystical certitude and revelations concerning the bond which joins all creatures in all-embracing unity with God and the world. This first stage, an intuitive process with the emotional background of young adolescent manhood, was nonetheless an authentic philosophical *point de départ* which stands among his *Three Encounters*. But at the age of twenty-five Soloviev deepened this exciting stimulus and in 1876 was exclusively engaged in studying the doctrine of Sophia, the primordial concrete living being created from all eternity. This universal outlook, seeing things not dissected by discursive reasoning but joined in all-embracing unity, constitutes the basis of his development of the religious conception of Divine Sophia held by the Orthodox Church. The book, *W. Solovjeff, Eine Seelenschilderung,*[15] sheds much light on Soloviev's departure from the study of physics and mathematics for the study of philosophy; but in my view the element of German materialism which dominated Russian intellectual life in his day played an even more important role in his early attainment of maturity, which is evidenced by his turning to the pantheism of Baruch Spinoza (1632-1677). Obviously, while such a conversion was based on will and reason, as Blaise Pascal (1623-62) says "Le coeur a ses raisons que la raison ne connait pas," Soloviev now beheld the secret of humanity and the secret of his own life, which was to become, in the endeavor to realize the divine harmonies in temporal existence, a prophet of divine humanity and of the union between God and man and the world, between Catholicism and Orthodoxy.

The West is inclined to see in Soloviev its occidental image because Soloviev saw clearly the weaknesses of the Russian mentality. Nevertheless Nicholas Alexandrovich Berdiaev (1874-1948), his disciple, calls him "our national philosopher."[16] The Occidental Man in Soloviev was first seen when he delivered, at the age of twenty-one, his inaugural lecture at Moscow University on the topic, *The Crisis of Western Philosophy*. The young Soloviev sees man as emerging from a heavy load of temporality and finding himself with *élan* of faith on the road when one could not even find a path of the ongoing process of divinization *(obozhenie)* in the concrete form of Logos. Earthliness and temporality do not constitute the final and complete man but are in opposition to his longing, his *desiderium naturale*[17] for a deeper and more universal world-embracing unity with humanity. Man struggles against drowning in the illusion of the passing moment as the ultimate mystery of his life.[18] This process of development in time merges into unconditional and unlimited surrender to the indubitable and profoundest certainty which is the Logos. Given this point of view, it is understandable that Soloviev in his work on *The Crisis in Western Thought* could state his conviction that Western Philosophy, confronted by intellectual chaos, was at the end of its course and plunging into a nothing-ness of verbalism. This intuitive vision of decline in Western Philos-ophy was perceived by Soloviev as a disease in the modern develop-ment of thought. Seeing this, Soloviev definitely proved that he, al-though wholly immersed in Western Philosophy, is not occidental, but a philosopher deeply rooted in Eastern Philosophy.

The most interesting element in Russian philosophico-theological or theologico-philosophical thought is a 'dissipation,' touching the threshold of new philosophical systems without creating genuine systems.

Spiritually, Soloviev was a pilgrim, wandering throughout Russia, spending his life in search of the Heavenly Jerusalem. Having no family, he had no permanent abode as he wandered across the entire world of his day. His "theology of the world" is expressed in his words to the Jesuit Paul Pierling touching upon his homeless condition: "Why do you not admit the idea that though I am not a monk, I have no 'abiding city here' like yourself?"[19]

In 1896 he visited the Trotsky-Serguevesky Abbey, intending to be-come a monk; a year later he wrote Archimandrite Antonius: "I would be now very much inclined to become a monk.... I am by no means in favor of unconditional freedom, but believe that between such free-dom and unconditional slavery, there must be an intermediate way, that is freedom conditioned by sincere submission to that which is holy and legitimate. However, will such freedom be accepted in our midst? Will they not demand everything without discrimination, no matter whether holy and legitimate or not?"

Soloviev depicts his life path:

> Once in the misty dawn with timid foot
> Towards a mysterious strand I walked alone...
> My soul engaged the host of dreams in fight
> and prayed to the Unknown.
> Now in the cold hard light I tread as then
> A lonely path, beside an unknown stream...
> The haven of my dream:
> But till the midnight hour with fearless foot
> I travel to the goal of my desires....[20]

Among Western philosophers Georg W. Hegel greatly influenced Russian philosophy. Boris Nikolayevich Chicherin (1828-1903), pupil of P. T. Redkins (1808-1891, professor at Moscow University), began with Hegel's philosophy but transformed it into a complex and original entire system of philosophy. S. S. Gogotsky (1813-1889, professor, Ukranian University at Kiev), changing the entire system of Hegel's philosophy, rejected Hegel's pantheism and defended individual im-mortality. Nicholas Gavilovich Chernyshevski (1828-89), Peter Lavro-vich Lavrov (1823-1900), Nicholas Konstantinovich Mikhailovski

(1842-1904) and Nicholas Nikolayevich Strakhov (1828-96) did not create philosophical systems because their creative philosophical reflections and studies were absorbed by the problems of daily life, resulting in journalistic, critical writing. Their audacious and original thought, passionately written, greatly contributed to the treasury of Russian thought with its profundity and intensity suitable for the erection of a new philosophical structure.

Kantian tendencies in Russian thinking were represented by Alexander Ivanovich Vvedenski (1855-1925), as was Russian positivism by Vladimir Viktorovich Lesevich (1837-1905), but more influential were those attached to a basic intuition of existence with the characteristic approach of ontologism. Soloviev's 'positive total unity,' Nicholas Onufriyevich Lossky's (1870-1965) 'organic whole,' Sergius Nikolayevich Bulgakov's (1887-1944) 'Sophiology' constitute the most important school of Russian idealists. Idealism characterizes the very being of 'Russian Soul,' while imported 'Dialectical Materialism' is an opposed ontological intuition in Russian philosophy showing the sharp conflict of the inner struggle in Russian thought. Vladimir Sergeevich Soloviev died on the threshold of the twentieth century, symbolically separating contributions of philosophers of the nineteenth century from those who developed their philosophy in the twentieth century. There is no connection between the philosophers in Russia who exercise the one-sided philosophy of dialectical materialism and the philosophers living outside Russia.

Secular tendencies, breaking with the Church, dominated Russian philosophy in the second half of the nineteenth century. The polarization became more sharply outlined and a systematic resistance to secularism emerged more clearly, but pure philosophy independent of the religious sphere never materialized. In Russian philosophy outside Russia, religious themes predominate. The same can be asserted in some way about the silent philosohpy inside Russia where a militant atheism prevails. While four decades ago the militant atheism confined only to philosophy inside Russia was considered by many only as a gateway into oblivion, subsequent years of political euphoria in Europe proved the opposite. Philosophy never was a sterile handmaid (cf. St. Bonaventura) of theology or vice versa. The Russian mind differs from that of the Western philosopher by not indulging in differentiations or distinctions. Eastern religious thought often employed mere reason to prove its claims while philosophical truth is often substantiated by revelation. Thomism never entered Russia as a system.[21] Consequently Russia on the one hand stood theologically in her childhood without making any progress; on the other hand, precisely because of this theological stagnancy, it seems to be much easier for the Orthodox Church to revert to the simplicty of the Gospel than for the sophisticated Western Church with its progressive philosophy. First Metanoia of greater proportions in Christian teaching occurred in the

Golden Age, when the Greek and Latin Fathers introduced Greek philosophical elements into Christian theology. In the thirteenth century
the process of this metanoia was completed. Now new philosophical
systems—Phenomenology, Existentialism, Process Philosophy—have
induced theologians to update theology in a dejudaization and dehelleni-
zation process in search of Christian identity notwithstanding accumu-
lated ambiguities throughout the history of the Church. Thus the intense resistance to rising secularism in Russia in the nineteenth century
became futile after the October Rvolution with its stormy and militant
atheism (which M. R. Stefanik prophetically called "a cancer of human society"). The intention of Soloviev to establish a new system,
exhibiting Christianity in the form of philosophy, like the efforts of
other philosophers, could not overcome the new political trends which
culminated in a revolution disturbing the whole tradition of Russian
spiritual life.

> A strange child was I then,
> And strange dreams did I dream . . .

wrote Soloviev of himself. 'Sophia' and mysticism played an important part in his life. K. V. Mochulski unjustifiably ascribed to these
strange dreams a decisive importance, which is just as bad as to ignore
them.

The religious concept in Soloviev's view is that of a religion transcending all limitations of the denominational Churches. In his struggle for unity, or, better expressed, for a true universal Christianity, he
states: "As long as we assert our religion, *first of all* in its denominational particularity and *only after this* as ecumenical Christianity, we
take away not only its sane logic, but moreover its moral significance;
thus transforming it into an obstacle on the path of man's spiritual
regeneration." Although Soloviev's universalism contains not only
Christian religions but also oriental, which he treats on a larger level,
his main concern is the Christian religions—Catholicism, Orthodoxy and
Protestantism—in which he advocates not absorption of any one by
the other but preservation of their formative principle. Touching on
this point in his work, *The Three Conversations,* he states explicitly in
1892 to Vasili V. Rofanov:

"I am as far removed from Latin limitations as I am from Byzantine
limitations, or the Augsburg or Geneva ones. The religion of the
Holy Ghost . . . is wider and of fuller content than all separate religions. . . ."[22]

The gradual acceptance of revealed truth continues to take place according to man's progressive development. In this connection Soloviev
rejected triumphalism linked with denominational vanity as a distortion of Christianity. To be a follower of Christ and yet be dedicated
to the triumph of one's truth over another's, defeats Christ's testament:
to love one another as he has loved us. Such a triumphalism does not

build Christian charismatic bridges between men, but the shameful walls of partition made by man's hand.

The Spirit of Christ can act through unbelieving social and political leaders as well as through militant atheists because the Spirit breathes where it will. Eschaton is a leading thought in Soloviev's final creative period. "The Short Narrative about the Antichrist" appended to his book *Three Conversations* represents an epoch of Christian religious imposters who hate Christ, His teaching, and His work. The Antichrist in his "parousia" is a social reformer,[23] a philanthropist who wants to gain the confidence of everyone. This Antichrist has even new "super-religious" ideals for Christians, if they would but follow him as their sovereign Master. Love he wants, hate he preaches. Only a small group remains faithful in expectation of Christ's parousia when the total union of Churches and mankind will be consummated.

Soloviev's attacks on political and religious triumphalism pretending to serve the people's interests evoked controversies and criticisms. Vasili V. Rofanov called him "a harlot, cynically playing with theology, a thief, having stealthily crept into a Church." Only after his formal confession of faith (1896) was he considered Catholic, Protestant rationalist, nihilist, and a Jew.

The age of enlightenment (Aufklärung) not only questioned the sacraments and their effects but reduced them to purely human symbols. This age also rejected the essence of Christianity, namely, the incarnation. Consequently, the resurrection fell heir to the same rejection. There was no difference between faith and science, and the death of Christianity was near. Thus, in retrospective reflection, these theological developments preceded the short-lived school of the "Death of God" (Thomas J. Altizer).[24]

Christianity in its all embracing love transforms the world and spiritualizes matter, but does not allow that the world materializes the spirit. This Vision creates a new heaven and a new earth through a mutual interpretation of all beings. Vladimir Soloviev makes of himself a new architect with the task of bringing to light the spiritual foundations of man's life on earth. This task is a complete realization and integration of both divine and human natures through the God-Man, theoanthropos in Christ. It becomes evident, then, that Nietzche, Malreaux, Sartre, Camus in their negative theistic approach awakened and deepened Christian thought and conscience.

Modern Western European thinkers developed out of Kant's, Fichte's, and Hegel's philosophy a new system which was primarily concerned with a study of the spiritual principles of reality. These spiritual principles were designated by the term Logos but not the Logos of a Living God incarnate in Christ. Soloviev and his followers attached to Logos a concrete living principle which gave to the world unity and definiteness. Furthermore, Soloviev emphasized the transfiguration of spiritualized deified matter and the resurrection of the body. The entire doctrine was worked out by Soloviev on a much wider basis than that of Fichte's idealism. In effect, Soloviev worked out "ideal realism." Thus this search for concrete principles was connected with the primary thought of I. V. Kireyevsky and A. S. Khomiakov while the influence of his teachers, Pamphilus Danilovich Yurkevich (1827-74) and F. W. Schelling lurked in the background.

One is tempted to see a pan-theistic current in Soloviev's system, particularly regarding the necessity he posited concerning the world and man for God. The difference which separates God from the world appears to be metalogical otherness. It was at this point that Soloviev advanced the idea of God as being only the source of Divine all oneness, which is attracted towards all beings. There, the fullness of man's life must be united through Christ with the fullness of God.

Religious feeling wants to possess nothing outside of God and because of this acceptable proposition Soloviev was influenced by Origen's thought on the human person. Yet, in his mature philosophical progress, he advanced his concept of substance and hypostasis. In his view substance could not be carried away by the river of time in the sense of Heraclitus' stream *panta rei*. Moreover, one must remember that Godfried Wilhelm von Leibnitz understood substance as creating its manifestations in spatio-temporality. From this point of view, then, the concept of substantial agent expresses better the manifestations of substance in time. However, Soloviev's system demanded the recognition of free will, but without the recognition of the ideal being and the supratemporality of the ego, the development of the doctrine of free will was hardly possible. In addition, Soloviev's doctrine of Sophia was vague and inconsistent. On one hand Sophia, as the Eternal Feminine,[25] was a being eternally perfect and invariably subjected to the will of God. On the other hand, Sophia[26] was the world soul temporarily fallen away from God and then reuniting again with Him in a gradual process. Teilhard de Chardin's doctrine of the world which points to the Omega Point, although not in any way the result of Soloviev's doctrine, could bring a new light on the development of Sophia in its different stages. Still, it must be noted that Soloviev was unjustly accused of introducing a feminine principle into the Concept of Deity. This happened primarily because he was aware of the many pitfalls associated with Sophianism as he, himself, mentioned in the preface of his collected poems.

D. N. Strémogukhoff[27] divided Soloviev's philosophical work into three stages: *theosophy, theocracy,* and *theurgy.* Theosophy consists in his Christian teachings which are mostly contained in his two works: *Lectures on Godmanhood* and *Spiritual Foundations of Life.*[28] Soloviev had hoped that the incarnation of Sophia, Wisdom of God, could have been achieved through a knowledge of God and God's relation to the world. This constitutes the first period of his philosophical activity which is correctly termed theosophy. After 1882 Soloviev made original advances in the field of political philosophy. He placed his hopes in a theocracy which would transform mankind in creating a just state and social order which, in time, would materialize in the establishment of Christian politics. To this period of theocracy belongs his major works: *The History and Future of Theocracy, The Great Quarrel and Christian Politics* and *The National Problem and Russia.* However, by 1890 Soloviev was absorbed in the problem of *theurgy,* a mysticism, which would create a new life according to Divine Truth. The major works belonging to this period of *theurgy* are *Justification of the Good*[29] and *The Meaning of Love.*[30] His "utopian" hopes for the achievement of good in man's terrestrial life were expressed in his best work, *The Three Conversations.* Yet, the search for a knowledge of reality as a whole and the concreteness of metaphysical conceptions (which were the most characteristic feature of Russian philosophical thought) are found in Soloviev's early works: *The Crisis in Western Philosophy,* written against the Positivists in 1874, *The Philosophical Principles of Integral Knowledge,* written three years later, and *The Critique of Abstract Principles* (1877-80). In these works, however, one finds that empirical theories did not satisfy Soloviev, since in such theories relations could be cognified only by thought, and consisted in the relationships of everything to the whole. It is an incorrect oversimplification to find Soloviev's Sophia to be only the operating Wisdom of God. Thus, the whole is understood as a systematic pan-unity and not as a chaotic multiplicity. However, experience is only concerned with the particular and never with the "all" or "unity," so that the knowledge which is attained in wisdom is not given in experience. Yet, experience is the foundation of knowledge as individual images collectively constitute the totality of a motion picture. Still, once the images are separated into individual pieces, stagnation begins. Where there was once life there is now death. Where there was motion, dynamism, dynamic religion and dynamic thought, there is now a quiet immovable stillness. This is verifiable in mystics whose lives flow like rivers of eternal time in contrast to the dying waters of the receding marsh.

Human personality is a verifiable entity which inchoatively is negatively absolute. It cannot be fulfilled with a limited content, but "it can attain positive absoluteness" and "possess the complete fulness of being." This attainment is realized through the perfect mutual interpenetration of all creatures who are united in love one with another and all with God. The world then, is the Absolute that becomes, while God is the Absolute Who is. The realm of earthly life stands midway between these two poles, the world and God. The life of beings separated from one another inevitably ends in death. Yet, the establishment of relation between men is defined as the struggle for existence, since the fullness of being is not to be found in this path but at its consummation.

The need for philosophical systems has been keenly felt in Russia for a long time. But the problems of daily life have preoccupied the thought of Russian thinkers and the profundity, as well as the intensity of Russian philosophical creativity has been obscured by concrete rather than theoretical thought. However, such thought has been expressed in professional journals and fostered elsewhere, so that the foundation on which structure-organic synthesis could be created has been present for some time. No new ideas are needed to construct philosophical systems but rather what is needed is a synthesis of already existing themes.

The role then of a synthesizer has not been to evaluate some preceding period and reinterpret existing thought but rather to integrate already existing themes into a system. In modern time, Gabriel Marcel proclaimed: Philosophy is not a system. He objected to being classified as a Christian existentialist. To this time no Russian thinker has traveled the road of neutrality; all have been influenced by religious thought.

II

PARAPHRASING the words of S. N. Bulgakov we can see that the world as a single whole cannot be compared to the Absolute because God is the unfading light and the world 'in becoming' is a fading darkness, thus the transition from Absolute Being to relative being is incomprehensible. This provocative thought led many Russian philosophers and theologians to the metaphysical conception of total-unity which at first was applied only to the cosmos and—by means of a third being—beyond the limits of the cosmos in which the Divine being, in Sophia, acquires other-being in the world. But the difficulty involved in the concept of total-unity carried followers of Soloviev into different directions as can be seen in Bulgakov's 'world-soul,' P. A. Florensky's Sophia, Lossky's[31] personalism and Berdiaev's prophecy of Orthodoxy. While leading Russian philosophers of our time derived from Soloviev chiefly his metaphysics of total-unity with intention to develop Soloviev's various philosophical themes into a system, they define their own path of new philosophic thought. Western European thinkers like Romano Guardini, Fr. Muckermann and in Central Europe Jan Mastylak, Jan Dieska, S. Tyszkiewicz, Theophil Spacil, Vincent Porizka, e.a. focused their attention on the encounter between East and West, between Moscow and Rome.

Moscow as a Third Rome envisioned by the messianic Russian thinkers was condemned by Soloviev in the figure of the Elder Ioann returned to the Idea of Holy Russia independent of the state. Russia suffered heavy defeat by the Japanese in 1905. In 1917 the Empire collapsed at the very moment when it was preparing to place the cross on the Cathedral of St. Sophia and realize the idea of the Third Rome. The proud idea of messianism, unification of all the Slavs in a uni-

versal theocracy under the Russian Third Rome, was untenable and
incompatible with the course of coalescing reality. V. Soloviev ascribed
his earlier worship of Russian greatness (1894) to "flatterers" quite
reminiscent of Aleksei S. Khomyakov: "From the example of old
Byzantium . . . you are the Third Rome." In 1896 V. Soloviev revised
his idea of the Third Rome[32] in his article "Byzantium and Russia."
He was convinced that if the first two Romes had failed to achieve their
destinies, Russia too was far from her goal. The final and decisive renun-
ciation of the Third Rome found in *Three Conversations* is veiled in
polemics against L. Tolstoy's anarchic conception of the Kingdom of
God on earth. The *Narrative about the Antichrist* echoes even earlier
Soloviev's prophecy (1894) of the defeat of Russia by the yellow races:

> O Russia, forget thy former glory!
> The two-headed eagle is o'ercome,
> And to a yellow children's game
> Have thy tattered banners come.

All the eschatology of *Three Conversations* leads to the idea that the
Kingdom of God is unrealisable. Vanishing "Holy Russia" in our
times is a sinful Russia where the religious-moral ideal of the Russian
national soul is changed into a concise formula of international militant atheism. No nation can witness such a total revolution as envisioned by V. Soloviev two decades before his death. French "la belle
France," English "Olde England," German "die deutsche Treue" still
express in some way their national love for the particular nation and
the people but the mystical' "Holy Russia" reversed its course into an
apocalyptic universal atheistic messianism. Does this change the destiny
of a Christian Nation or is it only a supernatural sign of the sword of
God for the nations of the world?

On January 16, 1973, a hundred and twenty years had passed since
the birth of Soloviev. In Central Europe, in Slovakia there were two
promising pioneers of Soloviev's work: Jan Mastylak, C.S.S.R., and
Jan Dieska, S.J. Twenty years ago with some others these two were
eager to proclaim the centenary of Soloviev's birth, but their voices
were silenced. Soloviev lived only 47 years, but he rose very early in
his life to a high level of achievement. He crossed the threshold of
eternity at the turn of the century. Symbolizing a beginning of a new
era, with his departure a great, promising work came to an untimely
end. The light of his torch was dimmed. And his age felt the loss
very keenly. It was—as he himself puts it in his short poem, "Near
Troy"—as if someone were singing a beautiful song and then suddenly
became silent. And his silence had an unusual effect upon future generations. There were those who were eager to follow in his footsteps.

When someone departs from his workshop, the rest of mankind feels
his presence for a long time, and his silence speaks in the places where
he moved. In such a way, with his silence, Soloviev speaks forcefully
to our own time.

Soloviev in the span of four years struggled from a young unbeliever to a confessor and proclaimer of Christ's mission. Already at the age of 20 he writes: "I dedicated my whole life and all my strength that this conversion (change) may be real ... I am no longer my own, I belong to this task, which I shall serve, and which has nothing in common with my personal inclinations, interests ... of my personal life."

Soloviev not only lost his faith through his theorizing, but also denied in practice for the span of four years all that he had believed before his fourteenth year.

After his conversion Soloviev wanted to become the philosopher of Christianity. He undertook the task of creating a new formula suitable to his new faith, the absolute religion. As a youth of twenty he did not possess an integrated system of thought, but during his three years' stay abroad, his system was reaching maturity, and in 1876 he presented his system in substantial outlines. The new formula after which he was seeking gradually acquired the appearance of a synthesis of theosophy, theocracy, and theurgy.

This synthesis is based on universal unity and embraces a triple sphere of the will, imagination, and feeling, which corresponds to the triune idea of one Absolute Being. The synthesis also includes the Idea of good, truth, and beauty which is true Wisdom (Sophia) and is realized in the integral "Incarnate Divinity" (Bogoceloviecestvo).

The young philosopher saw before himself a university lecture hall crowded with a not at all sympathetic and knowledge-thirsty audience, but rather opponents of liberal thought. Soloviev faced the possibility of being completely undone by his lecture, and his audience was already preparing to "whistle" him out of academic existence. But Soloviev captured the minds of his young audience for all times. His lectures were attended by F. M. Dostoevsky (1877-78) who at that time was 56 (died in 1887), and by L. N. Tolstoy who listened while Soloviev spoke on the Incarnation.

The Idea of Incarnation was not only the leading idea of his theocratic system, but also served as the basis for true Christian living. All activities of Soloviev radiated love toward God Incarnate. His theocracy and also his theurgia made use of this idea. The last two years of his life assume a tone of expectation for the Second Coming of the Incarnate God (Parousia).

In this study I wish to offer briefly the position which Soloviev's idea of Incarnation occupied in his debates with Tolstoy. This study exposes the dark side of the human soul and the present world with its eschatological meaning.

Similarly has Friedrich Muckermann compared Soloviev, Tolstoy and Dostoevsky. His claim is that Dostoevsky exposed the dark side of the human soul and Tolstoy a man of this world, stuck to the earth, which Soloviev, with the alacrity of an eagle, moved in the heights of the "God Incarnate" idea. Yet Soloviev climaxes his studies about the "God Incarnate" with the Resurrection of Christ, which was also the keystone in his debates with L. Tolstoy.

Soloviev writes very tactfully to Tolstoy: "I think that in your world view—if I understand your last works correctly—there is nothing that would stand in the way of accepting the truth about Jesus Christ's resurrection, but in fact, there is something in them that compels one to accept this truth."

In effect, Soloviev shows that it is possible to prove immortality and the resurrection about the redeeming death directly from the fullness of perfection and from the personal resurrection of the Logos.

Just as the idea of "God Incarnate" with Soloviev is the center of his thinking and of his unionistic apostolate, so logically the resurrection of the "God-Man" is the central sense of the world. Either the idea of the world makes no sense or else Christ did rise from the dead. Soloviev, as he himself indicates in his letter to Tolstoy, has not the least doubt about the resurrection of Christ, for he acknowledges that the history of the world and of the human race would not make sense without the resurrection.

Tolstoy presents a serious objection regarding resurrection: If we accept the resurrection, then Christians will have to depend for their salvation more upon God than upon their own moral efforts. To this Soloviev correctly answers in his letter: in reality, even though Christ has risen from the death, He demands man's effort, and for that reason there can be no question of quietism as far as sincere and conscientious Christians are concerned.

Whatever may be the consequences to Christ's resurrection, the question regarding its truthfulness is not thereby decided.

Soloviev with great earnestness speaks theoretically and practically about the resurrection of Christ, with which according to St. Paul, Christianity stands or falls. Soloviev worked long and hard to convince him, he strove in his last years to make Tolstoy in *Tri Razgovora* harmless. Soloviev's arguments were so strong that even the Holy Synod[33] could not overlook them and excommunicated Tolstoy from the Orthodox Church.

Soloviev's influence was powerful because he was a bearer of penetrating ideas regarding the Incarnation. He was not successful in covering the entire field of Christian philohophy and theology. Yet the ideas which he did communicate to the world live on, so that new thinkers constantly appear who, by reliving his "God-manhood," continue his work and make fruitful the drying furrows of human thought.

Soloviev died on July 31, 1900, on the estate of Prince Peter Trubetzkoy in Uzkoe near Moscow. Some fifty most devoted friends, other admirers, and several students escorted him on his last journey, August 3, from the University chapel to the monastery cemetery of Novodevic.[34]

Soloviev both in life and in death had many things in common with

Cardinal Newman and philosopher Henri Bergson. Soloviev, baptized in the Orthodox Church, embraced the Catholic Church four years before his death, keeping faithfully the entire Orthodox tradition.

Newman, an English Soloviev, pillar of the Oxford movement, lighted the candle from Shadows and Symbols to the Truth *(ex umbris et imaginibus in veritatem)* in a similar way as Soloviev—Russian Newman. Henri Bergson, French philosopher of Jewish origin, died without baptism of water and formal reception in the Church because he did not want to forsake his people during the nearing waves of anti-semitism and imminent persecutions of Jews. But Henri Bergson expressed his wish to embrace Catholicism four years before his death to Antonin Gilbert D. Sertillanges. Although he wanted to stay amidst those who would be persecuted because of their race, nevertheless he hoped that a Catholic priest would pray at his grave in the event that permission of the Cardinal-archbishop of Paris be given. In a negative case a rabbi must be summoned but without concealing *(sans cacher)* to him his moral adherence to Catholicism.[35] Bergson's desire to have a Catholic priest's prayer at his grave was not unfulfilled.

Newman professed his faith in words which remind Soloviev's profession. Bergson's desire was, four years before his death in 1941, differently expressed, nevertheless in the same spirit. The profession of these three giants of thought shows their answer to the call of the Master that "they may all be one" (Jn 17:21). Bergson's answer is mentioned above. Expression of Cardinal Newman's approach is epitomized in the words:

> Let us turn from shadows of all kinds—shadows of sense, or shadows of argument and disputation, or shadows addressed to our imagination and tastes. Let us attempt, through God's grace, to advance and sanctify the inward man. We cannot be wrong here. Whatever is right, whatever is wrong, in this perplexing world, we must be right in doing justly, in loving mercy, in walking humbly with our God.[36]

Soloviev based his profession on the venerable tradition of the Fathers and Doctors of the Eastern Church.

> As a member of the true and venerable Eastern or Greco-Russian Orthodox Church which does not speak through an anti-canonical synod nor through the employees of the secular power, but through the utterance of her great Fathers and Doctors, I recognize as supreme judge in matters of religion him who has been recognized as such by St. Irenaeus, St. Dionysius the Great, St. Athanasius the Great, St. John Chrysostom, St. Cyril, St. Flavian, the Blessed Theodoret, St. Maximus the Confessor, St. Theodore of the Studium, St. Ignatius, etc. etc.—namely, the Apostle Peter, who lives in his successors and who has not heard in vain our Lord's words: 'Thou are Peter and upon this rock I will build My Church' . . . .[37]

On the cross of Soloviev's tomb hang two ikons. One of mental behind a glass contains the image of Our Lady of Ostrobram or Our Lady
of Vilno (Wilno, Vilnius), and above are the words engraved in stone
from Psalm 111 (112) verse 7 "In memoria aeterna erit justus." The famous biographer of Soloviev, K. V. Moculskij, who dedicated his work
to Sergius Nikolayevich Bulgakov, writes: "On Soloviev's tombstone in
the Novodevic Monastery two ikons are placed by an unknown hand."

During my philosophical studies I read almost all the literature about
Soloviev. K. Jindrich, a great admirer of Soloviev, speaks about the
second ikon as his own. For a long time I could not put my hands on
this book which was put into print by Fr. Zak, S.J., until J. Mastylak
sent it to me in Holland. K. Jindrich, on page 281 in his book
Vladimir Sergejevic Soloviev, speaks of his participation in the burial of
Vl. S. Soloviev and about his many visits to his grave, on which he had
the ikon with the image of the Mother of God and the citation from
Psalm 111 placed. There are two ikons. Thus we know definitely the
origin of the second ikon and make known at least part of what K.
V. Moculskij calls "by the unknown hand."

Soloviev's vision expressed in his *Russia and the Universal Church*
written almost a century ago assumes new dimensions at the threshold
of the third millennium as evidenced in today's approach to unity of
all Christians and non-Christians alike. In the last several decades,
non-Catholic Christians of various communions are becoming increasingly conscious that the existing division among Christians is a grave
evil. For that reason they come together in various Congresses and
look for adequate solutions for the divisions. The Catholic Church
does ... follow with interest these efforts. As against this the highest
authority of the Church shows the correct path to unity of all Christians, and warns us against the fallacious ways of uniting, which would
be to achieve unity even at the cost of faith itself and of truth.

Since the division of Eastern and Western Christendom, the Holy
Pontiffs have all been interested in this re-uniting of Eastern Christians
with the Catholic Church. Even in this regard, these Holy Pontiffs
have continued to give directives as to how this re-union was to be
achieved. Pius XI, in his secret consistory Dec. 18, 1924, laid down as
the basis of success in this reunion, three conditions: the first concerns
the Catholics, who will have to free themselves of the mistaken views
which have had their genesis in the past centuries, i.e., mistaken views
with respect to the Eastern Christians.[38] The second condition concerns
the East itself, which is bound to understand that the faith of their
patristic Fathers of the East is identical with the faith of the Church
Fathers of the West. The third condition is that of Charity; that is
bound to be exercised on both sides.

And now let us proceed to consider how these conditions of the
Holy Pontiffs with regard to unity of East and West are being carried
out.

In their efforts for reunion the Sovereign Pontiffs have always united to their acts and their hopes fervent prayer. They have even more emphatically urged the faithful to do the same. Let me mention a few examples.

Leo XIII in his encyclical "Provida Matris," . . . recommends prayer to the Holy Ghost . . . for the accomplishment of union. . . .

Pius X in 1909 greeted and approved the world-wide Octave of prayers for the unity of the Church. . . .

Benedict XV . . . approved a new prayer for the unification of Eastern Christians. He ends the prayer with the words: "Preserve us from every mistake which would drive them further from us. . . ."

The extraordinary love of Pius XI towards a suffering Russia found an expression in material help and prayer. At the time of a cruel persecution of Christians in Russia Pope Pius XI, on the feast of St. Joseph, 1930, voiced a public protest and exhorted the whole world to prayer. . . .

Pope Pius XII concentrated in his own great heart the desire and effort of his predecessors for the renewal of peace amongst Christians.

Pope John XXIII in opening Vatican II opened the door for the union of Christians in a manner unprecedented in the annals of history, which was sealed in the embracement of Pope Paul VI and the Patriarch of Constantinople on the Mount of Olives. The Anglican-Catholic Statement raises substantially a new hope on the reunion issue. Thus the High Priest's prayer 'that all may be one,' arduously repeated in Rome by St. Cyril[39] eleven hundred years ago, is nearer to the ear of our times at the threshold of the third millennium.

In the physical order of the universe the manifestation of the Logos in flesh has no significance if in his faith one is not aware of the Spirit which was sent to man through the divine Logos. *Via ascensionis* means that the revelation of God in flesh leads man to the infinite personality of the Trinity and to surrender to the Infinite who descended upon and rendered man a spiritualized human. This *via ascensionis* results because the highest of God became the utmost of man in his utterance and expression of the Infinite. The Logos is the Word of God incarnated, passible unto death, glorified in resurrection, and guiding finite man to the Infinite. Such guidance makes man's life a witness to and echo of the eternal Logos in a created time. But the unfolding fullness of life is the working of the Spirit. Theology as a preliminary to the official teaching of the magisterium is not permitted to prolong its dwelling in the stage of theory anymore than the chosen people were permitted deliberation in their contact with the Word of God. Eschaton oriented towards the resurrection of flesh is a revitalisation of man's *desiderium naturale* in which resurrection is not relative but an unparalleled and unique event in man's eternal destiny. The necessitating dictums (Laws and principles) are raised to a higher plane from their applications of finite truth to the infinite manifestation of the Logos

which is in flesh and transcends the boundaries of the temporal. This
transcendence presents the whole Truth revealed in the openness of the
Logos because the thought of previous generations serves more than
a pillow for future thought.[40] The transcendent Logos is unique, and
his creaturely status is a function of his uncreated eternal Sonship,
which represents the Trinity in the world. The task of Theology lies
in the exploration of the extent to which the Logos represents the
Trinity in the created world.

Eschatology in Paul's dictum *Maranatha* is a source of reinvigorating
theology in various fields. The destiny of man lies in death. No man
can escape death. But the Christian knows that his death is an escape
to freedom to be with Christ whose death on the cross signaled a new
life for a new creature in the newness of Christ. Death is not a victory
over life. It is a victory over death. The mortal becomes immortal.
Credo in carnis resurrectionem, vitam aeternam is not a leap of *faculté
fabulatrice* (as Bergson says in his *Deux Sources de la Morale et de la
Religion*), a defensive reaction of nature against the intellect's representation concerning the inevitability of death, but it is a fulfillment of
Christ's promise: "I am the resurrection and the life. Whoever believes
in me will live, even though he dies; and whoever lives and believes
in me will never die" (Jn 11:25); "For if the dead are not raised,
neither has Christ been raised" (I Cor 15:16).

Although the Eschaton is not a biblical expression (the same may be
said about second Adam), nonetheless, it is easy to understand that the
remolding of theology by eschatology looks on Christ as the Eschaton
because the incorporation of man into Christ constitutes the foundation
of Eschatology.

Eschaton of the whole man in his course from birth to death must be
carried over into an entirely new dimension, which can be illumined
only by revelation and faith. Otherwise eschaton is inaccessible to the
thought manifested by God's revelation[41] particularly in his dealings
with the world because man's history and his world assumed new dimensions. Christ transforming man into a new creature gave eschatology a
new significance elucidating the mystery of the Church as a ferment in
the present order of things, which ferment will be understood fully only
in its final outcome. The eschatological element in ecclessiology has
been lacking since the sixteenth century and it has been presented in an
earthly fashion as a vague something behind the curtain of death. The
inapproachability of the All-holy, and the Christian attitude towards
the indissoluble unity of judgment[42] and redemption, is indicative of
the parousia in the Christian eschaton. The Eschaton interpreted chris-
tologically deepens decosmologized eschatology and leads to the integral faith revealed by Christ who is the resurrection and the life.

Eschatology takes in account the present understanding of man and
the world. Every epoch approaches the word of God in a new light
gained from a new understanding of the history of revelation. The

new insights may bring to light new aspects of eschatology previously obscured by a narrow regulative idea limiting pilgrim man's eschatological vision to the historical setting of the past. *Homo viator* of the present adduces greater dimensions in his search for higher states of religious thought. Many theologians aware of the difficulty avoid eschatology. Nevertheless, the doctrine of eschatology is most decisive for theology. There is a new encounter between theological and philosophical eschatology because supernatural transfiguration must include the perfections of natural transfiguration. The risen Christ is the fulfillment of the meaning of man and his world.

God is the divine basis of Creation and man.

If we consider the whole of the theoretical and moral content of Christ's teaching as expounded in the Gospels, the only thing in it that will be new and specifically different from all other religions is Christ's teaching about himself, his speaking of himself as the living, incarnate truth.

God as an integral being possesses both unity and, in His relationship to man, a plurality of substantival ideas.

The connecting link between the divine and the natural world is man.

It is necessary to distinguish a two-fold unity within the wholeness of the divine Being: the active or producing unity of the World's divine creativeness, and the produced or realized unity.

In order to exist really and actually, God manifests His existence, i.e., God acts in other beings; but God as manifested implies man. We are speaking of the ideal man who is not any less concrete or real than the visible manifestation of human beings.

Though man as an empirical fact is temporary and transient, in his essence he is of necessity eternal and all-embracing. An infinite existence after death does not logically tally with nothingness before birth. An intelligible essence is from its very meaning not subject to our temporal forms which apply to appearances only.

The central idea of the Gospel is the idea of the Kingdom of God —the complete realization of the divine in the naturally human through the Godmanhood of Christ. Man must manifest the Kingdom of God hidden within him; he must combine a deliberate effort of his free will with the secret action of the divine grace within him. The Kingdom of God is the union of divine grace with man, not as shut up in his own selfhood but with man as a living member of the cosmic whole in an all-embracing total-unity.

The view that man plays a merely passive part in the divine work must be recognized as a crude counterfeit of Christianity. Sons of the kingdom of freedom are called to conscious and independent cooperation in the work of the Father. Counterfeit Christianity is generally connected with denial of all progress and development in the Christian religion.

Societies that call themselves Christian must recognize it as their duty to harmonize all their political and social relations with Christian principles.[43]

The Godmanhood conception is so important for Soloviev's philosophy that it occupies a central position in the Russian metaphysics of the Spirit. His theadrism is a symphonic development of this *leit motiv* for his moral philosophy in *Justification of the Good* because Godmanhood is not simply a Christological but also an anthropological concept (which is evident in his philosophy on beauty and on art in the essay *The Meaning of Love*). V. Soloviev could have said with Nicholas of Cusa that the highest knowledge of God is the knowledge *of the unity of the Creator in the Creation and in the creatures.* 'All-unity' is Soloviev's call for the world's salvation to overcome the dividedness in an all-embracing harmonious unity. Soloviev expressed this very simply in one of his letters: "Not only do I believe in everything supernatural, but strictly speaking I believe in nothing else. . . . From the time that I began to think, the materiality has always seemed to me merely as a kind of nightmare of the sleeping humanity" (L., I, 33-34). Russian philosophy and the world had placed great hopes in Soloviev from the beginning of his philosophical career at the age of twenty one, when a great historian, A. A. Bestuzhev-Ryumin, said after Soloviev's defense of his thesis, *The Crisis of Western Philosophy:* "Russia may be congraulated upon a new genius."[44]

Here we touch upon Soloviev's moral philosophy, or, better expressed, on his philosophy of love, as treated in his *Justification of the Good* and *The Meaning of Love.*

Logos revealed to man what to do to achieve his eschatological goal *(finis)* but He did not tell him *how* to achieve it, therefore man is constantly fumbling on the way to his goal *(finis),* to the Kingdom of God, *"regnum cuius nullus est finis." Justification of God* is Soloviev's conamen to provide a norm to achieve the supernatural goal *(finis)* in man's economy of salvation. The word "norm" is commonly known in its definition as that which presents a standard by which something is gauged or judged. Therefore the moral norm of social life might be more simply restated as the moral standard of social life.

It is felt that the true definition of society as an organized morality does away with two contemporary false theories. The first is the view of moral subjectivism which prevents man's moral will from being realized in community life; the second, the theory of social realism according to which certain institutions are supreme in themselves. From the latter point of view, this or that certain type of social life is considered essential although attempts are still made to give it a moral justification. This search for a moral basis for human society indicates that neither the concrete form of social life nor social life as such is the utmost and final expression of human nature.

If man were described as a social animal the extension of the word would increase to include animals such as ants to whom social life is essential. It will prove interesting to go into this aspect a little deeper. There are three inner characteristics of the ant community: 1) a complex social organization, 2) a distinct difference in the degree of organization among communities, and 3) a gradual development of the various forms of "human" culture from hunting to the agricultural stage. Analogously to human life, there is also a great deal of division of labor; there are special ants for special jobs. At this time it is also known that ants have domesticated insects of their own just as humans have domesticated animals. It is continually remarked by John Lubbers, a great naturalist, that the greatest harmony reigns between members of the same ant community. This harmony he feels is exclusively conditioned by the common good. He has found through experiments that ants help each other when the project is for the good of all, but do not take heed when an individual ant gets into trouble on its own. The feeling of civic duty is paramount among ants.

We may thus state that social life is an essential characteristic of these insects as it is in man. Now the question arises as to how this fact relates to man and his social life. Unless we bestow upon ants the same rights as man it must mean that man has another and more essential characteristic, one that is separate from social instincts. This characteristic is expressed in the idea that man as such is a moral being, one who has worth in himself and apart from society, one who has a right to develop his positive powers.

No man under any conditions or for any reason may be regarded as only a means for purposes extraneous to himself. A person is not an instrument to be used solely for the good of another person or even a whole class of people. No claim can be made upon the man, only on his work, and on the extent to which it is being used for the good of the community. The rights of a person are unconditional by their very nature, but the rights of the community with regard to the person are conditioned by the recognition of individual rights.[45] Society therefore can or should compel a person to do something only through an act of his own free will. No social group or institution of any sort has a right to detain its members. A man's dignity does not depend upon specific qualities or social utility.

We have stated that often some animals are more virtuous than men; but it has never occurred to anyone to deprive man of some of his rights and give them to the more virtuous of animals, as that is not the human or the Christian way. We feel that man's great ideas and inventions shall have been sacrificed if we were to consciously and intentionally sacrifice the life of one single human being, be he savage or saint. The work of many great men shall have been considered immoral were we to admit that the end justifies the means. That which is really and truly good is for the good of all and therefore for the good of each and every individual in his turn, excluding none. For this very reason, if one's life be sacrificed it shall not have been for the good of all.

The only moral norm, then, is the principle of human dignity or of the absolute worth of each individual; in virtue of which society is determined as the inward and free harmony of all.[46] Soloviev feels that it is not difficult to show that religion, family, and property do not as such contain any definite moral norm in the rigid sense of the term.

A thing taken by itself may be either moral or immoral but this can only be judged by means of some external criterion. Therefore it cannot be a moral norm on its own account because it cannot yield something which is not contained within itself. (Nemo dat quo nam habet). It has often been said that religion is the moral norm and foundation of society. If this be true, it must have a moral fibre which agrees with the principles of morality. It is demonstrable that the final criterion is the principle, not the religion as such. But Christianity, because it does contain the moral principles within itself, is considered the norm. Furthermore, if these moral principles are abandoned, Christianity loses its significance.

The family may be summarized similarly. How can it become the norm of something when it has to receive its own standards of morality from something else?

Likewise, to think of property as the moral norm of society is completely illogical. Property in its own two fundamental historical forms was destroyed. This destruction was demanded and accomplished in the name of social morality. It would be illogical to consider property to be the norm of something which forced its eventual destruction.

Throughout history a distorted view of the essence of morality has persisted even though in its earliest stages there was no definite application. A good example of this can be found throughout the East especially in Russia where a man was said to have full personal rights, but such rights or dignity were ascribed to one man only, and he was a despot. Thus transformed into an exclusive and externally determined privilege, human right and worth lose their moral character. The moral principle demands that all men respect human dignity as such and that dignity be respected both in other people and in oneself. It is only through treating others as persons that the individual can himself be recognized as a person. The Eastern despots however did not adhere to this moral principle, which holds true for all mankind and society. They did not have personal moral relations with anyone and in turn lost their personal moral character.

Some of the communities of the ancient world such as Sparta recognized the human dignity of man only within the sphere or limits of civic union. This was not a society based upon moral principles because outside of this union the dignity of man was frequently rejected. But it at least approached a moral norm for society.

The reason is readily apparent why progress in this direction was very slow if not almost impossible in ancient times. There were many prohibiting factors, such as the threefold classification of men who were not recognized as bearers of any rights or objects of any duties. These were enemies, slaves, and criminals. They were primarily regarded as obstacles or impediments to the common good. Despite their utility, slaves were not afforded any recognition of worth as human beings. Similarly, all enemies were considered to be things unquestionably harmful which should be mercilessly exterminated. However, there was always respect for an enemy's force and fear of his revenge. With regard to criminals, there were no bounds to the cruelty to which they might be exposed in reciprocation for the real or supposed threat which they presented to society.

All of these facts were considered legitimate for people of the ancient world, in the sense that they followed logically the view held by all. This was the level of moral awareness of society at that time. If the worth of man as an independent individual and the fullness of his rights and dignity depended exclusively upon his belonging to a certain civic union, the natural consequence was that men who did not belong to that union, who were strange and hostile to it, or men who, though they belonged to it, violated its laws and constituted a menace to the common safety, were, by the very fact of what they were, deprived of human rights and dignity. With regard to such men all things were lawful.[47]

Since ancient times, however, this point of view came to be changed consequent upon two basic factors. 1) The ethical thought among Greco-Roman Stoics, followed by the work of Roman lawyers in an Empire which embraced many peoples and many nations, widened the theoretical and practical outlook.[48] 2) Contemporaneously in the East, Jewish and Christian prophets were expounding a religious doctrine which proclaimed a complete and absolute human dignity. In this milieu it was felt that the combination of these Greco-Roman and Judaeo-Christian forces would precipitate an entirely new order of things. Their anticipation of the imminence of a complete and absolute revamping of the physical world was obviously wishful thinking, for heathendom has persisted basically unchanged down to the present day. It is clear, as foretold in the Gospel, that the problem can only be solved gradually; for, despite the noticeable progress of the past few centuries, it is painfully evident that much yet remains to be done.

Indeed, man's attitudes toward the old foundations and beliefs of society are changing and are beginning to manifest themselves more and more in his way of life. He has reached a state of moral maturity and consciousness which is beginning to make it impossible for him to do things which to the ancient world were natural. Even individuals who do not aspire to faith adhere to moral principles which eschew the justification of collective crimes. Modern-day transportation methods are doing much to bring people together and to break down many social barriers which formerly existed. The fear of war has also become prominent in international affairs so that countries can no longer harbor plans of conquest as they once did. Slavery as it once existed has been abolished, although economic slavery still exists. The treatment of criminals has also definitely become more moral and more Christian. Change has been and will continue to be slow, but it is always and everywhere present.

It becomes more and more obvious that religion, property and family, as such, cannot be the norm of the moral foundation of society. These institutions should not be maintained as preserved in the *status quo*, but should flexibly reflect the one and only moral standard.

Soloviev feels that universal Christianity, free from all denominational peculiarities, is the embodiment of the absolute moral ideas. To be truly universal, religion must not separate itself from intellectual enlightenment, from science, from social and political progress. If a religion fears any of these things and yet claims to be the sole moral norm of society, it fails to fulfill the most elementary moral condition of being genuine.[49]

The family on the other hand may be in some respect considered the moral norm of society. Each member of the family is not only intended and meant to be but actually is an end for all the others. Each has a definite significance and each is irreplaceable. In this light, the family is the elementary constitutive cell of universal brotherhood, of human society as it ought to be. Care must be taken to see that the family does not fall into the embodiment of mutual egotism.[50]

Property in itself has no moral significance but the question of distribution of property does, and it is inconsistent with human dignity and with the moral norm of society that a person should be unable to support his existence,[51] as can graphically be seen in the sociological conditions of the poor of the world.

It should now be clear why none of the above considerations (apart from Christianity) may be said to be precisely the moral norm of society. In conclusion, then, we can state that all of human society (especially that which professes to be Christian) must, if it is to continue to exist and to attain to a higher dignity, conform to the moral standard of universal Christianity. What matters is not the external preservation of certain institutions, which may be good or bad, but a sincere and consistent striving inwardly to improve all institutions and social relations which may be good by subordinating them more and more to the one unconditional moral ideal of the free union of all men in the perfect good.[52]

While love could have a transcendental meaning as the notions *unum*, *verum*, *bonum*, beautiful in a strict sense cannot be considered as transcendental, because it does not add a new notion, it simply emphasizes *verum boni* and *bonum veri*. Jacques Maritain counts beautiful among the transcendental notions. In our discussion at Notre Dame he simply stated that there were more transcendental notions. My arguments against the transcendency of the beautiful in Thomistic teaching are the following: Thomas Aquinas speaks of the beautiful only in passing (incidentally). First, beautiful *quod visu placet* presupposes a matter, which is not transcendental. Secondly, St. Thomas' *splendor ordinis* could be considered as a transcendental notion but for bad reasons. God is simple, simplicity does not admit *ordo* even with a splendor. St. Thomas used this expression because, in his time, the expression was ascribed to Dionysius, a disciple of St. Paul. Now we know that it was the expression of Pseudo-Dionysius, who lived in the V century.

It is true that without "beautiful" the language would be impoverished, but, strictly philosophically, beautiful does not add a new notion to *bonum* and *verum*.

Mysticism employs this expression in ecstasies and raptures, and reflection on art participates in mysticism in a natural order. The material being can enter into the moral order only through spiritualization in the form of beauty. V. Soloviev approaches aesthetics, in its function of a link between art and nature, with a deeper insight into the artistic work, which is the continuation of the work begun by nature.

The usual answer to the question of the reduplication on canvas of beauty as it already exists in nature is that the aesthetic element of natural events after passing through the artist's consciousness and imagination is cleansed from all material elements and thus is intensified and seen more clearly. But the aesthetic connection between art and nature is obviously much deeper and more significant, for it consists not in the mere reception but in the continuation of the artistic work begun by nature.

Man as the most beautiful and most conscious of natural beings is not simply the result of the natural process but an agent in it who answers more perfectly its ideal purpose, i.e., the complete mutual interpenetration and free solidarity of the spiritual and the material, the ideal and the real, the subjective and the objective factors and elements of the universe.

Would it not be better to regard the cosmic process begun by nature and continued by man as the realization of truth and goodness rather than, from the artistic point of view, as the solution of some artistic problem? A strict moralist will say that to do good and to know truth is all that is needed. But the very existence of a moral order in the world presupposes its connection with the material order, a certain coordination between the two. To be secure a moral order must rest upon material nature as the medium and the means of its existence, but to be complete and perfect it must include the material basis of existence as an independent part of moral activity which becomes aesthetic, for material being can enter into the moral order only through spiritualization and enlightenment, i.e., only in the form of beauty. Beauty, then, is needed for the fulfillment of the good.

Should not art strive merely to clothe in beauty human relations alone and embody in sensible images the true meaning of human life, since the beauty of nature is merely a veil thrown over the evil life? For their true realization, goodness and truth must become a creative power in the subject, transforming the reality and not merely reflecting it. Every kind of evil consists at bottom in the violation of the mutual solidarity and balance between parts and whole; and all falsehood and ugliness can be likewise reduced. The same essential characteristics that determine evil in the moral sphere and falsity in the intellectual determine ugliness in the aesthetic sphere.

Anarchic multiplicity is as much opposed to goodness, truth and beauty as is dead crushing unity. The fullness of freedom for the whole as for the parts requires that there should be absolute solidarity between all that is, and that God should be all in all.

The fundamental aesthetic requirement is that there should be the closest and deepest interaction between the inner or spiritual and the outer or material being. Neither abstract spirit incapable of creature incarnation nor soulless matter incapable of spiritualization corresponds to ideal or worthy being and neither can be beautiful. True and perfect beauty requires 1) direct material embodiment of the spiritual essence, 2) complete spiritualization of the material appearance as the inherent and inseparable form of the ideal content, and 3) the mutual interpenetration of the spiritual content with the material appearance must become permanent and immortal.

Nature has not succeeded in realizing perfect beauty in the domain of physical life. Natural beauty expresses the idea of life not in its inner moral quality but merely in its external physical characteristics; true beauty does not wholly and inwardly pervade the chaotic nature of material. The task that cannot be fulfilled by means of physical life must be fulfilled through human creativeness.

Hence the threefold task of art is 1) to give a direct objective expression to the deepest inner qualities and determinations of the living Idea which nature is incapable of expressing, 2) to spiritualize natural beauty, and 3) through this spiritualization to perpetuate its individual appearances. Completely to embody this spiritual fullness in our actual world, to realize therein absolute beauty, or to create a universal spiritual organism is the highest task of art. Clearly the fulfillment of this task must coincide with the end of the cosmic process as a whole.

Every sensuous expression of any object or event, therefore, from the point of view of its final state, or even the light of the world to come, is a work of art.

The anticipation of perfect beauty in human art is of three kinds: 1) direct or magical, when the deeper inner states concerning us with the true essence of things and the transcendental world ... break through all conventions and material limitations and find direct and complete expressions in beautiful sounds and words; 2) indirect, through the intensification of the given beauty; 3) also indirect, consisting in the reflection of the ideal from an environment alien to it, intensified by the artist to make the reflection more vivid.

The complacency of men in comedies, wherein they are at variance with the ideal, constitutes the essential nature of the comical as distinct from the tragical element, where the characters are imbued with the sense of an inner contradiction between their given reality and that which ought to be.

The final task of perfect art is to spiritualize and transfigure man's actual life. The future development of aesthetic creativeness depends upon the general course of history, for art in general is the sphere of the embodiment of ideas and not of their original inception and growth. This expresses *par excellence* the teleology of man's eschaton transcending the present life in anticipation of a spiritualized transfiguration.

The central theme which Vladimir Soloviev relates in his essay on love and its relation to the Eschaton of man is that only through the experience of the sex-love relation can an individual embrace and be embraced by the All-one existence; by the individual transferring his significance or his center of being to the beloved, and ultimately to each and every particle of the whole, he experiences the truth—the unity of the All.

Soloviev when using the term "sex-love" does not mean the mere physical union of two sexes but "the exclusive attachment between persons of different sexes which renders possible the relation between them as husband and wife."[53]

The author views man as a creature with a dual nature, one material and the other ideal. The ideal nature is the actuality that man is made in the imge and likeness of God, that we are 'God-like.' Love is the living force which enables man to discern and realize the ideal image of the beloved in substance, and, in reaching for this higher nature, to surrender his egoism and transfer the center of his being to another. "Passion" is the term Soloviev uses to describe this all-encompassing desire for unification with the ideal nature, the God-like reflection of the beloved.

Only by experiencing sex-love can a person justify his true existence, where in true love he reaches out to the individualization of the reflection of the All-one and transfers the center of his being to another. In giving to another true significance he necessarily must recognize his own capacity to love and to enter a union with his own individualization of the reflection of the All-one, thereby confirming his individual significance.

Hence, the basis of love is realized as faith, "the assurance of things hoped for, the conviction of things not seen."[54] When man is reaching for the unity with the reflection of the All he necessarily is convinced of the existence of the All, which is not seen, or else he would not be attempting to achieve such union. In the words of Soloviev, "I can only acknowledge the unconditional significance of a given person, or believe in him, by affirming him in God, and therefore by belief in God Himself and in myself, as possessing in God the centre and root of my existence. This triune act is already a certain inward act and by this act is laid the first beginning of a true union of the man with his 'other' and the restoration in it, or in them, of the image of the triune God.[55]

In his consideration of the existence of true love in this world, V. Soloviev asserts that once the focus of the union is transferred from the ideal nature to any materialistic focus the true essence of the relation is destroyed. With this understanding it is readily seen that in the mere physical union where love is absent, the focus of the relation is on the material physical body denying the spiritual nature in defiance of the totality of the individual and is therefore no relation at all. Soloviev would term an interaction of this type a sexual abnormality in the same way society considers fetishism an abnormality.

The individual and independent significance of the sex-love may be seen in the mutual sexual impulses of the two individuals to unite with the reflection of the All in the beloved and in the achievement of this substantial union the complementary all in one is represented in the other.

The individual must realize that this single relationship is the fundamental unit, the stepping stone to the perfect All-oneness which necessarily demands "equivalence and equality of right between the one and the all, the whole and the parts."[56] For this perfect All-oneness to be realized the individual must perceive the reflection of the All-one in others (besides the beloved) and in nature and then actively confirm the individual significance of each part of the whole and the whole itself. Here can be seen the influence of Spinoza on Soloviev, from whom Soloviev "gained a living sense of God's reality and a clear experience of the total spiritual unity of the world."[57]

Soloviev states that in order to justify in reality the meaning of love "a union of two finite creatures is demanded as would create out of them one absolute personality."[58] From the individual's experience of the sex-love relation, he is capable of expanding the significance he gives to the beloved to all parts of the whole, and to the whole itself, where in this union not one ideal personality would be created but rather One Ideal Person, the perfect All-oneness.

The sex factor is connected not with reproduction as such (which may take place without it) but with the reproduction of higher organisms. The meaning of sexual differentiation (and consequently, of sexual love) must be sought for not in the idea of generic life and its reproduction, but only in the idea of a higher organism.

Among animals which reproduce themselves in the sexual way (the vertebrates) the higher we go in the organic scale, the less is the power of reproduction and the greater the force of sexual attraction.

In man the rate of reproduction is lower than in the rest of the animal kingdom, but sexual love attains the greatest force and significance, uniting in the highest degree the permanence of relations with the intensity of passion.

Thus sexual love and reproduction of the species are in inverse rates to each other: the stronger the one, the weaker the other. If then, at the two opposite poles of animal life we find, on the one hand, reproduction without any sexual love, and on the other, sexual love without any reproduction it is clear that each of them has an independent significance of its own. In human love especially sexual love acquires an individual character in virtue of which precisely this person of the opposite sex has an absolute significance for the lover as unique and irreplaceable as an end in itself.

There is a popular theory that with human beings it is not producing offspring or such that matters, but producing a particular kind of offspring, most suitable for world purposes. And since the given individual can produce such offspring, not with any individual of the opposite sex, but only with one particular person, that person must have for him or her a special power of attraction and appear exceptional, irreplaceable, unique and capable of bestowing the highest bliss.

If this theory were correct, if the individual and exalted nature of the love feeling had its whole meaning, reason and purpose in the quality of the offspring required for world purposes, it would logically follow: the more valuable the offspring, the greater the love between the parents, and, vice versa, the stronger the love between two particular persons, the more remarkable their offspring should be. It follows, therefore that if the cosmic will is extremely interested in the birth of some person, a world genius, for instance (Soloviev is not here insinuating genetic engineering, as the science of genetics was hardly in its inception in his time) it must take extreme measure to secure the desired result, i.e., it must arouse in the parents a passion of extreme intensity, capable of overcoming all obstacles to their union.

In reality there is no correlation whatever between the intensity of the love-passion and the importance of the progeny. The most intense love often remains unrequited and produces no offspring whatever.

Suicide because of unhappy love, which is generally exceptionally intense, disproves the theory that intense love is aroused solely for the purpose of producing descendants whose importance is indicated by the intensity of the love.

As a general rule from which there are hardly any exceptions, particular intensity of sexual love either altogether excludes reproduction or results in offspring the importance of which in no way corresponds to the power of the love feeling and to the exceptional character of the relations arising from it.

Both with animals and with man sexual love is the great consequence of the individual life.

Unlike the animal, where the highest pitch of intensity achieved by the individual merely profits the generic process, the human personality has absolute worth consisting in the rational consciousness inherent in him. He is able to know and realize truth in itself. That is why he is the highest being in the natural world and the true end of the process of world-creation.

Animals can know nothing of the geological and biological transformations that conditioned their actual appearance on the earth. Man, with the whole truth latent in his living consciousness, can know and realize the positive unity of all. In his spiritual progeny he manifests himself as the center of the universal consciousness of nature, as the soul of the world, as the self-realizing potency of the absolute all-unity; consequently only that absolute in its perfect actuality or its eternal being, that is, God, can be higher than man. Truth or universal unity can only triumph in the animal kingdom through the change of generations, the permanence of the species and the destruction of the individual life incapable of comprehending the truth. The human individuality, however, just because it is capable of comprehending the truth, is not cancelled by it, but is preserved and strengthened through its triumph.

An individual being must be not only conscious of the Truth, he must be *in* it. Until the living force of egoism meets in man with another living force opposed to it, his own being will remain outside Truth, like the animal, and disappear in its subjectivity. Truth as a living power taking possession of man's inner being and really saving him from false self-affirmation is called love. Although love is higher than rational consciousness, man, through the consciousness of truth, can sacrifice his egoism to love and preserve his individual being.

The meaning of human love is the justification and salvation of individuality through the sacrifice of egoism. The fundamental evil and falsity of egoism lie not in the recognition of the subject's own absolute significance and value but in the fact that he recognizes himself as a center of life and refers others to the circumference of his being, setting upon them only an external and relative value.

But it is precisely this exclusive self-affirmation that prevents man from being in fact what he claims to be. God is all. 'This' man may be 'all' only together with others. In affirming himself outside all else, man robs his own existence of its meaning, deprives himself of the true content of life and reduces his individuality to an empty form. Thus egoism is self-negation, emptiness and destruction.

Although physical and metaphysical, social and historical conditions of human existence modify and soften man's egoism, there is only one power which may and actually does undermine egoism at the root, from within, and that is love, and chiefly sexual love. The evil and falsity of egoism consist in ascribing absolute significance exclusively to oneself and denying it to others. Love abolishes this unjust relation. Through love we come to know the truth of another in reality and in so doing manifest and realize our own absolute significance, which consists precisely in the power of transcending man's actual phenomenal existence and of loving not in ourselves but also in another.

All love is a manifestation of this power. If egoism is to be undermined totally it must be counteracted by a love as concretely determined as is egoism itself. The relation of the individual being to the 'other' must be a complete and a continual affirmation of oneself in another, a perfect interaction and communion. Such fusion is to be found in sexual love. In all other kinds of love there is absent either the homogeneity, equality and interaction between the lover and the beloved, or the all-inclusive difference of complementary qualities.

Thus in mystical love the object of love is reduced in the last resort to absolute indifference that engulfs individuality. A living man and the mystic 'Abyss' of absolute indifference are so heterogeneous and incommensurable that the two cannot co-exist, to say nothing of being in any vital communion. In schools of mysticism where they do co-exist, the relations with the object of love acquire the clear and consistent character of sexual love.

Parental love and especially maternal love approximates sexual love both in the intensity of feeling and the concreteness of its object. But in maternal love there can be no complete reciprocity and life-long communion because the lover and the beloved belong to different generations. The parents cannot be the object of the children's life in the same sense in which the children can be the object of life for the parents. In maternal love, although a mother sacrifices her egoism, the recognition of another person's absolute significance is really conditioned by an external physiological bond—it is *her* child.

Intimate friendship between persons of the same sex becomes an unnatural substitute for sexual love because it lacks the all-around formal distinction between the mutually complementary qualities of the sexes. Patriotism and love for humanity cannot in themselves concretely and actually eradicate egoism. Neither humanity nor the nation can be for the individual man as concrete an entity as he himself is.

Love is important as the transference of man's whole vital interests from himself to another, as the transposition of the very center of his personal life—this is pre-eminently true of sexual love which alone can lead to the actual and indissoluble union of two lives made one. And two will be one.

The love-feeling demands such fullness of inner and final union but as a rule things go no further than this subjective striving and demand, and that too proves to be transitory.

The fact that love had not been realized in the course of the comparatively few thousands of years lived by historical humanity gives us no right to conclude that it cannot be realized in the future.

The task of love as set to man by his spiritual nature is to create such a union of two given limited beings who while preserving their formal separateness overcome their essential disparity and disruption as would make them one absolute ideal personality.

Love is a fact of nature and a gift of God, a natural process arising independently of man; but this does not imply that man cannot and must not stand in conscious relation to it and of his own will direct this natural process to higher ends.

Everyone knows that in love there always is a special idealization of the object of love which appears to the lover in quite a different light than it does to other people. Beside the material or immaterial content of his life every man contains the image of God. That image is known to man in the abstract and in theory through reason, and concretely and actually through love. The reinstatement of the image of God in material humanity cannot possibly happen of itself, apart from man. The passive respectivity of feeling is enough with which to begin, but it must be followed by active faith, moral endeavor, and effort in order to preserve, strengthen and develop the gift of radiant and creative love and by means of it embody in oneself and in the other the image of God, forming out of two limited and mortal beings one absolute and immortal personality.

The actual feeling of love is merely a stimulus suggesting to man that he can and must recreate the wholeness of the human being. In the feeling of love, in accordance with its essential meaning, we affirm the absolute significance of another personality and, through it, of our own. But an absolute personality cannot be transitory and it cannot be empty. If we love a human being and if love is the beginning of that being's spiritualization and enlightenment, it necessarily demands the preservation, the eternal youth and immortality of this particular person.

If the inevitability of death is incompatible with true love, immortality is utterly incompatible with the emptiness of life. True love not only affirms in subjective feeling the absolute significance of human personality in another and in oneself, but also justifies the significance of reality, actually delivers one from the inevitability of death, and fills one's life with absolute content.

On the lower levels of the animal kingdom individual entities exist solely in order to procreate themselves and then die. It is self evident that so long as man reproduces himself like an animal, he also dies like an animal. Mere abstention from the act of procreation does not in any way save one from death. To remain in sexual dividedness means to remain on the path of death. Only the whole man can be immortal, and if physiological union cannot reinstate the wholeness of the human being, it means that this false union must be replaced by a true union and certainly not by an abstention from all union.

In what, then, does the true union of the sexes consist and how is it realized? The three relations or bonds between the sexes, normal for the human being in its wholeness, do actually exist in the human world: the bond in the animal life according to the lower nature, the morally-civic bond under the law, and the bond in the spiritual life or union in God. But they are realized separately from one another, in an order of sequence contrary to their true meaning and interdependence, and to an unequal degree.

The animal physiological bond is regarded as the basis of the entire union while it ought to be only its final culmination. Many do not go beyond animal relations; others build upon this broad foundation the socially moral superstructure of the legal family union which becomes an involuntary channel of meaningless material life. As a rare exception there is left for the few elect pure spiritual love, robbed beforehand by the other lower bonds of all actual content.

True spiritual love is not a feeble imitation and anticipation of death, but triumph over death. False spirituality is the negation of the flesh; true spirituality is its regeneration, salvation, and resurrection.

The relation that God has to His creation and that Christ has to His Church, must be the relation of the husband to the wife. God gains no increase from the creature, but gives everything to it; Christ receives no increase from the Church in perfection, and gives all perfection to it; but He does receive from the Church increase in the fullness of His collective body. Finally, man and his feminine alter ego complete each other both really and ideally, attaining perfection through interaction only. Man can creatively reinstate God's image in the living object of his love only by reinstating that image in himself as well; but he has no power of his own to do it, he must receive it from God. Hence man is the creative and formative principle in relation to his feminine complement not in himself, but as a mediator of the divine power.

The work of true love is based on faith which means the affirmation of that object as existing in God and in that sense possessing infinite significance. To affirm an individual being in God means to affirm it not in its separateness but in the unity of all. God, in distinguishing all that is not, posits all as another unity distinct from His primary unity—a feminine unity.

The ideal unity towards which our world is striving is God's eternal 'other.'

The complete realization, the transformation of an individual feminine being into a ray of the divine eternal feminine, inseparable from its radiant source will be the real reunion of the individual human being with the Deity.

The object of true love is twofold: man loves the ideal entity which we must bring into our real world and we love the natural human entity which provided the real personal material for such realization. God wills that His 'other' should exist not for Him only but that it should be realized and embodied for every individual. The whole cosmic and historical process is the process of its realization and incarnation in an endless multiplicity of forms and degrees.

In sexual love rightly understood and truly realized this divine essence finds a means for its complete and final embodiment in the individual life of man. Love is the highest expression of the individual life which, in union with another being, finds its own infinity. The distortion of the love relation is the cause for losing infinity. When physical union is put in first place in inevitably becomes the moral grave of love.

To abolish this bad order the experience of faith is needed. In our material environment it is impossible to preserve true love except through understanding it and accepting it as a moral task. It is only together with all other beings that the individual man can be really saved. If the moral meaning of love demands the identification of one's own self with the other it would be contrary to this moral meaning to separate the attainment of our individual perfection from the process of universal unification.

True life means living in another as in oneself. The pattern of this life shall always be sexual or conjugal love. That love cannot be realized without a corresponding transformation of the whole external environment; the integration of the individual life necessarily requires the same integration in the domains of social and of cosmic life.

Just as in sexual love the individual 'other' is at the same time 'all,' so the social all . . . must appear as a real unity, as, so to speak, another living being completing him. Man should treat his social and cosmic environment as an actual living being with which he is in the closest and most complete interaction, without ever being submerged in it.

Every conscious human activity, determined by the idea of universal syzygy (compunction) actually produces or liberates spiritually material currents which gradually gain possession of the material environment, spiritualize it and embody it in certain images of the all-embracing unity. This is the meaning of love in Soloviev's eschatological doctrine.

The beauty in art is a dictate of love in the eschaton of man.

The "coming" of Christ is a process in which the whole of mankind is engaged and which offers to every man the orientation to see his place in this movement through time. This "coming" relates the end of history to the Christian and to every individual as well as to the whole creation. A Christian recognizes in everything a new step towards the final re-capitulation of all things in Christ, whose "coming" is not only in our eschatological future but also in the present moment in history because Christian past and present have assumed eschatological dimensions in Christ's coming, parousia. 'Last things' refers not only to the human-individual but also to the cosmic dimensions of eschaton confronted with the spirit of our time in a special nearness to our days. Eschaton does not constitute the final treatise of theology as it is constantly present and mysteriously active in man. Eschata are intimately related to the realities of faith and they are relevant in every theological treatise as it can be seen in the mysteries of redemption. Eschaton would lose its foundation if once the continuity of the individual life were interrupted. Eschaton postulates an immortality and the continuation of consciousness and awareness linked to God.

Soloviev's theandric doctrine with its eschatological conclusion greatly influenced Russian thinkers who, amid the chaos of the Russian Revolution, continued their testimonial to their great teacher Vladimir S. Soloviev till the forced exodus terminated their work inside of Russia.[59] Permission for them to leave Russia is mistakenly ascribed in the West to the intervention of the government of the United States of America and the Vatican. The truth is that Leon Davydovich Trotsky, trying to win for the newly formed Communist Government diplomatic recognition by Western powers, took this "generous" diplomatic step. Among the expelled were N. O. Lossky, former Marxist Nicholas Aleksandrovich Berdyaev, and theologian Serge Nikolayevich Bulgakov, a former admirer of Karl Marx who had become disillusioned with Marxist philosophy long before the 1917 Revolution.

As Serge N. Bulgakov was a dean of the Theological Institute in Paris from its founding (1925) until the end of his life (1944), where he taught dogmatics eschatologically oriented, it is proper to mention his turn from Marxism to religio-metaphysical problems under the influence of Vladimir S. Soloviev.

As a Cadet deputy in the 1907 Duma and as an active participant in the intellectual, spiritual and artistic revival that characterized the Russian intelligentsia at the turn of the Century, Serge Nikolayevich Bulgakov (1871-1944) became disillusioned with Marxist philosophy, and after the 1917 Revolution, he, along with a group of former Marxists—N. Berdyaev, Simon Lyudvigovich, Frank and Peter Berngardovich Struve—returned to the Crimea and to the Orthodox Church.[60]

> The turn from "Marxism to idealism" began a new period in Bulgakov's life. Here he was greatly indebted to Vladimir Soloviev, as he himself testifies in his essays—especially the article "What Solovyov's Philosophy Offers The Contemporary Consciousness" in the volume From Marxism to Idealism. "Solovyov's philosophy," Bulgakov wrote at this time, "offers the contemporary consciousness an integral and consistently Christian world-view." Bulgakov did not merely free himself philosophically from the doctrine of economic materialism, accepting the basic propositions of idealism; he also moved consciously and wholeheartedly toward a religious conception of the world. He and Berdiaev founded a journal, *Voprosy zhizni* [Questions of Life], and in it Bulgakov published a number of articles on religious and social themes. In 1906, he moved to Moscow, and was appointed to a chair in the Commercial Institute; the institute's director was P. I. Novgorodtsev. Bulgakov was a deputy in the second Duma, for the Constitutional-Democratic Party. He wrote a number of remarkable essays, which were collected in the two-volume work *The Two Cities*. During these years Bulgakov became very intimate with P. Florensky, who greatly influenced him. Bulgakov accepted Florensky's Sophiological conception, gradually

reworking it in his own way. In 1912 he published a book entitled *The Philosophy of Economics,* for which he received the degree of Doctor of Political Economy at Moscow University. It was in this work that he first developed his Sophiological conception.[61]

The Undying Light (1917) by Bulgakov recounts the story of his conversion. In 1918 he was ordained a priest, after which the Communist government prevented him from teaching at the University of Simferopol and in 1923 expelled him from the Soviet Union. After two years of academic work in Prague he was appointed professor of theology and dean of the newly established Russian Orthodox Theological Institute of Paris, where he died on July 12, 1944.[62] He was a friend of K. Kautsky.[62a]

His last twenty years were spent elaborating a system of theology known as sophiology, a doctrine centered on the concept of Wisdom *(Sophia).* Taken from the Old Testament, this concept was used by medieval mystics and more recently by modern Russian philosophers; besides Bulgakov, Paul Aleksandrovich Florensky and V. S. Soloviev produced a treatise on cosmology as the loving and organic unity revealing the Divine Wisdom. According to Bulgakov's teaching, *Sophia* is that link connecting God to the created world. But his theories met strong opposition among certain Orthodox hierarchs and theologians, and thus were condemned by the synods of Orthodox bishops.

The doctrine of the *eschata* regarding the individual and a universal eschatology finds its fulfillment in Nirvāna in the Buddhist religion. The Greeks developed an idea of separated souls in Hades. The Sumer-Babylonian conception of *kurnugea,* reminiscent of 'the land without return,' is pessimistic. The Celtic underworld is more optimistic and is nearer to the Germanic *Walhalla* reserved for gods and heroes. The Slavic piety for the dead veils the mystery of the final fate. The Egyptian religions developed a strong individual sechatology. The Day of Yahweh as the eschatological expectation of the Old Testament is not a one-sided, unbiblical spiritualized event but a *restitutio in integrum et novum.* In the New Testament the final eschatological fulfillment of individual and universal eschaton takes place in the Parousia of the Word in the person of Jesus.[63]

Death consequently must possess for man a personal and natural aspect. In the doctrine of the Church, the natural aspect of death for man is expressed in the proposition that death means the definitive end of our state. The universality of our death is an absolute proposition of our faith. Reason and faith teach that all men are subject to the law of death. All men are sinners therefore all men must die.

Only in the meaning of the statement of faith in the theological foundations from which its certitude derives can man understand that death will rule all future centuries and that its dominion will never be abolished. The natural causes of death are to be traced back to a prnciple in the moral and spiritual history of man.

Catholic doctrine describes death as separation of soul and body. The separation of the soul and body implies that the soul becomes acosmic.

The proposition of faith views death less existentially and more formally. It affirms that with bodily death, man's state of pilgrimage comes to a definite end. This means that the basic moral decision made by man in the finiteness of bodily existence is rendered definite and final by death. The "second option" is treated in another place.

Death is the beginning of eternity. It is also the end of biological life. Death is in part a consequence of sin. Death becomes the visible demonstration of the fissure between God and man which cleaves man's being to its very essence and which was opened at the very beginning of spiritual life. Man's death is the demonstration that he has fallen away from God in an alienation which embraces the imperfect world.

> Throughout both Testaments the Bible proclaims that history has meaning, that it is moving toward an encounter with God, and that God's judgment will definitively establish his holy people. The various depictions of the judgement are not meant to describe it so much as to summon men to the conversion in faith. Then, in Jesus Christ, they will receive the wondrous and mysterious salvation that God offers them.[64]

Today's society however refutes this concept of eschatology because of a genuine lack of understanding of its nature. Modern man has cast away most myths and with them their meaning. Theology has aided in devaluing the concept of eschatology by eclipsing the problem, rather than emphasizing the idea that descriptions of judgement are meant to bring men together in a preparation of faith. The theologians attempt to dismiss the concept completely, thereby losing the biblical message.

The problem of eschatology goes back much further than modern times. Among the second-generation Christians, the realization that there was a delay in the parousia was not yet a conscious problem but still the church was making adjustments in its day-to-day life to cope with it. Refusing A. Schweitzer's doctrine it is more accurate to say that the emphasis was shifted to having a longer time on earth and the buildup of organization helped to minimize the eschatological vision of Christian life. We can see in the writings of Saint Augustine that the city of God is the future, definitive shape of Church and State together; it will give heavenly bliss to redeemed individuals. "Augustine equates the visible form of the Catholic Church in history with this city of God."[65] After Augustine, though, this idea of "kingdom" in eschatology was lost. Through influences of hellenism the Church again became over-spiritualized. Today this spiritualization is mocked as primitive, un-enlightened religion. In the Middle Ages the elaboration of Canon Law led to new developments in the process of institutionalization and these times bore witness to an ever-widening chasm between ministers and people of God. However the old thrust of Christian eschatology took on new life.

In the twelfth century and first half of the thirteenth century, a widespread eschatological piety dominated Western Christianity, apparently for the last time. In modern times the unity and teleology of history remained the basic consideration in man's attempt to understand history. An eschatology oriented around salvation history had already been undermined in the patristic age. In the Middle Ages it was replaced by a view of history founded on divine providence. "The Renaissance revolutionized the whole emphasis. It was man, not God or his eternal plan, that gave meaning to history. Man was the one who gave unity and impetus to history."[66]

Our times are extremely complex and reality-oriented. Man lives now because of his technology rather than in creation of it, and the knowledge of science has elevated man's self-esteem. Salvation is not a pressing topic to the new generation. Like his life modern man feels his death too "will be taken care of." Any planning ahead is planning towards a future which, according to modern meaning is eternal. However what made twentieth century man so anxious about his terrestrial end is what makes twentieth century man so unconcerned of judgement ("After us, the Deluge"). Life has definitely improved with advanced technology but so too has the chance of death increased. Violation of ecology, and chemical, biological and nuclear warfare make the end seem close at hand rather than a distant possibility.

The hope then for the future of advancing eschatological thought is with man of today. The distaste for a materialistic society, the refusal of unnecessary competition are the premonitions of a new return to nature. With this return to his original natural state man will become more aware of his death, judgement and eternal place of rest. Man, who almost succeeded in masking his spiritual identity, will again become aware of his dual identity. His former concern for the mortal body will again be channeled into a concern for his everlasting life. Eschatological matters will take preference in philosophical thought. Awareness, though, is the key in eschatological matters for it is often easy to forget the eschaton. However when the eschaton is constantly brought to mind, and if a new eschatology emphasizes the hope, man can unite. If all men become aware of a destiny based on a judgement of love, then man could become of one mind, in God.

Do the people wish to believe in life after death? There are many reasons but perhaps paramount is our fear of death. There are many references in the Bible to death as an occasion of suffering and in Job (17:14) death is personified as the "King of Terrors." The Bible recognizes at least three kinds of death: physical, spiritual and "second" or eternal. The first kind of death, "physical," is the dissolution of the body, as described in Eccl. 11:7: "the spirit takes flight and the body passes back to dust from which it came." On a deeper level, spiritual death is a state of sin that alienates man from God, a death from which Christians believe we are saved by the redemptive death of Christ. The "second" or eternal death signifies the loss or an opportunity to repent and follow the Lord: the person who does not repent is presumed to be excluded from the presence of God in the life to come. Of these three types of death the most dreadful seems to be the physical kind, perhaps because of man's fear of the unknown which alone may have inspired in him the desire to somehow survive beyond the grave. Through the ages man has believed in many different kinds of immortality, the most current among which seem to be biological, influential, impersonal and personal immortality.

The idea of biological immortality resides in the hope of a 'racial' or 'genetic' continuity of oneself via one's offspring—which may explain why some parents try to force their opinions on their children: so that something of themselves may continue through the minds and deeds of their inheritors. Perhaps we can expect this idea of biological immortality, despite its egotistical base, to foster the growth of family importance in our society and counteract the spreading belief that the institution of the family is disintegrating.

The idea of immortality has a deeper and farther-reaching social impact and dimension which can be described as an extension of the individual through the ideas and thoughts of others; an "immortality of influence" is attested to by our remembrance of the great men in history (such as Socrates, Plato, Jesus Christ) and their profound influence on men of all ages, an immortality which finds eloquent expression in these lines by George Eliot:

> O may I join the choir invisible
> Of those immortal dead who live again
> In minds made better by their presence.

A third view of immortality, as being something impersonal, is much less acceptable to man because it means giving up his own individuality. This view insists that upon death the individual is absorbed into the Absolute and so absolved of mortality that there remains no memory of life as it was prior to death. Elements of this belief can be found in Buddhism in the search to become *one* with the impersonal Buddha.

The final but most important view, personal immortality, which is the belief held by Christians, affirms the continuation of the self after death. The Christian belief in eternal life is based on the personal immortality of Jesus, who suffered on the cross, died and rose again from the dead to be with God. It represents not a mere elongation of life but a continuation of a fellowship with God begun here on earth. This belief in personal immortality is held in common among Christians although opinions on the state of eternal life differ. This study *is* an attempt to understand the new approach to the old question of eternal life taken by modern Protestants.

The belief in eternal life is perhaps the best weapon humanity possesses to counteract the fear of death, yet in past ages it has been used to strike terror into the hearts of men. Among the leaders of the Reformation, for example, John Calvin believed that only a few people, an "elect," were destined to be saved while the rest of humanity were doomed to eternal damnation. And the earlier Medieval period abounds in such graphic representations as Dante's *Inferno*. From the time of the Reformation there have been adjustments in our conception of the state of eternal life but little doubt that some sort of after-life actually lay in store, the basis for this belief being Christ's own triumph over death. It was the destination of Christ's life to die and be resurrected. As Karl Barth puts it, on Easter morning our wages of sin which caused our death were paid by Jesus through his death and resurrection. Those who believe in Christ will receive God's gift of life, as promised in John 5:24:

> I tell you the truth: whoever hears my words, and believes in him who sent me, has eternal life. He will not be judged, but has already passed from death to life.

Despite this common belief, there are many differences of opinion on the state of this after-life. Will man possess a body or just be a soul or spirit? Proposed answers to these questions have differed over the years among the theologians of Protestant Christendom.

The Greeks believed that the human body and the soul would separate at death, that the body decays but the soul is eternal, a view which gave rise to the notion that the body is an impediment to the soul. The Hebrews, on the other hand, believed that the body and spirit were connected through eternity. The Christians attempted to combine in some way these two views. In doing so they laid down the following conditions:

1) the soul of each individual is created by God;
2) upon death this soul goes to a place to await judgement;
3) at final judgement body and soul are rejoined and assigned to live either in heaven or in hell through eternity.

The second condition stated above is not accepted by Protestants but is the basis of the Catholic doctrine known as Purgatory.

The question as to whether the body and soul will be united after death is a subject of heated debate. The traditional belief, as stated above, that the body and soul will be rejoined, has been advocated by St. Augustine.

Today there are still many theologians who accept this idea of a reunion of body and soul, as indicated, for instance, in the *Presbyterian*

Westminster Confession, which affirms the resurrection of the body no matter what the state.

The Union of the Churches meant universality of the mystical whole of Creation, hence of universal brotherhood. Russia was not conscious of this, but, according to Soloviev, the idea of a nation is not that which it thinks of itself in time, but what God thinks of it in eternity. This entire concept greatly influenced the Russian Catholic movement.

Soloviev's ethics is based on a religious metaphysics. Man's goal is the unification of mankind in history, the realization of the one ideal mankind. This is possible because God is the energy within man, and since God works in each individual, it follows that each has absolute value, but also that free will exists only in the irrational choice of evil. Evil is separateness—to exist is man's duty and the means to salvation.

> Society is the completed ... individual, and the individual is .... concentrated society. If we can have no absolute moral solidarity with those who have died, there can be no ground for such solidarity with those who certainly will die.

The Orthodox was influenced by the doctrine of "God—humanity" (of the God—Man as the center of Christian anthropology) and of the incarnation of the Trinitarian principle in the visible world—metaphysical and moral and social applications. Soloviev based his social outlook on the principle of the divine essence embodied in humanity and in each man in particular. He believed that man is not an ordinary being of flesh and blood, but a transcendent being, inhabited by the Trinity; he is the "otherness" of God. This concept of Christian anthropology proclaims the dignity and unique value of the human person and its sacred character. These many faceted eschatological concepts and philosophies of Soloviev are of vital perspective in order to fully understand his most basic and overriding study involving eschatology—the union of Churches which is essential in order to achieve the universal Church which is established as one of the last things of man.

Soloviev's notable words, along with his many universal concepts and philosophical views, have provided valuable insight, especially in the area of the man's eschaton to the people of the world.

Let us turn now to his last vision of the eschaton of man as he saw it before he reached his own eschaton in the Maranatha in the words of the venerable John: "For us the dearest thing is Christ ... for in Him dwells the fullness of Divinity."

III

APPROACHING the last work of Soloviev one must bear in mind that it is the work of a mature philosopher and a theologian who leaves his legacy to the world shortly before his death.

A philosopher of greater proportions ends his work with the idea of society as a culmen of his philosophical thought bringing a synthesis to his previous works which served as a preamble to his lasting vision.

A theologian does not reiterate his philosophical synthesis as his legacy to human society; he transcends his philosophy and his own system and enters into the last mysteries of God and man in the world[67] because his past philosophical process and language are not satisfactorily equipped for the question of relationship of God *over* all in order to be "all in all"—in other words, the question of relationship of the transcendence of God to his immanence. The vision in Ostia is an impressive witness to the longing of man for the transcendent God of an ever increasing immanence and self-communication. The longing of man for a *Deus absconditus* who emptied, *exinanivit,* himself in Christ and in each man in whose form God opened himself to the world, is man's *desiderium naturale.* "He (Son of God) always had the very nature of God, but ... of his own free will ... took the nature of a servant" (Phil 2:6-7). *Deus absconditus* became a visible God in Christ. God and man are over against one another *(gegenüber).* God is the All but transcending the All and in his transcendence and infinity he is the All. Thus the transcendent God *absconditus* is at the same time God immanent. Transcendence does not exclude immanence: on the contrary, transcendence includes immanence, which is fully realized in Christ: that God is not becoming God but rather God is becoming *our* God.

In the informative analytical and projective process of Teilhard's Omega point in the Incarnation, Christ, principle of all vitality, so transformed everything in his conquest that *God* shall be all in all.[68]

In Teilhard de Chardin's doctrine evolution does not cease with the appearance of man, rather it continues in the sphere of *noogenesis,* in the sphere of thought, to make man participant in the completion of the universe because man is a willing co-creator with God of the world's destiny and future. Just as the cosmos tends towards cosmo-genesis, so man *(anthropos)* in his fidelity builds from the elements of the earth a new way towards anthropogenesis as "the arrow pointing the way to the final unification of the world in terms of life."[69]

The Christ of revelation and the Incarnate Logos have the same end, dynamic, not static, moving towards the completion of maturation in the Parousia.

Vladimir Soloviev has pointed out the fundamental task of bridging the gap between the eternity of God and the eschatological course of man and his universe on different grounds.

V. Soloviev was primarily a scholar and he carried over his scholarly rigour into his philosophical investigations. The inseparability of the philosopher from the theologian is clearly evidenced in his intellectual penetration of the eschaton of man at the threshold of the third millennium. Everything in the world which is not worthy of eternity is in revolt against God and must be recognized as ontological limits of history. Even Satanism, which recalls the teaching of Gregory of Nyssa, is exhaustible. But this ontological postulate flowing from the metaphysics of total-unity is a mystery.

V. Soloviev's eschatological message to modern man and the modern Christian, summed up in *A Short Narrative about the Antichrist,* is timeless, above all in its finding a way out of many impasses, of reopening passageways of unity for an apocalyptically disturbed world.

Soloviev concludes his prophetic narrative with the decisive words of the venerable John, full of Christian hope: "For us the dearest thing in Christianity is Christ Himself—He in His person . . . for we know that in Him dwells bodily the fullness of Divinity."

This prophetic vision could be implemented with modern images and the writer may be encouraged to do so, but not the translator. Nevertheless, here too the first duty of a translator is to convey what the author wrote. It would certainly be inappropriate to give the form of the translation precedence over the meaning.

At the turn of the twentieth century Vladimir Soloviev, shortly before his death, thus prophetically envisions the eschaton in the forthcoming historical events of human society (here follows a condensed translation of Soloviev's vision of the eschaton as described in his last work *A Short Narrative About the Antichrist*).[70]

> Pan-mongolism! A mystical premonition,
> As it were, of the glorious providence of God.

The twentieth century after the birth of Christ was the period of the last great wars, and revolutions. The very greatest of foreign wars had its remote cause in the rise of Pan-Mongolism which occurred in Japan at the close of the nineteenth century. The adaptive and clever Japanese, with astonishing speed, successfully copied some forms of European culture and adopted certain European ideas of order. Having learned from news magazines and historical manuals about the existence in the West of Pan-hellenism, Pan-germanism, Pan-slavism, and Pan-islamism, they proclaimed the great idea of Pan-mongolism, (and today ideologically anticipated Pan-socialism in a new form of a global Pan-communism) i.e., the union, under their leadership, of all the peoples of Eastern Asia with the purpose of making a resolute struggle against foreign intruders (Europeans). In the beginning of the twentieth century, Europe was engaged in a final and decisive struggle with the Moslem world. The Japanese began the realization of a great plan (first, by occupying Korea and then Peiking) where, with the assistance of the revolutionary party in China, they deposed the ancient Manchurian dynasty and put in its place a Japanese. The Chinese Conservatives acquiesced with this agreement. They saw that the lesser of two evils was that blood was thicker than water and they necessarily chose in the spirit of family ties, the Japanese, as their brothers.

The government of China had not the power to hold its independence and would have unavoidably succumbed to either the Europeans or to the Japanese. But it was clear that the Japanese sovereignty, abolishing the external forms of Chinese dominion (which seemed trivial) would not interfere with the basic foundations of national life. On the other hand the predominance of European powers, which, for political reasons, supported the Christian missionaries, would have threatened the deep spiritual foundation of China. The former national hatred of the Chinese toward the Japanese developed at a time when neither the one nor the other had known Europeans, although this enmity of two racially related peoples took place in the presence of Europeans and became a mere civil dissension, losing its significance. Europeans were entirely alien, merely enemies, and their domination could in no way be flattering to racial pride. While in the hands of Japan, the Chinese saw the delightful lure of Pan-mongolism, which, moreover, in their eyes did away with the sad inevitability of European influence. The Japanese urged: "You see, obstinate brothers, that we take the weapons of the Western dogs, not from any love for them, but simply to destroy them with their own devices. If you join us and accept our practical guidance we shall soon be able not only to drive the white devils out of our Asia, but we shall fight them in their own countries and establish a real Middle Empire over the whole world. You are right in your national pride and contempt of Europeans, but it is vain to keep alive these feelings on dreams alone without a sensible action. In this we are far in advance of you and we must show you the way of our common welfare. Otherwise, see for yourselves what your policy of self-assurance and distrust of us, your natural friends and defender, has given you: Russia and England, Germany and France have almost divided you up among themselves, leaving you nothing, and all your tigerish plots show only the harmless end of a serpent's tail."

The sensible Chinamen found this sound, and the Japanese dynasty was firmly founded. Its first care, of course, was the creation of a powerful fleet and army. A great part of the Japanese force was brought to China, where it served as the nucleus of an enormous new army. Japanese officers speaking Chinese acted as instructors far more successfully than the dismissed European, while the countless populations of China, Manchuria, Mongolia and Tibet provided a sufficient supply of excellent military material. Already the first Chinese Emperor of the Japanese dynasty was able to make a successful test of the arms of the revived Empire by driving out the French from Tonkin and Siam, the English from Burma, and by including in the Middle Empire all of Indo-China. His heir (Chinese on his mother's side) united in himself both the cunning and tenacity of the Chinese with the energy, mobility, and enterprise of the Japanese, and mobilized in Chinese Turkestan an army of four million. At the time when the Tsun-li-Yamin confidentially informed the Russian Ambassador that this force was intended for the conquest of India, the Emperor appeared in Central Asia, having collected there all the inhabitants. He moved swiftly across the Ural mountains and overran with his armies all Eastern and Central Russia, while the Russian armies, mobilized in great haste, (from Poland,

Lithuania, Kiev, Volhynia, Petersburg, and Finland) were hurrying to meet them. Owing to the absence of a prearranged plan of campaign and the enormous numerical superiority of the enemy, the fighting by the Russian forces ended in a defeat with honour. The swiftness of the invasion left no time for necessary concentration, and army corps after army corps was annihilated in desperate and hopeless battles. The victories of the Mongols also involved great losses, but they easily replaced their losses, having control of all the Asiatic railways. The Russian army of two hundred thousand, for some time concentrating on the Manchurian frontier, made an abortive attempt to invade a well-defended China. Having left a part of his forces in Russia to prevent the forming of new armies in the country, and also for the pursuit of guerilla bands which had increased in number, the Emperor with three armies crossed the German frontiers. Here they had succeeded in making preparations so that one of the Mongol armies was annihilated. At this time, however, the party of a belated revanche was in power in France and a million hostile bayonets soon appeared at the rear of the Germans. Finding itself between the anvil and the hammer, the German army was forced to accept honorable terms of surrender proposed by the Chinese Emperor. The jubilant French fraternizing with the yellow men were scattered throughout Germany, and soon lost every appearance of military discipline. The Emperor ordered his soldiers to kill the allies who were no longer useful. This slaughter was carried out with Chinese punctiliousness. Simultaneously in Paris an uprising of working men *sans patrie* took place, and the capital of western culture joyfully opened its gates to the Conqueror of the East. Having satisfied his curiosity, the Emperor set out for Boulogne, where, protected by the fleet which had come from the Pacific, he speedily prepared transports to convey his fleet to Great Britain. But he was short of money and the English bought their freedom with a sum of a million pounds. In a year all the European States submitted themselves as vassals of the Chinese Emperor, who, having left a sufficient army of occupation in Europe, returned to the East, where he began preparations for a naval expedition against America and Australia. The Mongol yoke lasted for half a century in Europe. In the domain of thought, this epoch was marked by a general confusion and mutual permeation of European and Eastern ideas, a repetition *en grand* of the ancient Alexandrian syncretism. In the practical way of life, three facts became most characteristic: the great influx into Europe of Chinese and Japanese labour, and consequent on this acute social-economic problems; the series of palliative attempts to solve this question, which were prolonged by the ruling classes; and lastly the increasing international activity of secret social organizations which resulted in an organized European plot to expel the Mongols and to re-establish the independence of Europe. This colossal conspiracy, which was supported by the local national governments in so far as they could evade the control of the Imperial viceroys, was prepared in a masterly manner and succeeded brilliantly. At an appointed hour began the massacre of the Mongol soldiers and the murder and expulsion of the Asiatic workmen. In various places secret staffs of the European troops suddenly appeared, and a general mobilization took place according to a previously prepared and circumstantial plan. The new Emperor, the grandson of the great Conqueror, hastened from China to Russia, but here his innumerable hordes suffered a crushing defeat by the all-European army. Their scattered remnants returned to the interior of Asia, and Europe became free again. If the half century of subjugation to the Asiatic barbarians was the result of the disunity of the States, who thought only of their separate national interests, a great and glorious liberation was attained by the international organization of the united forces of all the peoples of Europe.

As a natural consequence of this obvious fact it followed that the old traditional organization of divided nations everywhere lost its former importance, and almost everywhere the last traces of monarchical institutions gradually disappeared. Europe in the twenty-first century presented an alliance of more or less democratic states —the United States of Europe. The progress of material civilization, somewhat interrupted by the Mongolian subjugation and war of liberation, again went forward. The problems of inner consciousness, however, such as questions of life and death, the ultimate destiny of the world and of mankind, complicated and confused by latest physiological and psychological discoveries, remained as formerly, unsolved. Only one important negative result was made clear—the absolute bankruptcy of theoretical materialism. The representation of the universe as a system of floating atoms, and of the life as the result of a mechanical conglomeration of slightest alterations of matter was a notion which no longer satisfied even a single thinking being. Mankind had forever outgrown this stage of philosophical infancy. But it was clear on the other hand that it had also outgrown the infantile capacity of a simple and unconscious belief. The idea that God created the universe out of nothing was no longer taught even in elementary schools. A certain general and higher level of representing such matters had been worked out, and dogmatism could not risk falling below it. And if the vast majority of thinking people remained entirely unbelievers, the few who believed became of necessity thinkers, fulfilling the commandment of the Apostle: be children at heart but not in your mind.

There was at this time among the few people believing in spiritual things a remarkable man—called by many a superman—who, however, was equally as far from being intellectual as from being a child at heart.

> ... and he thought of himself to be second only to God in his origin as the only son of God. In a word, he avowed that he was, in reality, Christ. But this consciousness of his supermerit, in practice, defined itself in him not as any moral obligation of his towards God and the world, but in his right and prerogative at the expense of the others, and, more than all, before Christ in particular. He had no ill feeling towards Jesus. He recognized His Messianic significance and merit, and he really saw in Him his own greater precursor. The moral grandeur and absolute one-

ness of Christ were not understood by a mind clouded by self-love. He reasoned thus: "Christ came before me; I appeared second, but that which appears later in time is, in essence, first. I shall come last at the end of history because I am the absolute and final saviour. The first Christ is my forerunner. His mission was to precede and prepare my coming."

In this sense the great man of the twenty-first century applied to himself all that was said in the Gospel about the Parousia, the Second Coming, proclaiming that this Coming is not a return of the same Christ but a replacement of the previous Christ which is final, that is, he himself.

On this point the coming man does not yet present much that is characteristic of an original feature. He regards his relation to Christ in the same way as did, for instance, Mohammed, a truthful man, whom it is impossible to accuse of any evil design.

The self-loving preference of himself to Christ was justified by this man with such an argument as follows:

"Christ, preaching and proclaiming moral welfare, was the re-former of humanity, whereas I am called to be benefactor of that same humanity partly incapable of being reformed. I shall give to all men all that is necesary for them. Christ as a moralist divided all people by the notion of good and evil; I shall unite them by blessings which are necessary both to the good and the evil. I shall be the real representative of that God who causes the sun to shine upon the good and the bad, and the rain to fall upon the just and the unjust. Christ brought a sword; I shall bring peace. He threatened the earth with the Day of Last Judgment. But I shall be the last judge, and my judgment will not be a judgment only of justice, but also of mercy. There will be justice in my judgment; not a retributive justice, but a distributive one. I shall make a distinction for all, and to everybody I shall give what he needs."

And behold, in this magnificent frame of mind he awaits some unmistakable divine call for a new salvation of humanity....

.... "It is I, it is I, and not He. He is dead, is and will ever be. He has not—He has not risen!..."

.... On the following day...having locked himself up in his own study, he wrote his famous work entitled "The Open Way to Universal Peace and Well-Being."....

.... In the second year of his reign the Universal World's Emperor issued a new manifesto. "Peoples of the earth, I promised you peace and I have given it to you...."

.... The great majority of the council, among which were included almost all the hierarchy of the East and West, were on

the platform. Below there remained only three groups, now more
closely brought together and pressing about Elder John, Pope
Peter and Professor Paul.

The Emperor turned to them and addressed them in a grieved
voice: "What more can I do for you? . . . . tell me what it is that
you value most in Christianity?" Then, like a white candle, the
venerable John arose and in quiet voice answered: "For us the
dearest thing in Christianity is Christ Himself—He in His person
. . . . for we know that in Him dwells bodily the fullness of Divinity."

This is Soloviev's prophetic eschatological answer to the persistent
question of humanity. Soloviev answered this question dramatically
at the turn of the twentieth century, four years before his death, and it
echoes his early doctrine given in his twelve lectures on God-manhood,
in the words of the venerable John, Christ is the dearest thing in
Christianity.

NOTES

[1] Joseph Papin in *New Catholic Encyclopedia* (McGraw-Hill, New
York, 1967), vol. XIII, pp. 423-24.

[2] A difference between Julian and Gregorian calendar.

[3] See Note 2.

[4] K. Mochulsky, *Vladimir Soloviev Zhizn i Uchenie* (Life and Doctrine), (Paris, 1951), p. 64 ff.

[5] Vladimir Soloviev, *Lectures on Godmanhood* (London, Dennis
Dobson, LTD Publishers, 1948). In Russian: *Sobranie Socinenij Vladi-
mira Sergeevicha Solovieva (Collected Works of Vladimir Sergeevich
Soloviev)* (St. Petersburg, 1877-84), vol. III, pp. 1-151.

[6] Joseph Papin, "Soloviev on Godmanhood" in *Almanac of Slovak in
America*, ed. Jan Okal (Chicago, 1956).

[7] V. V. Zenkovsky, *A History of Russian Philosophy* (New York:
Columbia University Press, London: Routledge and Kegan Paul LTD,
1953) p. 476.

[8] Bernhard Schultze, *Russische Denker, Ihre Stellung zu Christus,
Kirche und Papstum* (Thomas-Morus-Presse im Verlag Herder, Wien,
1950) p. 274.

[9] ibid., p. 276.

[10] Vladimir Solovyev, *Russia and the Universal Church* (Geoffrey
Bles, The Centenary Press, London, 1948).

[11] Joseph Papin, "Modern Christian Maturity of the Pilgrim in the
World: Encounter between East and West" in *The Pilgrim People:
A Vision With Hope*, vol. IV, (The Villanova University Press, 1970)
p. 13.

[12] "A Short Narrative about the Antichrist" in *Collected Works of
Vladimir S. Soloviev* (in Russian), vol. VIII, (1889-1900), pp. 556-
582.

[13] Joseph Papin, "Soloviev on Godmanhood," see note 6.

[14] M. d'Herbigny, *Un Newman Russe* (Paris, 1911).

[15] "V. Solviev, The Portrait of a Soul."

[16] V. S. Soloviev in his Letters (Pisma) III, 187, April 8, 1866: "I shall never become a convert to Latism" and after his trip to Zagreb, Coratia, he wrote Archimandrite Anthony (later Metropolitan): "I returned to Russia, if I may so express it, more Orthodox than I left." Ibid. p. 189.

[17] Cf. Brisbois' "desiderium naturale."

[18] S. Tyszkiewicz, *Moralistae Pravoslavi Russi* (Copisterie "Velox," Rome, 1935), p. 197.

[19] N. O. Lossky, *History of Russian Philosophy* (International Universities Press, Inc., New York, 1951), p. 89.

[20] Pisma (Letters), I, 171.

[21] E. Denissoff touches on this point. *L'eglise Russe devant le Thomisme*, (J. Vrin, Paris, 1936), p. 15.

[22] V. V. Zenkovsky, o.c., p. 477.

[23] "*A Short Narrative about the Antichrist*," see note 12.

[24] Joseph Papin, "Post Conciliar Perspectives" in *The Dynamic in Christian Thought* (Villanova University Press, 1970), p. 3.

[25] N. O. Lossky, o.c., p. 103.

[26] Bernhard Schultze, o.c., p. 261.

[27] D. N. Strémooukhoff, *V. Soloviev et son oeuvre messianique*, (Strassbourg, 1935), pp. 8-9.

[28] V. S. Soloviev, *Duckovniya Osnovy Zhizni (The Spiritual Foundations of Life)*, Collected Works, vol. III.

[29] ———, *Opravdanie Dobra (Justification of the Good)*, Collected Works, vol. VII (1894-1897).

[30] ———, *The Meaning of Love, (Smysl lubvi)* Collected Works, vol. VI, pp. 364-418.

[31] Joseph Papin, *Doctrina de Bono Perfecto eiusque in Systemate N. O. Lossky Personalistico Applicatio* (J. E. Brill, Leiden, 1946).

[32] Alexander V. Soloviev, *Holy Russia* (The Netherlands; Mouton & Co., The Hague, 1959), p. 58.

[33] Joseph Papin, *New Catholic Encyclopedia* (New York: McGraw-Hill, 1967), vol. VIII, pp. 104-105.

[34] Cf. Joseph Papin, Narod Supplement, Chicago, March 3, 1957, pp. 2. 11.

[35] "Sans lui cacher, et sans cacher à personne mon adhesion morale au Catholisme, ainsi que le désir exprimé par moi d'abord d'avoir les prières d'un prêtre catholique" (Fl. Delatre Etudes Bergsonnienes p. 16, Presses Universitaires de France, 1942).

[36] William R. Lemm, *The Spiritual Legacy of Newman* (Milwaukee, 1934), pp. 7-9.

[37] Vladimir Soloviev, *Russia and the Universal Church*, translated by Herbert Rees (London, Geoffrey Bles, 1948), pp. 34-35.

[38] Piero Chiminelli, *Vladimiro Solovieff* (Unitas, No. 2, 1957), p. 6. "O l'autorita vincolante della Chiesa, oppure la intellectuale o morale."

[39] "O Lord God, who has created all the orders of angels, who has stretched forth the heavens and established the earth, bring all together in unity; establish all Your chosen ones in harmony, and inspire in their hearts the word of Your hearing, so that they may bind themselves together to do what is good and pleasing to You." Quoted by Joseph Papin in the invocation at the opening session of U.S. Senate, July 9, 1963. The Senate met at 12 o'clock meridian, and was called to order by the Vice-President, Lyndon B. Johnson. Cf. Congressional Record, vol. 109, No. 103, Washington, July 9, 1963, p. 11537. (At the occasion of the Eleventh Centennial of SS. Cyril and Method.)

[40] Hans Urs von Baltasar, *Word and Redemption* (Herder and

Herder, New York, 1965), p. 18.
41 ――――, *ibid.*, p. 153; Yves Congar in RSPTh, 1949, 436, and in *Le Mystère de la Mort et sa celebration* (Paris, 1951).
42 "Christus ... cuncta examinans ... secundum ... indistinctum judicium in uno momento ..." Nicholas de Cusa, *De Docta Ignorantia*, III, 9.
43 Karl Pfleger, *Geister die um Christ ringen* (Anton Pustet), *Wrestlers with Christ*, translated by E. I. Watkin (Sheed & Ward, New York, p. 222 ff. and J. Papin in LThK (Herder), vol. III, pp. 394-395.
44 *A Soloviev Anthology*, arr., S. L. Frank, Translated from the Russian by Natalie Duddington (New York: Scribner's, 1950), p. 9.
45 V. S. Soloviev, *Justification of the Good*, in Collected Works in Russian, o.c., vol. VII, p. 273 ff.
46 Ibid., p. 281 ff.
47 Ibid., p. 194 ff.
48 Ibid., p. 404 ff.
49 Ibid., p. 418 ff.
50 Ibid., p. 77 ff.
51 Ibid., p. 421 ff.
52 Ibid., p. 673.
53 Vladimir Solov'ev, *The Meaning of Love* (London: Geoffrey Bless, 1946), p. 30, *Smysl Lubul* in *Collected Works*, vol. VI, pp. 364-418.
54 Ibid., p. 59.
55 Ibid., pp. 59-60.
56 Ibid., p. 74.
57 Joseph Papin, "Solov'ev Vladimir Sergeevich," *New Catholic Encyclopedia* (New York: McGraw-Hill, 1967), p. 423.
58 *Meaning of Love*, o.c., p. 33.
59 Joseph Papin, "Exiled Dean of Russian Philosophy Dies in Paris," *The Catholic Standard and Times* (Philadelphia, February 19, 1965), p. 5, and J. Papin in New Catholic Encyclopedia, vol. VIII, p. 1002.
60 "Serge N. Bulgakov," *Chamber's Encyclopedia*, 1950 ed., II, 670.
61 V. V. Zenkovsky, *A History of Russian Philosophy*, pp. 891-892.
62 Cf. note 60.
62a J. Papin, "Karl Kautsky" in *New Cath. Ency.*, vol. VIII, p. 137.
63 O. Cullmann, *Christus und die Zeit* (Zürich, 1946), p. 28.
64 Edward Schillebeeckx, *The Problem of Eschatology* (New York, 1969, p. 23.
65 Ibid., p. 27.
66 Ibid., p. 36.
67 Piet Schoonenberg, "Evolution and Theology" in *L'origine dell'Uomo* (Rome: Colloquio Internationale, Accademia Nazionale dei Lincei, 1973), N. 182, p. 331 ff.
68 R. L. Faricy, *Teilhard de Chardin's Theology of the Christian in the World* (New York: Sheed and Ward, 1967), p. 92 ff.
69 Pierre Teilhard de Chardin, *The Phenomenon of Man*, translated by Bernard Wall (New York: Harper Torchbooks, 1959), p. 223.
70 Vl. S. Soloviev, "A Short Narrative About the Antichrist," from *Sobranie Socinenij Vladimira Sergevitcha Solovieva*, (Collected works of Vl. S. Soloviev), vol. VIII (St. Petersburg, 1897-1900), pp. 556 ff., a condensed translation from Russian by Joseph Papin.

SELECTED BIBLIOGRAPHY

Alis, Adhemar: *The Russian Newman Wladimir Soloviev*, New York,

1933, *Thought*, v. 8.

Amerozaitis, K.: *Die Staatslehre W. S. Soloviev*, 1927.

Amfiteatroff, A.: *V. S. Sololviev, Nekrolog, Dwe Vstrechi, Tri Vstrechi, Zametchaniya i Lektsii*, Literaturnij Albom, 1907.

Augustinus: *Das Antlitz der Kirche*. Trans. by Hans Urs von Balthasar. Köln: Verlagsanstalt Benziger & Co. AG. Einsiedeln, 1942.

Astafjev, K.: *K Sporou s V. S. Solovievim, Russkij Vestnik, St.* Peterburg, 1890, v. 210.

Balishov, V.: *Vsled za Solovievym*, Slovo Istiny, 1913, January 1.

Belotsvetov, N.: *Das Raetsel von Valdimir Soloviev*, Das Goetheanum 1933.

Berdjajew, Nicolai: *Slavernij en Vrijheid*, Antwerp: Uitgeverij Pantheon N.V., Amsterdam: L. J. Veen's Uitgeversmaatschappij N.V., 1947.

————. *The Destiny of Man*. Trans. by Natalie Duddington. New York: Harper Torchbooks, 1960.

————. *O Kharaktere Rouskoi Religioznoi Mysli 19-go Veka*, Sovremennyia Zapiski, 1930, T. X211.

Berg, L. (Dr.): *Die Roemisch-katholische Kirche und die Orthodoxen Russen*.

Bezobrazova, S. M.: *Byl li V. S. Soloviev Katolikom*, Rousskaya Mysl, Moskva, 1915. *Vospominania o Brate V. Solovieve*, Minouvshie Gody, St. Peterburg, 1908.

Bokovneff, Pavel: *Die Erkenntnisstheorie Solovievs*, Der Russische Gedanke, Bonn, 1934, Ergenzungsbau, N. 3.

Bosforoff, M. S.: *Ne skelko Slov o Znatchenii V. S. Solovieva*, Vera i Rodina, 1925, Nos. 20-22 Avgust i Sentiabr.

Bulgakov, N. S.: *Chto Daet Sovremennomu Soznaniu Filosofia V. Solovieva*, Voprosy Filosofii i Psichologii, Moskva, 1907.

Butler, Chr.: *Solovief*, Downside Review, Exeter 1932, v. 50.

Chalupny, E.: *Pravny Filosofie V. S. Solovieva*, Vys Myto (s.d.)

Chulkoff: *Poezia V. Solovieva*, Voprosy Zhizni, St. Peterburg, 1905.

Dániel, Joseph: *Doctrina Posttridentina de Formatione Primae Mulieris*. Rome: Pontificia Universitas Gregoriana, 1959.

Davidoff, N.: *Iz Vospominanij o Vl. Solovieva*, Golos Minuvshego, Moskva, 1916, T. 12.

Deiner, I.: *Prorok Sv. Edinstva*, Slovo Istiny, 1914, Janvaria 1-go.

Della Seta: *Nationalismo e Cosmopolitanismo nell Etica di Vladimiro Soloviev*, Conferenze e Prolusioni, 1914.

Duddington, N.: *The Religious Philosophy of Vl. Solovieff*, Hibbert Journal, Boston, 1917, v. 15.

Engelghardt, N.: *Idealy Vl. Solovieva*, Rousskij Vestnik, St. Peterburg, 1902.

Fedotov, G. P., ed.: *A Treasury of Russian Spirituality*. London: Sheed & Ward, 1952.

Florovsky, Otets Georgii: *Novya Knigi o Vladimire Solovieve*, Izvestia Odesskago Biograficheskago Obschestva, Odessa, 1913.

Gerrard, Th.: *Soloviev the Russian Newman*, Catholic World, New York, 1927.

Gizetti, A.: *O Mirosozertzanii Vl. Solovieva*, Zavety, St. Peterburg, 1914.

Goetz, F.: *Ob Otnosheniakh Vl. Solovieva k Evreiskomu Voprosou*, Voprosy Filosofii i Psychologii, Moskva, 1904.

d' Herbigny, M.: *Vladimir Soloviev a Russian Newman*, 1918.

Hessen, S.J.: *Borba Outopii i Avtonomii Dobra v Mirovozrenii Dos-*

toevskago i Vl. Solovieva, Sovremenniya Zapiski, Parizh, 1931, T. 45, 46.

Hieromoine, Pierre: *L'union de l'Orient avec Rome*, vol. XVIII. *Orientalia Christiana* (Rome).

Iz Literatournago Proshlago, Saltykoff—Vl. Soloviev, Bulleteni Literatoury i Zhizni, Moskva, 1913.

Iz Vospominanij o Vl. Solovieve, Vestnik Evropy, St. Peterburg, 1913.

Jankelevitch, J.: *Quelques tendances de la pensée philosophique Russe, Wl. Soloviev philosophe spiritualiste et mystique*, Revue de Synthèse Historique, Paris, 1912, v. 24.

Janko, Lavrin: *Vladimir Solovyev*. Slavonic and East European Revue, London, 1930-1931, December 9th, June 10th.

Jugie, Martin: *Theologia Dogmatica Christianorum Orientalium*. Paris: Letouzey et Ané, Ed., 1930.

Kireyeff, A.: *Neskolko Zametchanij na Statyu Vl. Solovieva 'Velikji Spor'*, Moskva, 1883, Journal Rous.

Kochevnikoff, A.: *Die Geschichtsphilosophie Vl. Solovievs*, Russische Gedanke, Bonn 1930, Jahrgang I.

———. *La Metaphysique religieuse de Vladimir Soloviev*, Revue d'Histoire et de la Philosophie Religieuse, 1934, et 1935.

Koni, A.: *Vl. S. Soloviev*, Vestnik Evropy, T. I.

———. *Vl. S. Soloviev v Ego 'Na Zhiznenom Puti'.*. Revel, 1923, T. 4.

Kousmin-Karavaieff: *Iz Vospominanij o V. S. Solovieve*, Vestnik Evropy, St. Peterburg, 1900, T. 206.

Kozloff, A.: *Vl. S. Soloviev Kak Filosof*, Znanie, St. Peterburg. 1875.

Krukovsky, A. V.: *Vladimir Soloviev Kak Myslitel i Tchelovek*, 1905, Rousskij Pochin.

Lopatin, L. N.: *Filosofskoye Mirosozertzanie Vl. Solovieva*, Voprosy Filosofii i Psychologii, Moskva, 1901.

Losski, N.: *Die Lehre Wl. Solovievs von der Evolution*, Bonn, 1930, T. I.

———. *The Philosophy of Vl. Soloviev*, Slavonic Revue, V. 2, London, 1923-1924.

Lourie, Ossip: *Vladimir Soloviev*, Revue Philosophique, Paris, 1914, v. S.

Lukjanoff, S. M.: *O Vl S. Solovieve*, Petrograd, Gosud. Tipofrafia, 1921.

———. *Yunosheskij Roman Vl. S. Solovieva v Dvoinom Osvestchenii*, Journal Ministerstva Narodnago Prosvestchenia, Petrograd, 1914.

———. *Zametki o Teoreticheskoi Filosofii Vl. S. Solovieva*, Journal N. Prosvestchenia, St. Peterburg, 1909.

Maksheyeva, N.: *Vospominania o V. S. Solovieve*, Vestnik Evropy, St. Peterburg, 1910, T. 264.

Matveieff, P.: *V. S. Soloviev*, Rousskij Vestnik, St. Peterburg, 1903, T. 288.

Medvedsky, K.: *Pamiati Vl. S. Solovieva, Istoritcheskij Vestnik*, Dekabr 1903.

Milioukoff, P. N.: *Po Povodu Zametchanij Vl. Solovieva*, Voprosy Filosofii i Psychologii, Moskva, 1893.

Mochoulski, K.: *Vladimir Soloviev*, Zhizn i Outchenie, Y.M.C.A. Press, Paris, 1936.

Mokievski, P. V.: *Dobro Vl. Solovieva* Rousskoye Bogatstvo, St. Peterburg, 1897.

Morozoff, F. (Archimandrite): *Religiosno-Filisofskoie Mirovozrenia*

Vl. S. Solovieva, Warszawa, 1928.

Muckermann, Fr.: *Abendland und Morgenland bei Soloviev*, in: Stimmen der Zeit, Freiburg, Breisgau, 1924, Jahrgang 54.

Muckermann, R. P.: *Soloviev und das Abenland*, Grünewald, Mainz, 1926.

Neumann, O.: *Wladimir S. Soloviev*, Deutsche Monatsschrift, fuer Russland, Reval, 1913.

Nikiforoff, N.: *Peterburgskoye Studentchestvo i Vlad. S. Solovyev*, Vestnik Evropy, St. Peterburg, 1912, God 47, T. I.

Novgorodzeff, P.: *Ideia Prava v Filosofii Vl. S. Solovieva*, Voprosy Filosofii i Psychologii, Moskva, 1901.

O'Connor, Edward D.: *Faith in the Synoptic Gospels*. University of Notre Dame Press, 1961.

Papin, Joseph in *New Catholic Encyclopedia*, 1967
————. *Almanach of Slovak in America*, Chicago, 1956.
————. *Narod Supplement*, Chicago, March 3, 1957, pp. 2, 11.

Petrovski, A.: *Pamiati Vl. Solovieva*, Voprosy Filosofii i Psychologii, Moska, 1901.

Pogodin, A. L.: *Vl. S. Soloviev i Episkop Strosmajer*, Rousskaya Mysl, Praga, 1923-1924, Kniga 9-12.

Pypina-Lyatskaya, V.: *V. S. Soloviev Stranitchka iz Vospominanij*, Golos Minouvshago, Moskva, 1914.

R. G.: *V. S. Soloviev* Rousskij, Vestnik, St. Peterburg, 1900, T. 268.

Rachinski, G. A.: *Vzgliad V. S. Solovieva na Krasotou*, Moskva, 1901.

Radlov, E.: *Estetika Vl. Solovieva*, Vestnik Evropy, St. Peterburg, 1907, T. 243.
————. *Charakter Tvortchestva Vl. S. Solovieva*, Journal Min. Nar. Prosv., St. Peterburg, 1909.
————. *Mistitzism Vl. S. Solovieva*, Vestnik Evropy, T. 236, St. Peterburg, 1905.
————. *Sobranie Sotchinenij V. S. Solovieva*, Journal Min. Nar. Prosv. St. Peterburg, 1905, T. 6.
————. *Vl. S. Soloviev Nekrolog*, Journal Min. Nar Prosv. St. Peterburg, 1905, T. 6.
————. *Vl. S. Soloviev Zhizn i Outchenie*, St. Peterburg, Obrazovanie, 1913.

Rappoport, S. J.: *The Russian Philosopher V. Solovyev*, Contemporary Review, New York, 1913, v. 108.

Robič, Paul.: *Solovjevs Auffassung von der zentralen kirchlichen Autorität*. Rome: Pontificia Universitas Gregoriana, 1944.

Ronon, M. V.: *Vl. Soloviev, a Russian Newman*, Irish Ecclesiastical Record, Dublin, 1916, Series 5, v 8.

Rosanoff, V.: *Iz Starykh Pisem*, Pisma Vl. S. Solovieva, Zolotoe Rouno, Moskva, 1907.
————. *Ob Odnoi Osobennoi Zaslouge V. S. Solovieva*, Novy Puti, St. Peterburg, 1904.
————. *Otvet Vl. Solovievou*, Rousskij Vestnik, St. Peterburg, 1894, T. 231.
————. *Pamiati Vl. Solovieva, Mir Isskoustva*, St. Peterburg, 1900, T. 4.

Sacke, Georg: *W. S. Solovievs Geschichtsphilosophie*, Ost-Europa Verlag, 1929.

Sbornik-Pervy: *O Vl. Solovieve*, Moskva, Puti, 1911.

Sbornik Statei Pamiati Vl. S. Solovieva, Izdanie Pouti, Moskva, 1910.

Schmemann, Alexander.: "Church and State: The Orthodox Christian Experience with a View Towards the Future." *Christian*

54   THE ESCHATON: A COMMUNITY OF LOVE

Action and Openness to the World, ed., Joseph Papin, vols. II-III.
The Villanova University Press, 1970.
————. "Crisis in Orthodox Theology." *Wisdom and Knowledge:*
Festschrift in Honour of Joseph Papin The Abbey Press, 1973.
Schweigel, J.: *Die Hierarchien der getrennten Orthodoxie in Sowjet-*
russland, vol. XIII. *Orientalia Christiania* (Rome).
Sikorski, J. A.: *Nravstvennoe Znatchenie Litchnosti Vl. Solovieva*,
Rechj, 1900. Otcherk iz Voprossov Nervno-Psicho-logicheskoi-
Meditziny, T. 6.
Skobtzova, Vl.: *Mirosozertzanie Vl. Solovieva*, Parizh, Y.M.C.A. Press,
1929.
Slonimski L.: *Vl. Soloviev*, Vestnik Evropy, St. Peterburg, 1900, T.
205.
Solovyev, Vladimir S.: *La Russie et l'Eglise Universelle*, Paris.
————. *Lectures on Godmanhood*. Introduction by Peter Zouboff. Lon-
don: Dennis Dobson, LTD, 1948.
————. *Sobranie Sochinenij* Pod redaktsiej S.M. Solovieva i E. L.
Radlova. St. Peterburg, Knigoizdatelstvo Prosveshtchenia, 1911
goda. Tom 1, 2, 3, 4, 5, 6, 7,8 i 9 dopolnitelnij.
————. *Stikhotvorenia* (Poems).
————. *Pisma* (Letters) Tom, 1, 2, 3.
Spáčil, Th.: *Doctrina theologiae Orientis separati de SS. Eucharistia*,
Orientalia Christiana, 47 (Rome).
————. *Doctrina theologiae Orientis separati de s. infirmorum unctione*,
Orientalia Christiana, 74 (Rome).
Spassovich, V. D.: *Vl. S. Soloviev Kak Poublitzist*, Vestnik Evropy,
St. Peterburg, 1901, T. 207.
Strakhoff, H. N.: *Poslednij Otvet Vl. Solovievou*, Rousskij Vestnik,
St. Peterburg, 1889. T. 200.
Stremoukhoff, D.: *Vl. Soloviev et Son Oeuvre Messianique*, Paris,
1935.
Struve, P.: *Pamiati Vl. Solovieva, Mir Bozhiy*, St. Peterburg, 1900.
Szylkarski, Wladimir.: *Das philosophische Werk von Wladimir Solo-*
wjew. Krailling vor München: Erich Wewel Verlag, Druck:
Fränkische Gesellschaftsdruckerei in Würzburg, 1950.
————. *Deutsche Gesamtausgabe der Werke von Wladimir Solowjew*,
vol. II. Freiburg im Breisgau: Erich Wewel Verlag, 1957.
————. *Deutsche Gesamtausgabe der Werke von Wladimir. Solowjew*,
vol. III. Freiburg im Breisgau: Erich Wewel Verlag, 1954.
————. *Deutsche Gesamtausgabe der Werke von Wladimir Solowjew*,
vol. VII. Freiburg Breisgau: Erich Wewel Verlag, 1953.
————. *Solovievs Philosophie der All-Einheit*, Humanitariniu Mokslu
Fakultetas, Kaunas, Lietuvos Universitetas. Humanitariniu
Mokslu Fakulteto Rastai, Kaunas, 1932, vol. 9. Anhang: Wl.
Solovievs religioese und philosophische Lyrik.
Tavernier, E.: *A Great Russian Philosopher*, The Nineteenth Century,
1916.
Troisfontaines, Roger: *I Do Not Die* (New York: Descles, 1963).
Troubetskoy, S. N.: *Osnovnoye Natchalo Outchenia V. S. Solovieva*,
Voprossi Filosofii i Psychologii, Moskva, 1901.
————. *Smertj Vl. Solovieva*, Vestnik Evropy, St. Peterburg, 1900,
T. 205.
————. *K. Voprossou o Mirosozertzanii Vl. S. Solovieva*, Voprossy Filo-
sofii i Psychologii, Moskva, 1913.
————. *Kroushenie Teokratii v Tvoreniakh Vl. S. Solovieva*, Rouss-
kaya Mysl, Moskva, 1912, Janvar.

————. *Mirosozertzanie V. S. Solovieva*, Moskva 1913 Mamontov.

————. *E. L. Radlov o Vl. Solovieve*, Rousskaya Mysl, Moskva, 1913.

————. *V. S. Soloviev i L. Lopatin*, Voprossy Filosofii i Psychologii, Moskva, 1914.

————. *Zhiznennaia Zadatcha Solovieva i Vsemirniy Krisis Zhizni Ponimaniia*, Voprossy Filosopfii i Psychologii, Moskva, 1912.

Truhlar, Karel Vladimir: *Der Vergöttlichungsprozess bei Vladimir Solovjev*. Rome: Pontifiica Universitas Gregoriana, 1941.

Tzertelev, D. (Knaiz): *Pamiati Vl. Solovieva* Voprossy Filosofii i Psychologii, Moskva, 1901.

von Balthasar, Hans Urs: *A Theological Anthropology*. New York: Sheed & Ward, 1967.

————. *A Theology of History*. New York: Sheed & Ward, 1963.

————. *Prayer*. Trans. by A. V. Littledale. New York: Paulist Press, 1967.

————. *Science, Religion and Christianity*. Trans. by Hilda Graef. London: Burns & Oates, 1958.

————. *The God Question and Modern Man*. Trans. by Hilda Graef. New York: The Seabury Press, 1967.

————. *The Moment of Christian Witness*. Trans. by Richard Beckley. Glen Rock, N.J.: Newman Press, 1969.

————. *Theologie de l'histoire*. Trans. by R. Givord. Paris: Librairie Plon, 1953.

————. *The Theology of Karl Barth*. Trans. by John Drury. New York: Holt, Reinhart and Winston, 1971.

————. *Warheit: Ein Versuch*. Zürich: Verlagsanstalt Benziger & Co. AG. Einsiedeln, 1947.

————. *Who Is a Christian?* Trans. by John Cumming. London: Burns & Oates, 1968.

————. *Word and Revelation*. Trans. by A. V. Littledale with the cooperation of Alexander Dru. New York: Herder and Herder, 1964.

Vvedenski, A.: *O Mistitzizme i Krititizizme v Teorii Poznania V. S. Solovieva*, Voprossy Filosofii i Psychologii, Moskva, 1901.

Wesseling, Theodore: *Vladimir Soloviev*. The Eastern Churches Quarterly, 1937.

Winklhofer, Alois: *The Coming of His Kingdom: A Theology of the Last Things*. Trans. by A. V. Littledale. New York: Herder and Herder, 1963.

Yeltzova, K.: *Sny Nezdeshniye K 25-Oi Kontchine Solovieva*, Sovremennye Zapiski, Parizh, 1926, Kn. 28.

Z. S.: *Filosofskoe Vozrenie Vl. Solovieva*, Novy Putj, St. Peterburg, 1903.

Zdzinchovski, M.: *Le Dualisme dans la Pensée Religieuse Russse* Vladimir Soloviev, Cahiers de la Nouvelle Journée, N. 8 L'âme Russe, Paris, 1927.

Acknowledgements

Besides those mentioned in the previous volumes, I wish to express my sincere thanks to our efficient panelists: Eulalio Baltazar, John D. Caputo, Frederick E. Crowe, Edmund J. Dobbin, Avery Dulles, Edward Gannon, Monika K. Hellwig, Mary B. Mohowald, Michael J. Scanlon and Barbara E. Wall for their invaluable service to the Institute and especially to John Cardinal Krol for his gracious hospitality to our guests-speakers.

J. Papin
DIRECTOR of the INSTITUTE

On Earth as it is in Heaven -- Dynamics in Christian Eschatology

Krister Stendahl

"ON Earth as it is in Heaven: the Dynamics of Christian Eschatology." The phrase—as we all recognize—comes from the Lord's Prayer, which is perhaps the most interesting compendium or summary of Christian eschatology. And we shall give detailed attention to that very prayer. Since it has become so central a piece in the Christian life, the Christian tradition, and Christian piety, we know that eschatology is at the center. Thus I welcome the theme of this institute: The Eschaton—A Community of Love.

Actually, as a biblical scholar, I hesitate to speak about the Eschaton, for the New Testament never uses the adjective in that fashion. But there are many things in the world that are not in the Book. So we should not perhaps be too concerned about it. It is just that we have no *second* Adam in the Bible. He is called the *last* Adam. And little observations like that may help us so that we do not make into too frozen concepts what at the biblical stage is still rather playful use of words or concepts which are still in the process of forming.

There can be no doubt that the eschatological mode of thinking dominates early Christian thought. But an eschatological mode of thinking is not peculiar to Christianity, not even peculiar to Judaism and Christianity, nor is it the only way of thinking about life and the world. There are people who use the word *eschatology* so as to have it apply to absolutely everything that becomes related to things ultimate, things divine. I would rather like to define the eschatological mode of thinking—and let us not forget the speaking, witnessing, singing, dancing, and worshipping—as a habit of thought where the models of history supply the basic concepts and the basic structure to transcendence. Eschatological thinking is thus an historical mode of thinking. The historical process or the historical chain of events can then be affirmed or transcended or exploded; but the basic vehicles

by which one thinks and feels are concepts of time, so that the Greek
word *telos* always retains a connotation of time. When we say "to
what end, to what *telos?*" the ambiguity of the term is of course there:
the *telos* does not only mean *purpose,* it means *end.*

Perhaps the latest decades of biblical studies have overdone the
historical dimension of biblical thought.[1] But it is still true that most
theology in the New Testament is done by the structuring of history.
Think about Stephen's speech in Acts 7. His way of communicating
and his way of theologizing consist of a clever, anti-cultic periodization
of history. He draws the lines, he sets up the periods, he structures
history in order to make his point. The same is true with the Epistle
to the Hebrews. And I guess that Conzelmann is right after all in
saying that the same is what happens in the Gospel of Luke, as one
of its basic messages is communicated by the structuring of history.
It does not matter whether it is what the Germans call *Heilsgeschichte*
or other kinds of history. The point is that there is only one history,
God's and ours.

1) Apocalyptic thought is not an alternative, but a subtype of
eschatology. I am getting rather tired of listening to—let alone explaining—the various kinds of distinctions that are made between
eschatology and apocalypticism. There is a lot of plain apologetics out
of embarrassment with apocalyptics in such distinctions. It seems to
me that apocalyptic thought can be best understood as an intensified
and radicalized form of eschatology. Or better to say that when one
has really given up on this world and understands its situation as
totally beyond mending by tinkering, then one turns apocalyptic: "Let
this world go to pieces and let your kingdom come," as the church
prays according to the Didache. That is apocalyptic thought because
it is totally convinced that the only future is in the smashing of the
system. It is an anarchist's stance. It is one that is even similar to
the real hard-core revolutionary stance. The apocalyptic and the revolutionary both encourage things to get worse before they can get better,
see e.g. Lk 21:25-28. Apocalypticism is a kind of eschatology which
from the point of view of all kind of hope for the standing order has
gone over the deep end, as we establishment people say. And this
apocalyptic, anarchistic stance where there is no other future for this
world than its destruction, takes on, for reasons that historians can
well understand, an increasingly cosmic dimension. Frank Moore Cross
has shown how at the time of Second Isaiah, the Canaanite mythology,
so fiercely fought by Israel at an earlier stage, was now innocent enough
and not any longer a cultic threat to the life of Israel and the life of
the Temple. Hence the religious values of creation myths and divine
kingship myths and other Near Eastern myths could be used afresh and
positively so as to yield religious intensity and glory.[2]

And so the cosmic dimension of eschatology toward the apocalyptic
comes into the stream of the biblical tradition. There you are with

the whole glory of the Urzeit/Endzeit pattern: as it was in the beginning so it will be in the end. The cosmic creation motifs now come back. This is syncretism, but syncretism is a very complicated problem. My teacher H. S. Nyberg always said that any religion that is sure of itself is syncretistic, because it is not afraid to lay all kinds of thought structures under its domain. It is only during the uptight, scared periods in the history of theology that one becomes purist and afraid of what we call syncretism. In the creative periods of theology, the amalgamation, the absorbing, the claiming of new thought patterns, or of all thought patterns ready to be claimed, is a well-known phenomenon in the history of Christianity. The apocalyptic movement thus is a specific form of eschatology, intensified and radicalized. The key to apocalypticism is what I might call the anarchist's stance, or the stance of despair, as to the possibility of the mending of this world.

2) What is eschatology about? That is perhaps our most important question today at this conference. Why be concerned about the end, about where things are going? I think I am right in saying that within the whole spectrum of biblical thought, Old Testament and New Testament, the basic concern for eschatology lies in the concern for God's victory and for the vindication of those who are righteous in the eyes of God. The question of eschatology is not what is going to happen to little me—that is a Western preoccupation. Augustine, I am sorry to say in this institution, is one of the most intelligent chief sinners in turning man in on himself. As we say, he is the first one who wrote an autobiography. And narcissicism has not gone out of our Western system ever since. But glorious insights have appeared. Even so, it is important to note that biblical eschatology is not answering the question of the future of the individual but has its searchlight, its laser beam, on the question of God's victory. In more general terms, the issue is the theodicy, the question how this world, if ruled by God, is such a miserable world and how one is to understand the power of God, the almightiness of God, the promises of God, and in eschatological terms, the ultimate victory of God and the vindication of his own. That I think is what biblical eschatology is about.

Thus the question is one about the moral universe, whether the universe is a moral universe, or whether crime pays. In a way, it is the problem of Job. Even more, it is the question of Fourth Ezra, where we find perhaps the simplest expression of one of the main types of Christian eschatology and Jewish eschatology. There the question is raised about why it is that the righteous suffer and the evil are fat and happy. The answer is: I will tell you the secret. There is not one world, but two—i.e. there is no way of solving the problem within the structure of this world (7:50-51).

The vindication of the righteous is, furthermore, the root of the faith in the Resurrection, the crucial, central point in Christian escha-

tology. I think it is important to show that the origin of the idea of
the Resurrection lies in the problem of martyrdom. When resurrection
is first spoken of, there is no general resurrection, but there is the
assurance that *the martyrs* will somehow be vindicated and restored.[3]
The Resurrection is the vindication of the righteous martyr. That is
the very web out of which also Christ's resurrection has to be understood in eschatological terms. And how closely they are related you
know from that early tradition which does not quite fit into the system (Mt 27:52): On Good Friday—not on Easter day—at the earth-
quake the tombs were opened and many of "the holy ones who had
fallen asleep" rose in the cosmic event of the great vindication of the
righteous. I take this to mean that the focus for eschatological thought
in New Testament thinking, and in this case based also in the Jewish
tradition, is the question of God's victory and the vindication of the
righteous.

3) Jewish and Christian eschatology knows of two types of resurrection. There is the resurrection of only the righteous, while the rest
remain in Hades or Sheol. Nothing is said about them. They are in
non-existence. And side by side with that you have a double resurrection where everybody is raised, and some are judged, and some are
glorified. That became the mainline of the Christian tradition. But we
also have Christian texts which still retain only the vindication of the
righteous. Variations of that kind are the best tools by which to figure
out what the issue was, what the question was that had to be answered.
If the issue were to know what happens to everybody who dies, then
such a variance is unbearable, because it has to be either one way or
the other. But if the question is the vindication, then whether you do
it with a vengeance, which is really what the double resurrection is, or
if you do it without the vengeance, is a matter of style and feeling and
emphasis. So eschatology is about God's victory and the vindication
of his own.

4) Where is Jesus in all this? Did he take eschatological language
and thinking and feelings and moods and modes for granted? Did he
operate within it but really not associate himself with it in a serious
way? Was it the *lingua franca,* the *vulgata* of his time, so that we
should read his message through the eschatology, as Rudolf Bultmann,
for example, is inclined to do in a very peculiar way? For Bultmann
the meaning of eschatology is an attitude of being on tiptoes in an
existential manner; but all the rest is just scaffolding. Or should we
rather read the message of Jesus as primarily an eschatological message?
Should we see Jesus as an apocalyptic prophet? My answer to that
question will be in three parts. First, it seems clear that one of the
central messages of Jesus is that the Kingdom is at hand. Jesus speaks
to the timetable and assesses the timetable of eschatology.

Secondly, however, it is worth noting that when Jesus speaks about
the Kingdom being at hand, he sees it as an opportunity to call for

repentance. It is not a naked announcement; it is not a piece of information for its own sake. The Kingdom of God is at hand; therefore, repent. And it seems that this repentance rather than the assessment of the time is where the accent lies. In calling for repentance, in assessing the time-table, how desperate was Jesus? How apocalyptic was he? How much was he convinced that this world was totally beyond repair? That is a tricky question. And I wonder if the simple answer to the question is not: As most men, he sometimes despaired and sometimes hoped. Only pedantic scholars decide that those two things have to come from two different sources. How is that possible? Shouldn't at least Jesus know?

That leads us to a third observation. The first is that the Kingdom is at hand. The second is that it is an occasion for speaking for repentance. The third point is the most important of all when one deals with true prophets and prophets of apocalypticism and doom: A true prophet always prays intensively that he will be proven wrong. Here is the easiest way of separating the true prophets from the false ones—those who are on an ego trip—like Jonah. Isn't that what the story of Jonah is about? You remember that strange story. He prophesied doom and he called for repentance, for *metanoia,* and, lo and behold, it worked. So Jonah proved to be a fool. And he could not take that, but he sat there sulking under the plant. Now, I mean this rather seriously. I have thought about that in my courses when I come to that difficult passage in Mark 9:1 where Jesus says to his disciples that there are some of them that will not taste death until the Kingdom has come in its power. And I just cannot quite satisfy myself with that as a particular reference to Pentecost—or even to the Catholic Church. It sounds rather as if Jesus, according to that saying, expected the end of the world, the cataclysmic coming of the new age, within the lifetime of some of his followers. But perhaps Jesus was one of those prophets who in speaking about doom called for repentance, and in his love hoped that he would be proven wrong. That is a more interesting way to renew what is often despised in biblical scholarship —namely, the reference to the delay of the parousia by God's misericordia, by God's compassion. In the psychology of the true prophet, he is proven true by his sometimes successful call to repentance.

5) In eschatological thinking, history is transcended, not abolished. Now what do I mean by that? I guess I mean that eschatology is a way of dealing with transcendence, retaining the models of history, not getting nasty against history, not stepping out of it by some kind of eschatological leap, not by a via negativa, but as so often in Christian theology, by a via positiva, intensifying and thereby transcending the experiences and patterns of history. In the more general study of religion and from a phenomenological point of view, the main Christian way is exactly this—maximalizing and thereby transcending, as over against the spiritualizing tendency. There are both tendencies.

There are both possibilities. I have thought about this often in the very obvious sense in which, for example, Christian theology relates to sacrifice. The Jewish tradition took hold of the needs and patterns of sacrifice inherited from times immemorial. There is a way of saying that sacrifice is an ugly thing, a way of thinking that is not commensurate with the nature of God or the sane handling of man's religious life. Or one spiritualizes "sacrifice" to the utmost. But in Jesus Christ, the sacrifice, the gory, ugly earthiness of sacrifice is instead taken up and transcended as is perhaps best expressed in the Epistle to the Hebrews, but also in the whole mainline of the expression of Christology in sacrificial terms. So it is also with eschatology in relation to history. When one thinks about eschatology, one uses the patterns of history and pushes them to a point where they are transcended but not abolished. This tendency, this non-spiritualizing tendency, I would call by the inverted words of our title for today: In Heaven as It Is on Earth. That is to say that the earthly patterns and earthly experiences are projected into heaven in an unabashed way; in an unabashed way which will always irritate the spiritualists.

That is one way in which biblical language retains its mytho-poetic, its poetic character. I have always loved to think about heaven as a city of gold, the city of gold and pearly gates and a lot of angels around. Some people feel that we should rather speak about the existence beyond existence in existing non-existent existence. Or something that sounds a little more reputable. The only trouble with such abstract language is that some people in the church might get the idea that we are really transcending the imagery and saying how it really is, which we can't. Abstract imagery is only duller than concrete imagery. But both are imageries.

6) This observation is very important for the understanding of eschatology. Eschatological language is a playful language, it is a metaphorical language, the base metaphor being history. We apply the metaphor of history and transcend it. How ugly and how dangerous this can be can be exemplified in a passage which I love and hate; and that is the end of the Twelfth Chapter of Paul's Epistle to the Romans, in which we are instructed by no less than the Apostle Paul —the writer of the love hymn in First Corinthians 13—that when we are persecuted or wronged, then we should not seek our own vengeance. But we should leave the vengeance to the Lord; for, says Paul, if your enemy is hungry give him to eat, and if he is thirsty, give him to drink. And in so doing, you are collecting coals of fire on your enemy's head.[4] Augustine was bothered by this one. In so many other respects, he was the first western man, as I have said, with all the needs and instincts of the Western Christian. So he managed to come up with some exegesis so that he could get out of the ugliness of the situation. But there is no doubt that what Paul really says here is consistent and continuous with the very ugly thought

which can be well-documented from the Manual of Discipline from Qumran. The thought is this: With the atomic blast around the corner, the Christian should not pursue the enemy with his own little toy gun. He does as Jesus is said to have done in First Peter: When reviled, he does not revile in turn. But he leaves his case in the hands of him who judges justly (2:23).

I am sorry to tell you and myself that this is not really love. This is non-retaliation combined with a perfect hatred of God's enemies. This is one of the "less attractive" sides of eschatological thought. It is well covered over in the tradition, because the Gospel writers are the civilizers of the radical teaching of Jesus; just as Josephus was the civilizer of the Essene sect. The passage I am referring to in the Manual of Discipline (1QS 10.17-20) describes also these covenantors out in the wilderness as those who hold their hatred "in secret," not warning their oppressors so that perchance they might repent. We can compare this with 2 Macc 6:12f. Here God tells Israel that the trouble they have had was a sign of mercy, because by trouble they have been warned toward repentance; while the fat-eyed enemies run to their destruction unwarned. So the Qumranites kept their hatred secret, piling up coals of fire on the enemies. It is striking that when Josephus describes exactly this their attitudes—and he writes, as you know, to the Romans in order to give a good picture of the moral quality and standards of the Jewish nation—he describes them as "righteous controllers of wrath, being masters of their temper, champions of fidelity, very ministers of peace," (Wars 8:6). That sounds rather nice. And has it ever crossed your mind that there is only one passage in the New Testament where it says love your enemies, and that is in the end of the Fifth Chapter of Matthew in the Sermon on the Mount: You have heard that it was said to the men of old love your neighbor but hate your enemy; but I say to you, love your enemies . . . Otherwise, the hotter the love language becomes in the New Testament, the more that love is confined to the brethren. And the climax is reached in the First Epistle of John which is soaked in love in all kinds of directions—God's love for us, our love for God, God's love for Christ, Christ's love for God, our love for the brethren—love is pulsating in the whole blood system. But you read that Epistle and you will find very clearly that there is no love spilling outside the community, at least not consciously. This whole conference is going to end up with "the community of love" by anticipatory eschatology or something, and rightly so. Even so, in that passage of love, love your enemies, I have an eerie feeling that Matthew (5:43-48) again has civilized pretty crude eschatological language. You know how it goes. It speaks of how the Lord lets his sun rise over both the bad and the good and lets it rain over both the righteous and the unrighteous. So you should also be *teleioi*, which can be translated you should also be *end-minded*. You should also keep your eyes on the coming of the

Kingdom, although we usually translate it *perfect,* and it can have
that meaning also. If you really think about what that might mean,
is it not rather similar to that idea that God does not warn the evil
ones? The sun goes up over both good and bad ... so the evil ones
are not warned. And yet there will come a day of reckoning when
there will be a difference between those who are equally treated with
the glorious sunshine and the gracious rain. Now we should not shrink
away from the starkness of eschatological thought because it is really
very much part and parcel of early Christian life.[5]

As we deal with such thinking we must remember that the enemies
here spoken of are not *"my* enemies." It does not have to do with the
kind of thing which we hear about in Mt 5:23-26: When you come
to the altar and remember that your brother has something against
you ... That is not an "enemy," that is a "brother"; and I find
that very interesting. As a matter of fact, we cannot find a single
passage in the New Testament where the world "enemy" is used for
a fellow Christian. Enemies are the enemies of God; the enemies
are the suppressors and oppressors of the world. It is not the question
of feeling, but it is the question of how in the drama and the tragedy
of the world God's justice will finally come true. And within that
setting this eschatological thought says: don't seek your own vengeance,
because, as we say in Swedish, it is pathetic to hear mosquitoes cough.
Don't seek your own vengeance, but leave it in the hands of God.
Paul summarizes his thinking in Romans 12:21: "Be not overcome
by evil, but overcome evil by good." Paul has no illusions that the
goodness of the Christians will "change the world" or have much
impact on the cosmic drama. But he urges a stance of non-retaliation.
Christians are called to be an agent of God's vengeance. By doing
good, they leave room for God's judgment, God's victory, the victory
of goodness. Evil cannot drive them into retaliating "in kind," but
it drives them into kindness.

7) The hot eschatological material in the Sermon on the Mount is
one of the most significant sources for our understanding of early
Christianity. We are most fortunate in having it preserved by the
faithful Matthew. It is most interesting, however, that Matthew has
preserved this "hot" material in "cool" form. Here he has similarities
to his contemporary Josephus. We mentioned how Josephus presented
the hot eschatological stance of the Qumranites in a most civilized
manner, having it sound most attractive to his Roman audience. The
"practitioners of concealed hatred" turned into "masters of temper"
and "ministers of peace." In Matthew the eschatological intensity of
the received material seems to be presented as examples of a superior
ethic, superior especially to the Jews in the synagogue across the street,
whose achievements of righteousness, i.e. ethical achievement, are
found wanting and superficial (Mt 5:20).[6]

8) Even so, the material is there; and when read in a hot eschato-

logical key, we find here that the disciples of Jesus are given the Messianic License. By that I mean that they are given permission to practice the life-style of the Kingdom in a world that is not yet ready for such living. They are allowed to live "on earth as it is in heaven." When they turn the other cheek, they certainly undermine the established order. When they practice celibacy (Mt 19:12), they de facto break the commandment of procreation. But they are allowed to do so "for the Kingdom's sake." So close is the Kingdom that it is now permissible to live "on earth as it is in heaven."

It is important to note that such behavior is not commanded; it is *allowed* for those who find themselves called to such action. We have here an invitation to and a license for eschatological living. The Catholic tradition recognized this by its distinction between the commandments and the evangelical counsels. That was a sound insight. But when that distinction became institutionalized in monasticism, and by the distiction between "religious" and "secular," much of the dynamics of this eschatological urge was lost.

If I were to modernize the issue here at hand, I would say that the messianic license—the Operation Headstart for the Kingdom—has something to do with "the fear of precedents." It has been my experience, especially as an administrator, that often a group of people see quite clearly what love and compassion demands; but then someone raises the question: What if this action we consider became a precedent? And right then and there the spirit evaporates and the compassion cannot be afforded and we stay with defending status quo.

In such situations, we can sudy the dynamics of the Messianic License. It means the permission to be less afraid of the precedent. For the Kingdom is at hand. But just as we said about Paul's thinking in Rom 12:21, so also here. There is no illusion that acts of love or self-denial performed for the Kingdom's sake would impress the world or change its course very much. Such acts are performed because we have to do so, driven by our eschatological urge, heightened by Jesus. But the world is not ready yet. Hence it will not be impressed. It will rather accuse us of unrealistic idealism or romanticism or of being revolutionaries or anarchists.

9) This dynamic of eschatology is a central theme in Paul's thinking and experience. He is constantly reminding his congregations that he and they still live in a fallen and unredeemed world. He and they still groan with the enslaved creation (Rom 8:22); and the fact that "we have received the Spirit" does not change that fact. He describes the Christian as one who *has* died with Christ and *will* be raised in due time. In the certainly Pauline epistles, the resurrection and the salvation is always future (cf. Col 2:12, 3:1). He is afraid of those who think that the eschatological drama has proceeded further than it actually has. That fear is what dictates his discussion of resurrection in 1 Cor 15. Here he criticizes those Christians who think that the

resurrection has happened already (cf. 2 Tim 2:18, and Justin's Dialogue 80).

We could even say that he is criticizing the main tendency of the Gospel of John. For in John the eschatological timetable has been collapsed and the eternal life is already here through faith: Jesus says to Martha: "I am the Resurrection and the Life. He who believes in me will not ever, ever die" (11:25-26). And "he who hears my word . . . has eternal life and does not come to judgment but has transferred from death to life (5:24)."

In this Johannine way of thinking, the tension between the "now" and the "then" has been translated into a timeless tension between the quality of eternal life and the inferiority of a hostile world. Paul recognizes this type of thinking as dangerous to the eschatological tension. He is afraid of an implicit feeling of spiritual superiority. He stresses instead the "not yet." To him the Kingdom is future and only so can he preserve the dynamics of eschatology. That is also why he stresses his weakness as the trait in his life which he wants his congregations to emulate (e.g. 2 Cor 4:7-16, 13:4). To him the "Johnnine" theology has great dangers of triumphalism.

10) If we accept such distinctions within New Testament thought, we may ask who is right. But I would rather suggest that there are situations and perhaps even periods in the history of the church when one of those emphases is the one most needed. The hermeneutical question then is: Are we more in the danger of triumphalism—or of using the *theologia crucis* as an excuse for our lack of faith. Let each person answer for himself. But it could be suggested that the weak and the suppressed and oppressed, those without power, are entitled to triumphalism, while the strong certainly do not need it. For them the Pauline gospel is *the* gospel. And that is not so strange, since Paul fought all his life with his arrogant ego. He knew he was great and outshining all others in insight and theological acumen . . .

In the Old Testament, we note that Israel is named "chosen" when beleaguered. But when its chosen status gives it excuses from judgment, the prophet Amos tells the people that they will not be given preferential treatment on the day of judgment. The Day of the Lord will be darkness rather than light (5:18). And so God uses his grace to equalize the power of the beleaguered lest they be overcome by despair. He throws his weight on the side of those who hunger and thirst for justice, those who are poor in spirit and body, the meek and the persecuted. They are declared "blessed" (Mt 5:3-12).

And so we are back almost where we began, in the Sermon on the Mount. That is where we find the Lord's Prayer. That prayer is the most concentrated expression for the eschatological dynamics of Christianity. For in its original setting, it must be seen as a cry for the coming of the Kingdom. Through usage, and partly through translations, it has lost much of its stark eschatology. But I would like to end by rendering a paraphrase that captures what I consider the original intentions and connotations of that prayer. In so doing, I find myself summarizing my whole topic: On Earth as It Is in Heaven: The Dynamics of Christian Eschatology.[7]

> O Father of us who follow Jesus
> Let that day come soon when the whole creation honors You as God. Let your Kingdom come.
> Let your plan of salvation and liberation[8] be realized also on earth as it is now in heaven where Christ sits on Your right side ready for the judgment.[9]
> Let us already here and now take part in the Messianic Feast.[10]
> And forgive us what we have done wrong to our brothers and sisters, as we have forgiven[11] what they have done wrong to us—
> For only the mutually forgiven community can celebrate that anticipatory banquet.
> And do not bring us to trials beyond our capacity, but supply your emergency exit.[12]

NOTES

[1] Krister Stendahl, "The Role of the Bible in the Theology of the Future" in *The Dynamic in Christian Thought*, vol. I, ed., Joseph Papin, (The Villanova University Press, 1970) pp. 44-51.

[2] "New Directions in the Study of Apocalyptic," *Journal for Theology and the Church* 6 (1969). The whole volume deals with "Apocalypticism" and is of much significance.

[3] On these matters, see G. Nickelsburg, "Resurrection, Immortality, and Eternal Life in Intertestamental Judaism." *Harvard Theological Studies* 26 (1972).

[4] For an exegetical discussion, see K. Stendahl, "Hate, Non-Retaliation and Love," *Harvard Theological Review* 55 (1962), 343-55.

[5] Sammy K. Williams (*Jesus Death as Saving Event*, Harvard University Ph.D. Thesis, 1972) has recently shown conclusively how this motif of God's leaving the sinners and/or Gentiles unpunished also solves a classical exegetical problem. For it is within such a pattern of thought that Rom 3:25-26 can be best understood. Here Paul states how God's new act of salvation in Christ contrasts with how God in his restraint *(anoche)* had left unpunished *(paresis)* the previous sins.

[6] For more detailed discussion and references, see K. Stendahl, *The School of St. Matthew*, 2nd ed. (1968), pp. xi-xiv.

[7] For a more detailed argument, see K. Stendahl, "Prayer and Forgiveness," *Svensk Exegetisk Aarsbok* 22/23 (1957/58) pp. 75-86. The article is in English.

[8] God's will is not his commandments that we should obey but his intentions of salvation.

[9] Cf. Acts 3:21.

[10] Cf. Mt 8:11, Lk 13:29, 22:28. The Greek word *epiousios* (KJV, etc.: "daily") clearly means "anticipatory," "the bread of the future," "the bread for tomorrow." This alternative was known to the Fathers, but they consciously avoided that understanding.

[11] So in all the best manuscripts, instead of "as we forgive." cf. Mt 5:24.

[12] For this non-heroic stance, see 2 Cor 11:32-33. For "emergency exit," see Paul's word *ekbasis* in 1 Cor 10:13.

The Church as Eschatological Community

Avery Dulles

A DECADE AGO, Emilien Lamirande remarked that the problem of the relationship between ecclesiology and eschatology has thus far "occupied an exteremely restricted place—lest we say none at all—in scholarly theology, at least in the manuals."[1] In large measure this generalization still holds true. The considerations set forth in the following pages will therefore of necessity take on the character of somewhat tentative gropings rather than that of a finished product. The subject is all the more intriguing because of its elusiveness.

The term "eschatology" in the title plunges us immediately into ambiguities. To what theory of eschatology do we subscribe? Are we "realized eschatologists," convinced that the eschaton has in fact been brought by Jesus Christ, or do we hold, with the futurists, that the eschaton will not arrive until history comes to a close? Or do we accept an intermediate "both-and" position; namely, that the eschaton has initially broken into history with the event of Jesus Christ, but that it will not be complete and manifest until the final consummation? On this last theory one might still inquire about the relationship between the partially realized eschaton now within history and the final realization to which we still look forward. Is the latter the natural outgrowth of the former, or does it require a new and discontinuous intervention of God, determined simply by his own free choice?

Each of these types of eschatology brings with it a distinct vision of the Church. A fully realized eschatology would best harmonize with the doctrine that the Church as we experience it is already the eschatological community. An exclusively futurist eschatology, on the other hand, would imply that the Church as we know it cannot be eschatological except insofar as it preaches and looks forward to the coming consummation. If, finally, the eschaton is already partly realized, the Church may best be conceived as the place where the provisional divine

69

irruption into human history is confessed and celebrated, and where men strive to subject themselves more perfectly to God's lordship in Jesus Christ. According to the way in which one conceives the relationship between the partially and finally realized eschaton, one will have a different view of the status and mission of the Church. When the heavenly consummation comes, will the Church be carried forward into the divine glory, or will it be dissolved and replaced by the Kingdom of God? Must the Church on earth wait passively for God's free decision to bring history to a close, or does it play an active role in bringing about the advent of the "new heavens and the new earth"?

In order to approach these questions with a firm basis in Scripture and tradition we shall, in Part I of this paper, survey the New Testament data and the history of Christian theological views. Then in Part II we shall approach the questions more thematically.

PART I

1. NEW TESTAMENT

To avoid preempting the subject matter of another paper in this series, I shall omit the question of Jesus' own eschatological thinking. It may be enough to quote the opinion of Jeremias: "The only significance of the whole of Jesus' activity is to gather the eschatological people of God."[2]

In their discussion of the Church, the New Testament writers agree that it belongs to the end-time, but they have different points of view regarding its relationship to the consummation. The early chapters of Acts represent the Church as an eschatological reality within historical time. Peter is portrayed as claiming that the Pentecostal outpouring of the Spirit on the disciples is the fulfillment of Joel's prediction concerning the messianic age (Acts 2:14-36). The signs and wonders in the Church are seen as the immediate prelude to the final consummation. The earthly Church is thus the dawning of the final Kingdom. Possessing the Holy Spirit, it has within itself the anticipation of the end. In Acts 20:32 Paul is represented as telling the elders of Ephesus that God's grace is at work building up their community so as to give them "the inheritance among all those who are sanctified."

In the letters of Paul, the "Church of God" is seen not simply as a continuation of the Old Testament qahal, passing through the earthly desert, but as an anticipation realization of the assembly of the saints existing in the court of God (cf. Dan 7:27, Ps 89:6-8, Wis 5:5, etc.). The Christians as saints are chosen to have a share in God's power of judgment even over the angels (1 Cor 6:1-3). Already here on earth God has transferred us to the Kingdom of his beloved Son and has qualified us to share in the inheritance of the saints in light (Col.

1:12f.). Relying on texts such as these, Prof. Harald Riesenfeld has shown that Paul, building on the doctrine of Dan 7:27 concerning the saints of the Most High, regards the Church primarily as the eschatological community.[2a]

In the Pauline Captivity Epistles, which represent the high point of New Testament ecclesiology, the Church is seen as a reality that already exists with a certain density and stability on earth, but which also looks farward beyond historical time to its own final consummation. According to one image, the Church is a living and growing Temple, the "dwelling place of God in the Spirit." Of this Temple Christ Jesus is the main cornerstone, and upon him the entire structure must be aligned (Eph 2:20-22). According to another image, closely intertwined with that of the Temple, the Church is the body of Christ. The gifts of the Spirit are virtually at work in this Body causing it to "grow up in every way into him who is the head, into Christ. . . ." (Eph 4:15). For Paul, one may say, the transcendent arrival of the Kingdom will not destroy the Church but rather will consecrate and complete its development.[3]

The ecclesiology of Hebrews is founded not on the image of the Body or Temple but rather on that of the People of God. The author insists that in Christ God has established his new covenant, rendering the Mosaic covenant with all its ordinances obsolete (ch. 8). The people of this new covenant must practice patience and perseverance as they live in exile among trials and persecutions, "for we have here no lasting city, but we seek the city which is to come" (13:14). Allready here on earth Christians belong to the heavenly Jerusalem and to the "assembly (Church) of the first-born who are enrolled in heaven" (12:23). They are hastening to the goal of the Sabbath rest (ch. 4). Thus in Hebrews one finds essentially the same elements as in Acts and Paul, but with different emphasis. The accent in Hebrews is less on what God has already done for the Christian community, more on what he has promised to do.

Apocalyptic expectation dominates several of the New Testament ecclesiologies, including First Peter and, even more, the Apocalypse. "The theme of the eschatological community of salvation not only stands at the beginning and end of the Apocalypse, but also constitutes the center of its composition."[4] The letters to the churches in the opening chapters of the Apocalypse refer frequently to the necessity of patient endurance until the Lord returns. The true Temple, the city of God, and the new Jerusalem are eschatological realities to which the Christian still looks forward in hope. "He who conquers, I will make him a pillar in the temple of my God; never shall he go out of it, and I will write on him the name of my God, and the name of the city of my God, the new Jerusalem which comes down from my God out of heaven" (3:12). The Apocalypse closes with the climactic vision of the final consummation in which the glorious Church is depicted under the images of the holy city, the new Jerusalem coming down out of heaven from God, and the bride adorned for her husband (Apoc 21:2, 9-10). The ecclesial character of the heavenly Jerusalem in these passages is undeniable, for we read, "the walls of the city had twelve foundations and on them the twelve names of the twelve apostles of the Lamb" (Apoc 21:14). Thus we may say that according to the last book of the Bible the Church on earth is a token of that to which we look forward at the end-time; it is a community of hope that does not yet enjoy, except in anticipation and in promise, the blessings of the messianic age. The perspective of the Apocalypse is thus quite different from that of Acts and even from Paul, who speaks frequently of the gift of the Spirit as the first fruits (*aparchē*, Rom 8:23) and the earnest (*arrabōn*, 2 Cor 1:22, 5:5) of the life of glory. For the Apocalypse the blessed are those who have endured trial upon earth and have arrived at the heavenly rest (Apoc 14).

Summarizing the New Testament vision as a whole, one may say that the Church on earth possesses only the down payment of the Holy Spirit; it will not fully enter into the Sabbath rest until the parousia. But at that time the children of God who are dispersed will be gathered into perfect unity, and that which is present in a mysterious and hidden way in the Church will at length become manifest. The true and ideal form of the Church will then be achieved; the Church, purified through judgment, will then be fully justified in its witness and in its work. It will proclaim with one voice the glory of God and of the Lamb[5]

2. THE PATRISTIC AND MEDIEVAL PERIODS

A T the dawn of the Patristic era the Church was seen as being essentially ordered towards its consummation in the realized Kingdom. This eschatological orientation is clearly attested in the *Didache*. At the consecration of the bread the community is bidden to pray:

> As this broken bread was scattered over the hills and then, when gathered, became one mass, so may Thy Church be gathered from the ends of the earth into Thy Kingdom. For Thine is the glory and the power through Jesus Christ forever.[6]

The celebrated communion prayer of the *Didache* is still more evidently eschatological:

> Remember, O Lord, Thy Church, deliver her from all evil, and perfect her in Thy love, and from the four winds assemble her, the sanctified, in Thy Kingdom, which thou has prepared for her. For Thine is the power and the glory for evermore.[7]

The same eschatological inspiration penetrates the eschatology of

the *Shepherd* of Hermas. Commenting on this work, a modern scholar
writes: "In Vision III and Similitude IX the Church is represented
under the form of a tower under construction. It is not yet finished,
and will not be until the last day, at the time of the Parousia, which,
moreover, is imminent. This Church will be the society of saints;
it is an eschatological reality."[8]

To trace the relationships between ecclesiology and eschatology in
the various writings of the Fathers would be a complicated task, far
exceeding the possibilities of this essay. It may be permissible, for
present purposes, to concentrate on Augustine of Hippo as the theologian who investigated this theme most profoundly. Augustine preserves a dynamic tension between recognizing the present value of the
Church, as a place where the Lordship of Christ is provisionally realized, and a futurist orientation, which stresses the disparity between
the tribulations of the pilgrim Church and the blessed repose of the
heavenly kingdom. While the reign of Christ is still in some sort
present in the Church, a vast distance separates the *ecclesia qualis nunc*
from the *ecclesia qualis tunc,* the Church in this present age ("in hoc
saeculo," or "huius temporis") from the Church of eternal life ("ecclesia vitae aeternae").[9] Although in this present state of exile, we dwell
in tents, still we have a share in the reign of Christ.

In the view of some modern scholars, such as Dietrich Ritschl and
Rosemary Ruether,[10] Augustine unduly diminished the eschatological
tension by identifying the visible Church too closely with the Kingdom
of God. Others, however, holds that "With the whole ancient Christian tradition, he [Augustine] is convinced that the community in the
process of gathering by no means represents the future Kingdom of
God."[11] For a balanced position that seems to do justice to both aspects
of Augustine's thought, one may quote Ernst Bloch:

> *Civitas Dei* is an ark and often a mere catacomb, hiding over and
> over; it will not be revealed till the end of what has been history
> thus far. Which is why even the Church is not wholly identical
> with the City of God, at least not since its right to forgive sins
> has been extended to mortal sins, including (since the Decian
> persecution) even apostasy, and it has thus come to comprise a
> rather mixed group. Only as *corpus verum,* as the number of the
> elect, is the Church entirely *civitas Dei;* the existing Church, the
> *corpus permixtum* of elect and of sinners, is not identical with it,
> only bordering upon it as a preparatory stage. The existing Church
> is identical, however, with Augustine's millennium, as the first
> awakening, the first resurrection before the second, definitive one
> (Rev 20. 5f.).[12]

Although modern exegesis does not follow Augustine in his identification between the age of the Church and the millenium of the
Apocalypse, his views concerning the "time of the Church" in many

ways foreshadow those of modern proponents of salvation history. At
the conclusion of a searching comparison between Augustine and Cullmann, Lamirande maintains that of all the ancient doctors Augustine
is the best equipped to assist us in our rediscovery of the eschatological
dimension of the Church. In the view of Augustine, he writes:

> To speak of the eschatological character of the Church is to affirm
> with him that the Church is inconceivable except in relationship to
> the return of Christ, the resurrection of the flesh, and reunion with
> the angels—but also that the messianic blessings are already present
> in germ and that the Kingdom has been inaugurated. We live,
> if not in the 'last times,' at least in the period that precedes them.
> The Church is the Kingdom in its initial phase and we enjoy its
> blessings, but with a precarious claim on them and under veiled forms.
> The messianic times have begun, but the present Church is not the
> Kingdom in its fullness; it is not the term but the last stage, the
> sixth age of the world before the eternal Sabbath. It is the people
> of God on the march toward the definitive and plenary possession of
> the Promised Land. Hence it has an essentially 'tendential' and
> incomplete character.[13]

If Augustine is compared with the New Testament and even with
the *Didache,* it seems fair to say, with H. Richard Niebuhr, that the
concept of the *regnum Dei* has been made more teleological and has
in fact been subordinated to that of the *visio Dei.* The central concern
is with the beatific vision as something to which we are tending, rather
than with the sovereign initiatives of the God who powerfully estab-
lishes his reign. The entire middle ages, influenced by Augustinianism,
will be impressed by God's changeless perfection rather than by his
freedom and power. God is represented as being at rest and man
as in movement toward him.[14]

The early middle ages, in the Latin West, is dominated by the Augustinian vision of a Church that is primarily heavenly, but exists already as an anticipatory realization of the City of God within history.
In this view, the heavenly Church is no mere appendage of the earthly.
On the contrary, the Church is defined from above downward. It is
the heavenly Jerusalem that descends toward earth, but is never present
in its fullness here below. The sacramental symbol and the heavenly
reality to which it points are not separable; together they make up a
single whole.[15]

The seventh century Councils of Toledo express in very typical
form the medieval concept of a Church that is at once heavenly and
terrestrial. In the decrees of the sixth Council of Toledo (A.D. 638)
we read:

> We believe also that the holy catholic Church—without spot in its
> reality (*in opere*) and without wrinkle in its faith (*in fide*) (cf.
> Eph 5:23-27)—is the body of Christ Jesus and will possess the

Kingdom with its all-powerful head when this corruptible nature has put on incorruptibility and when this mortal nature has put on immortality (cf. I Cor 15:53), so that God may be all in all (*ib.,* 15:28). By this faith hearts are purified (cf. Acts 15:9), by this faith heresies are extirpated, and in this faith the whole Church glories—both as situated in the heavenly Kingdom and as still dwelling in the present world—and there is no salvation in any other faith, 'for there is no other name under heaven given among men by which we must be saved.[16]

For all his emphasis on the pilgrim status of the Church, Augustine and his followers never lose sight of the mysterious presence of eternity within time. It is of the very nature of time, Augustine holds, to be fragmented and thus remote from the concentration of eternity. On the other hand the time of the Church is the locus where grace shines through, manifesting itself to the eyes of faith. "The constantly self-realizing point of intersection between transient time and salvation time causes the duration of the Church to appear as an ever-present dramatic event which, precisely because of the indwelling of the eternal in it, can never be seen as a whole."[17]

This Augustinian sense of the mysterious presence of eternity in the heart of time was intensified in medieval monasticism. Augustine's ecclesiology of charity became in Bernard of Clairvaux an ecclesiology of the mystical life. The monastery as conceived by Bernard is a place where men enjoy on earth, in company with the angels, the blessed citizenship of heaven. The nuptials of the Lamb for Bernard are not exclusively reserved, as perhaps they were for Augustine, to the consummation of all things. In Bernard's mystical theology the soul that is spiritually united with the Word becomes, even here on earth, the Spouse of Christ. According to Yves Congar,

> The association of angels and men is less eschatological in St. Bernard than it was in Augustine: it achieves itself strictly in the Church at present. The mystery of the Church appears as lived par excellence in the monastic life, and the angels are, so to speak, inserted in it. To us it seems scarcely doubtful that these themes of Bernard, whose influence was vast, contributed to blur the differences, already unclear in Augustine, between the Church and the City of God. They favored the development of the idea, already present in Augustine, that the City of God achieves itself in the historical and earthly Church.[18]

Even in the lifetime of Bernard, another development was occurring which contributed in a very different way to the de-eschatologizing of the Church. The preachers of the Crusades, including Bernard who preached the second Crusade (1146), depicted the earthly Jerusalem as a focus for the life here below. Gradually the life of the Church here on earth began to achieve a certain autonomous consistency. About the middle of the twelfth century one begins to encounter in several authors the term "ecclesia militans," which designates a unit distinct from, although totally relative to, the *ecclesia triumphans* for which it is a preparation.[19] But the change of perspective is important. In place of the one Church, some of whose members are still in exile and on pilgrimage, the authors of this period speak almost as if there were two churches, face to face with each other. The order of consideration, moreover, is reversed. Instead of defining the earthly Church in terms of the heavenly, theologians begin to define the latter in terms of the former. The way is thus prepared for thinking of the heavenly goal as a mere reward for a life well lived, as an item in the list of "last things" to which the Christian may look forward if he wishes to speculate curiously on the blessings of the world to come.

The treatise on the Church, as a special discipline in theology, began to take shape in the later middle ages in answer to movements such as Gallicanism, Conciliarism, and the spiritual ecclesiology of Wyclif and Hus. To these considerations was subsequently added the need to reply to the denials of Protestantism, secularism, and Modernism. Shaped by the exigencies of controversy, ecclesiology became almost exclusively concentrated on defending the Church as a system of hierarchical meditation; it became, in Congar's famous term, "hierarchology."[20] The manuals and tracts of this long period, stretching from the fourteenth century into the twentieth, dealt by preference with institutional elements, and most of all with the primacy and powers of the Roman see. Even where some attention was given to the laity, as in Bellarmine's *Controversia de Ecclesia militante,* the Church was regarded almost exclusively as a visible society in this world, parallel to the secular state. Viewed as institution *(Heilsanstalt)* rather than as community *(Heilsgemeinschaft),* the Church was defined in terms of the threefold deposit of faith, sacraments, and ministerial powers. These means of grace, at least as we know them, were given to the Church only for its functioning in the present life. Thus concentration on these features inevitably tended to crowd out the idea that the Church is, in its deepest reality, and eschatological entity. If ecclesiology had continued to look upon the Church primarily as a community of persons, the idea of the heavenly Church might not have receded so totally from view.

Not surprisingly, the same period that saw the juridicizing of ecclesiology witnessed also the individualizing of eschatology. Compared with the early medieval councils of Toledo, mentioned above, the later medieval Councils (such as Lyons II and Florence), as well as the famous constitution "Benedictus Deus" of Benedict XII (A.D. 1336),[21] practically eliminate the social aspects of salvation. Beatitude came to be considered as consisting essentially in an individual encounter between the separated soul and God, a naked vision of the divine essecne. Neither the humanity of Christ nor the society of other men seemed capable of playing any intelligible role in this encounter; they belonged at most to the "accidental" aspect of beatitude—an addendum which might be admitted but was quite unnecessary. Only by the sheerest of metaphors did it seem possible to designate the aggregate of blessed souls as a community or "ecclesia."

3. MODERN PROTESTANT THEOLOGY

WHILE Roman Catholic ecclesiology was being increasingly juri-dicized, liberal Protestant theology became moralized. The eschatological teaching of Scripture, for Kant, was a purely symbolic portrayal of the ideal to be approached through the practice of pure rational religion. The Kingdom of God established itself invisibly within the souls of those who followed the precepts of pure reason. The true Church was viewed as an invisible community of persons obedient to the categorical imperative. The Church as an external visible organization, in Kant and his disciplines, came to be regarded as a merely sociological entity, devoid of theological interest.

"In the neo-Kantian theology of Albert Ritschl," according to Rose-mary Ruether, "this interpretation of the Kingdom of God as a this-worldly moral kingdom of the brotherhood of men, which was ad-vancing to an inevitable victory through the progressive forces of history, established itself in the heart of the new liberal orthodoxy itself."[22] In this theology the Kingdom of God was secularized by being severed from its ecclesiastical encasement and detached from the supernatural expectation of the second coming.

In twentieth century Protestant theology this Ritschlian conception of the Kingdom of God as a moral order to be realized within history met with strong opposition from New Testament scholars. Johannes Weiss, in his study of *Jesus' Preaching of the Kingdom of God* (1892) opened the bombardment by demonstrating that the ethico-religious use of the concept of the Kingdom in modern theology is totally un-justified in appealing to the gospels, where the term designates an absolutely supra-worldly factor standing in total contrast to every institution within history.[23] For Albert Schweitzer, likewise, "Jesus' eschatology and the existence of the Church stood in absolute separa-tion and opposition."[24]

Accepting the results of Weiss's and Schweitzer's eschatologism, and combining it with the existential dialectics of Kierkegaard, Bult-mann proposed a new eschatological vision of the Church. For him eschatology has to do not with the ultimate future of man and the world, but with the presence of eternity. "Jesus Christ is the eschato-logical event not as an established fact of past time but as repeatedly present, as addressing you and me here and now in preaching."[25] "Every instant has the possibility of being an eschatological instant and in Christian faith this possibility is realized."[26]

From this existential point of view, Bultmann can strongly affirm that the Church, although it looks forward to no future consummation at the end of history, is nevertheless an eschatological reality. "Like the word itself and the apostle who proclaims it, so that Church where the preaching of the word is continued and where the believers or 'saints' (i.e., those who have been transferred to eschatological existence) are gathered is part of the eschatological event."[27] "For the Church is the eschatological congregation of the saints whose identity with a sociological institution and a phenomenon of the world's history can be asserted only in terms of paradox." [28] Bultmann, therefore, seeking to safeguard the eschatological character of the Church, practically denies that it is a visible social and corporate community.[29]

Karl Barth, who began with an existential philosophy similar to Bultmann's, gradually combined this with a more incarnational view of history. In his earlier writings Barth stressed above all the difference between the Church, as a visible society of men here on earth, and the Kingdom of God, which is inseparable from God's eternity. Between time and eternity there could only be an unbridgeable gap, an "infinite qualitative difference." Barth's later work, however, increasingly stressed the fact that the guilt is, in some sort, miraculously bridged from God's side. The Church may therefore be described as "the existential form of the Kingdom of Christ in the interim between the Ascension and His second coming."[30] The *basileia* is paradoxically present in the Church, notwithstanding the Church's weakness and failures. The task of the Church, until the parousia, is to provide a credible representation of the eschatological community.[31]

The relationship between time and eternity, between history and the eschaton, is not for Barth one of simple succession. The end of history, in his view, "does not mean the termination of the historical process, as though calendar time should one day stop and leave eternity by itself, thereby annihilating all history. Time is not dissolved by eternity, but it is marked by it as finite, and this is a great difference.[32]

This qualitative understanding of the relationship between time and eternity enables Barth to speak in very positive terms about the eschatological character of the pilgrim Church. In the period between the Ascension and the Parousia, the eschaton is present as an inner moment of time itself—the eternal in the temporal, the divine in the human. In this perspective the Church may be called "the eschatological fact par excellence."[33] Returning to a more Augustinian vision than has been current since the middle ages, Barth looks upon the heavenly Church as the center and presupposition of the earthly:

> The *ecclesia militans* and the *ecclesia triumphans* are not two Churches but one Church.... Always and everywhere the Church exists in these two dimensions.... The *ecclesia triumphans* is 'with Christ' (Phil 1:23). With Him, the Head of the body, it takes part

in the glory which is still hidden from the *ecclesia militans.* But for that reason it can never be far from it. Christ Himself is not far from it. As the heavenly Head of His whole body on earth He is in the midst of it. And with Him the *ecclesia triumphans* is also with it and in the midst of it.... Therefore the Church which was and the Church which will be will still be the one Church. 'All live unto Him' (Lk 20:38): not only on that side, but on this; not only on this side, but on that. And because they live in Him, they are one community.[34]

Oscar Cullmann, following a path similar to Barth's, returns, on the basis of biblical exegesis, to a basically Augustinian view. For him the Church possesses the blessings of the messianic period in a provisional and tendential way. The Spirit has been given to the Church as a pledge and foretaste of the kingdom to come. Within history, the Church is the point where the Kingdom of Christ becomes visible and the center from which that Kingdom spreads outward. On several points, however, Cullmann differs from Augustine. He accepts the Barthian distinction, unknown to the Fathers, between the Kingdom of Christ (to be realized within historical time), and the Kingdom of God (an object of eschatological hope). Further, as already mentioned, Cullmann rejects the Augustinian identification of the age of the Church with the millenium. Like other contemporary theologians, he is on guard against what he calls a "Catholic absolutizing of the period of the Church."[35]

In the World Council of Churches considerable attention has been given to the relationship between the Church and the eschaton. Edmund Schlink, one of the leading theologians of the ecumenical movement, gave important addresses on this subject to the Faith and Order conference at Lund in 1952 and to the Second Assembly of the World Council of Churches at Evanston in 1954.[36] The Lund Conference, in its final report, clearly affirms that the union between Christ and the Church will be consummated when, at the end of time, Christ comes to meet his Church. But even in its present condition, the report goes on to say, the Church is an eschatological reality:

Through the indwelling of the Holy Spirit the new age of the future is already present and through union with the risen Christ the Church on earth is already given to participate in the power of the resurrection. The Church of Jesus Christ in history is at once the congregation of sinners and the new creation, for although it continues to live and work within the brokenness and estrangement of this world and to share in its divisions, the Church belongs essentially to the new age and the new creation. As such the Church is summoned to perpetual renewal, to put off the old life, and by the renewal of its mind to be conformed to Christ, looking beyond its historical forms to the full unveiling of its new being in the coming Lord.[37]

The Evanston Assembly likewise asserts the essentially eschatological nature of the Church. "In all the Church's life there is being manifested not simply the activity of mortal men, but the life of the whole
Church, militant on earth, triumphant in heaven, as it has its unity
in the one Lord of the Church, who is its life."[38] With regard to the
divisions of the Church, the Assembly takes consolation in the fact that,
from an eschatological perspective, they may be seen as merely provisional. "It is certain that the perfect unity of the Church will not be
totally achieved until God sums up all things in Christ."[39]

This last statement gave rise to remonstration on the part of the
Orthodox delegates. "The 'perfect unity' of Christians," they asserted,
"must not be interpreted exclusively as a realization at the Second
Coming of Christ. We must acknowledge that even at the present age
the Holy Spirit dwelling in the Church continues to breathe in the
world, guiding all Christians to unity. The unity of the Church must
not be understood only eschatologically, but as a present reality which
is to receive its consummation at the Last Day."[40]

4. VATICAN II

WHILE Protestant theology has sometimes tended to minimize the
value of the earthly Church, with its attributes of unity, holiness, catholicity and apostolicity, Roman Catholicism, in modern times,
has so concentrated on the earthly Church as to neglect the end-time.
Since the Councils of Toledo in the seventh century, the doctrine of
the heavenly Church all but disappeared from official ecclesiastical documents, and indeed from the works of private theologians, until Vatican II effected a remarkable reversal.

The original schema of the Constitution on the Church, presented
to the Fathers at the first session in 1962, contained no treatment of
eschatology. This omission evoked protests from several Fathers, including Cardinal Frings and Bishop Hermann Volk. Pope John
XXIII, more concerned with worship and piety, directed Cardinal
Larraona, Prefect of the Congregation of Rites, to prepare a text on
the veneration of the saints to be included in the Constitution on the
Church.[41] As this text was woven into the document, it developed
into the present Chapter VII, entitled, "The Eschatological Character
of the Pilgrim Church and her Union with the Heavenly Church."
Paolo Molinari has well said: "It is one of the outstanding merits of
this chapter to have offered, for the first time in the history of dogma,
a full and organic exposition of our union with the Church in heaven
and to have placed it in its proper Christological and ecclesiological
setting."[42] The eschatological dimension of the Constitution on the
Church was further strengthened by some alterations in Chapter I,
including the addition of article 5, which deals with the Kingdom of
God.

In its final form, *Lumen gentium* clearly teaches that the Church on earth is totally ordered toward the final Kingdom to be established at the eschaton. "Its goal is the kingdom of God, which has been begun by God himself on earth, and which is to be further extended until it is brought to perfection by Him at the end of time."[43] The Church on earth "strains toward the consummation of the kingdom, and, with all her strength, hopes and desires to be united in glory with her King" (*LG* 5, p. 18). As yet the Church is distant from her goal. On earth she is in exile (*LG* 6, p. 19; *LG* 14, p. 32). She has here no lasting city, but she seeks one that is to come (*LG* 44, p. 75). In the final Kingdom, the Church will achieve her glorious fulfillment (*LG* 2, p. 15), she will attain her full perfection (*LG* 49, p. 78). Thus there will be in heaven a consummated Church, the Church of heavenly glory. All the just will be gathered with the Father in the universal Church (*LG* 2, p. 15). This final gathering of the people of God will include many who, as yet, have not come to know Christ. (*LG* 69, p. 96).

The Church on earth is related to the heavenly Church in hope and desire (*LG* 5, p. 18). But its relation to the final goal is not merely passive. It prays and labors that the whole world may become the People of God, the Body of the Lord, the Temple of the Holy Spirit (*LG* 17, p. 36f.). All members of the Church, including the laity, are called to spread and intensify the Kingdom of God in the initial form in which it exists in this world. Inspired by the vision of the final Kingdom—a kingdom of truth and life, holiness and grace, justice, love and peace (*LG* 36, p. 62), Christians seek to animate the world with the spirit of the beatitudes, and to be signs and witnesses of the resurrection (*LG* 38, p. 65). In a special way the religious state foretells the resurrection and shows forth the power of Christ the King, wonderfully at work in the Church (*LG* 44, p. 75).

The Church does not simply bear witness to the Church or point to it as something absent. In the Church the Kingdom of Christ is already present in mystery (*LG* 3, p. 16). By its unity the Church is already a harbinger of the peace of Christ (*LG* 13, p. 32). In the holiness of the Church the final age is already anticipated in some real way (*LG* 48, p. 78).

The relationship between the Church on earth and the heavenly Church is not simply that between a real society and an anticipated goal. The heavenly Church already exists in the saints, and especially in Mary, in whom the Church exists without spot or wrinkle (*LG* 65, p. 93). Mary is the "image and first flowering of the Church as it is to be projected in the world to come" (*LG* 68, p. 98). Between the brethren in heavenly glory and those still laboring on earth there exists an intimate fellowship in charity (*LG* 51, pp. 83-84), so that the wayfarers and those who already sleep in Christ are united in the Holy Spirit to constitute a single Church (*LG* 49, p. 81). The present fellowship in cult and charity is a foretaste of the liturgy of consummate glory, when the splendor of God will brighten the heavenly city and the Lamb will be the lamp that enlightens it (*LG* 51, p. 84).

The Constitution on the Church does not attempt to set forth the meaning of the eschatological consummation in the categories of modern thought—a task that would call for considerable efforts on the part of systematic theologians. The Constitution, moreover, restricts itself to the ecclesiological aspect of eschatology; it does not treat, except in passing, of the eschatological consummation of the entire cosmos, a theme discussed more directly in the Constitution on the Church in the Modern World. If one bears in mind the limits which the authors set themselves, certain criticisms that have been made regarding the eschatology of *Lumen gentium* lose much of their force.

For further insight into the doctrine of Vatican II on our theme, attention would have to be given to the Constitution on the Liturgy,[44] the Decree on Ecumenism,[45] the Decree on the Missionary Activity of the Church,[46] and, most importantly, the Pastoral Constitution on the Church in the Modern World.[47] We shall touch on each of these four documents very briefly.

The Constitution on the Liturgy views the Church as a Temple still in the process of being built until Christ's full stature has been achieved (*SC* 2, p. 138). It finds in the liturgy a foretaste and pledge of the heavenly Jerusalem toward which we journey as pilgrims (*SC* 8, p. 141); it views the Lord's Supper, in particular, as a "proclamation of Christ's death until he comes" (*SC* 6, p. 140, cf. 1 Cor 11:26) and as a pledge of heavenly glory (*SC* 47, p. 154).

The Decree on Ecumenism shows a profound appreciation of the manner in which an eschatologically oriented ecclesiology makes it possible to achieve better relations with the separated Christian churches. It sees the ecumenical activity of Christians not simply as a method of relating the existing churches to one another, but as a way of contributing to the fullness with which Our Lord wishes his body to be endowed as it grows toward its final perfection (*UR* 3, p. 346; *UR* 24, p. 365). The Decree reflects an appreciation of the fact that none of the churches, in its present institutional form, adequately embodies the blessings that Christ intends for his Church.

The Decree on Missionary Activity, consistently with this approach, views the apostolate toward the unevangelized as a means whereby the Church advances toward the time of completion and grows to the mature measure of the fullness of Christ (*AG* 9, p. 596). In an official footnote the Decree refers to the opinion of Origen that the gospel must be preached to all the notions before the final consummation can come *(ibid.)*.

In the Pastoral Constitution, *Gaudium et spes,* similar principles are applied to the relationship between the Church and the modern world. The first draft of this Constitution, according to Father Barnabas

Ahern, labored under excessive dichotomies between the spiritual and the material, the sacred and the secular.[48] Cardinal Meyer of Chicago, in an intervention of Oct. 20, 1964, objected: "Nowhere does the schema explicitly propose that element of Christian revelation which dispels every kind of false dualism: namely that the entire world is not only the means by which redeemed mankind perfects itself but it is itself—just as our bodies are—an object of redemption."[49] In the revised schema, this defect was remedied. As a result, the Constitution goes far to overcome the common impression that the Church's ministry to the secular needs and concerns of mankind is secondary or incidental or one that must be subordinated to the Church's primary and essential task, which is to prepare men for eternal happiness. Rather, the Constitution teaches that the Church's service toward mankind in this life is an integral part of its labor for the final Kingdom. The body of the new human family grows here on earth; the Kingdom is already present here in mystery—and it is the same kingdom as that which will flower when the Lord returns in glory (GS 39, p. 237).

Underlying all these conciliar documents is the idea of the Church as sacrament of universal salvation. The Church is not the final Kingdom, but it is a true anticipation of this, and everything that authentically expresses the Church is a sign of the Kingdom that is to come. The Kingdom is a universal one that knows no divisions of race or color; hence the Church too must strive to become universal in actual fact.

5. SINCE VATICAN II

SINCE Vatican II the eschatological point of view has so strongly established itself both in Roman Catholic and Protestant theology that the necessity of defining the Church in terms of the final kingdom of God is scarcely contested. This may be illustrated on the Roman Catholic side from Hans Küng, Karl Rahner, Edward Schillebeeckx, and Johannes Metz, and on the Protestant side from Wolfhart Pannenberg and Jürgen Moltmann.

Hans Küng, in his major work, *The Church*, devotes a chapter to the theme, "The Eschatological Community of Salvation." In this community, he asserts, the coming of Jesus is recognized as the decisive eschatological action of God.[50] Several pages later he writes:

> For this Church—and here all parallels with later Judaism and with the Qumran communities break down—the decisive eschatological turning-point has already begun with Jesus the Christ. The promises of God have been fulfilled, his faithfulness affirmed: 'But when the time had fully come, God sent forth his Son' (Gal 4:4). The eschatological time of salvation has begun and will soon be consummated. This eschatological period between fulfilment which has come and consummation which is to come is the

temporary, interim period of the Church. It is precisely its expectation of the coming parousia which unites the Church and gives
it its distinctive form. Precisely because the Church confesses Jesus
as Lord, it has confidence that the Lord himself during this interim
period will lead the new community and with it the world to its
predestined goal. Hence the Church from the very beginning saw
itself as an eschatological phenomenon.[51]

Karl Rahner, in an important article on "The Church and the
Parousia of Christ,"[52] describes the Church as the eschatological salva-
tion-community which lives off the confidence that God has completely and irrevocably given himself in Christ, although the fullness of the
Kingdom is still to be awaited. Thus the Church is eschatological not
only in the sense that God has definitely established it in Christ but
also in the further sense that it is totally oriented toward the absolute
future. "The essential nature of the Church," writes Rahner, "consists in pilgrimage towards the promised future."[53]

Edward Schillebeeckx takes a similar position. "The Church on the
way," he writes in his book, *God the Future of Man,* "is not yet the
kingdom of God. She proclaims it, and it is only in this way that she
is permitted to anticipate, in a specific manner, the kingdom of God
whose powers are already actively effective in her and in the world."[54]

Johannes Metz, our fourth witness, stresses the interaction between
Church and world, as both move toward the promised future of God:

> The Church is not Non-World (*Die Kirche ist nicht Nicht-Welt*).
> For it is *that world* which attempts to live from the promised
> future of God, and to call *that world* in question which understands
> itself only in terms of itself and its possibilities. The decisive
> relationship between the Church and the world is not spatial but
> temporal. The Church is the eschatological community and the
> exodus community. Its institutional and sacramental life is based
> on this eschatological character. The Eucharist is the sacrament
> of the Exodus....[55]

In its new eschatological emphasis, Roman Catholic theology has
advanced in step with recent Protestant theology, especially in Germany.
Particularly important for this development has been the theologians
of hope, Wolfhart Pannenberg and Jürgen Moltmann. Pannenberg
insists that the Church, since it lives totally through Christ as the presence of God's future with men, must strain towards the ultimate consummation:

> Theology is challenged by the sad appearance of the empirical
> Church as a hangover from another historical period. The appro-
> priate response to this challenge is to be found in a new emphasis
> upon the Church as an eschatological community pioneering the
> future of all mankind.[56]

Moltmann, who stands at the center of the new movement of hope
theology, is strongly critical of the individualism that would depict
man's faith-relationship to God exclusively in terms of an inner spiritual relationship and would radically demythologize the futurist eschatology of the New Testament. In the concluding chapter of his *Theology of Hope,* entitled "Exodus Church," Moltmann seeks to restore
the biblical emphasis on the future expectation of the Church for a
renewed society in a renewed cosmos. He writes:

> It is generally recognized today that the New Testament regards
> the Church as the 'community of eschatological expectation,' and
> accordingly speaks of the gathering in and sending out of the
> community in terms of a horizon of eschatological expectation....
> This eschatological orientation is seen in everything from which and
> for which the Church lives....[57]

After substantiating this statement by some consideration of the
word of God, the Holy Spirit, baptism, and the Lord's Supper, Moltmann concludes: "Thus Christianity is to be understood as the community of those who on the ground of the resurrection of Christ wait
for the kingdom of God and whose life is determined by this expectation."[58]

On the basis of assertions such as those here quoted from leading
Roman Catholic and Protestant theologians of the past decade, we
may, I think conclude that there is a widespread consensus that Barth
was correct in his declaration that the Church is "the eschatological
community par excellence." It is generally agreed that the Church
cannot correctly be defined or understood without reference to the
eschatological Kingdom of God. But within this basic agreement there
are sharp differences of opinion as to how the relationship between
the Church and the eschaton is to be conceived. Some of these dis-
agreements will be considered in Part II of this paper.

PART II

1. HERMENEUTICS AND ESCHATOLOGY

THE eschatological nature of the Church cannot be adequately discussed in isolation from the problems surrounding eschatological
assertions in general. What do we really know about the "last things"?
The traditional Christian ways of speaking about the end-time are
strongly influenced by the language of the Bible; Church pronounce-
ments and theological speculations have not been able to escape from
their dependence on the biblical starting point. In the Bible, however,
the future is described in parabolic terms, through poetic images such
as Christ's coming on the clouds of heaven, the sounding of trumpets,
the general conflagration, and the opening of graves. These images are
rich, appealing, and suggestive. The poetic style of presentation appeals

to the heart and imagination; it grasps the whole man. But the truth-content is difficult to pin down. If one attempted to take all the figures literally, one would fall into self-contradiction. How, for instance, could those who are "like the angels of heaven" (Mt 23:30) sing hymns (Apoc 19)? How could those who have "spiritual bodies" (1 Cor 15:44) feast at the marriage supper (Mt 22:1-14)? How could the holy city come down as a bride adorned for her husband (Apoc 21:2)? Obviously the metaphors have to be unraveled, but in unraveling them we seem to strip them of their power. And we are faced with grave uncertainties as to how to draw the line between the literal meaning and the metaphorical dress. If we are not to be committed to an illusion, we seem to require some key for unlocking the reality-content of the images.

Several modern authors have correctly, in my opinion, proposed a Christological starting point.[59] The Christian faith stands or falls with the assertion that God has definitively and unsurpassably given himself to man in his Son, Jesus Christ. Jesus, therefore, is in some sense the end; in him the eschaton has already come. God's salvation is already given to man in Christ, though only in an inchoative or anticipatory way. The expected future, therefore, must be the completion of the realized present. As Karl Rahner puts it, "The *Sitz im Leben,* the setting of eschatological knowledge, the real original source of eschatological assertions is therefore the experience of God's salvific action on ourselves in Christ. It may be said in general that the event of revelation, the action of God on us in history, is the experience of his action on us in the grace of Christ."[60] Eschatological knowledge therefore reaches us under the form of the action that God has already begun in us—an action that tends dynamically to a fulfillment and thereby brings with it an obscure but genuine knowledge of the fulfillment to which it tends. The eschatological assertions of the Bible, therefore, take the form of a projection or extrapolation into the future of that which is contained in the revealed present. Eschatology, as Rahner defines it, is the opposite of apocalpytic—and by apocalyptic he understands an interpolation of the future into the present.[61] To interpret the eschatological assertions of Scripture as if they were descriptions of future phenomena, therefore, would be to mistake them for apocalyptic. While the sacred writers may not have consciously distinguished between these two modes of speech, the systematic theologian, proceeding from dogmatic Christological principles, seems to be justified in so doing.

The Christological principle just considered may easily be extended so as to yield an ecclesiological principle. The Church, insofar as it is a community gathered in the name of Christ, consciously experiences the saving grace of Christ. The eschatological character of that grace confers an eschatological character on the Church itself. It is a community that tends in hope and expectation toward the consummation of the supernatural life that brings it into being. As a community of grace, the Church obscurely experiences by anticipation the communal salvation toward which it aspires. The content of the Church's hope must therefore be the consummation of that communal grace which already sustains and animates it during the time of its earthly pilgrimage.

In eschatology one may fruitfully apply the "threefold way" excogitated by the medieval scholastics for speaking about God—the *via causalitatis,* the *via negationis,* and the *via eminentiae.* In the first place, we must affirm of the eschaton whatever is already present in a participated way in the earthly life of the Church as a source of its joy, vitality, and hope. The final Kingdom must therefore be viewed as one of life, peace, joy, and mutual sharing of the divine blessings. But there is also an element of negation: we must purify these notions of the limitations we experience in them by reason of our present condition of "exile from the Lord." Many of the most powerful biblical eschatological statements are negative. "We impart a secret and hidden wisdom of God ... 'What no eye has seen, no ear heard, nor the heart of man conceived, what God has prepared for those who love him ...'" (1 Cor 2:9). "He will wipe away every tear from their eyes, and death shall be no more, neither shall there be mourning nor crying nor pain any more, for the former things have passed away" (Apoc 21:4). As Rudolf Otto points out in his classic analysis of the element of the *fascinans,* we commonly read statements of this sort without adverting to their entirely negative character.[62] Though their language is negative, they unaccountably succeed in conveying a positive impression, for they are read against the background of an unthematic, numinous contact or encounter with the God who gives himself to us in love.

This "negative theology" of the eschata therefore blends imperceptibily into a theology of "eminence." The metaphors express what is in a superabundant way—whether formally or virtually—present in the fulfilled Kingdom. When we read that every tear will be wiped away, we are to understand a total satisfaction that leaves no room for sadness. Though we cannot grasp the positive content of that bliss except through remote analogies, we may rely on what is positively signified by the concepts of a meal, a wedding, a hymn of joy, a splendid vision of sparkling jewelry. These images serve a purpose similar to that which Plato assigned to myth—to convey something sufficiently like the reality so that we are not misled by acting as if the images were exact descriptions.[63]

2. THE SURVIVAL OF THE CHURCH

THE venerable doctrine of the *ecclesia triumphans* is by no means obsolete. The faithful of many denominations cherish the familiar hymn, "The Church's One Foundation," including the stanza,

'Mid toil and tribulation,
    And tumult of her war,
She waits the consummation
    Of peace forevermore;
Till with the vision glorious
    Her longing eyes are blest
And the great Church victorious
    Shall be the Church at rest.

In some contemporary theology, however, this notion of the "victorious . . . Church at rest" is unacceptable. It has become common, within the past decade, to describe the Church as a merely provisional earthly society, and to deny that it will remain in existence once Christ has returned to establish the final Kingdom. Pannenberg, for instance, affirms that "Christ points the Church towards the Kingdom of God that is beyond the Church."[64] "Indeed," he writes,

it is quite possible to conceive of the Kingdom of God without any Church at all. The Kingdom of God is that perfect society of men which is realized in history by God himself. In Revelation, Saint John the Divine envisions a society in which there is no need for church or temple.[65]

In a similar vein the contemporary Catholic theologian, Hans Küng, warns against the specter of an *ecclesia gloriae*. In contrast to the hymn we have quoted he affirms quite starkly, "The Church is called to pilgrimage, not to rest."[66] Amplifying this statement, he draws a series of sharp antitheses between Church and Kingdom:

While ekklesia is something essentially of the present, something finite, basileia is something which, although it has irrupted into the present, belongs fundamentally to the future. Ekklesia is a pilgrimage through the interim period of the last days, something provisional; basileia is the final glory at the end of all time, something definitive. Ekklesia embraces sinners and righteous, basileia is the kingdom of the righteous, of the saints. Ekklesia grows from below, can be organized, is the product of development and progress and dialectic, in short is definitely the work of man; basileia comes from above, is an unprepared action, an incalculable event, in short is definitely the work of God.[67]

These statements, although they can easily be paralleled by others in contemporary Protestant and Catholic theology, cannot be taken as irrefragable. The biblical foundation for this position is insecure. As we have seen, many of the biblical images of the Church—such as people of God, body of Christ, heavenly Jerusalem, the Spouse of the Lamb—apply equally well, and in fact better, to the time of final consummation. The Temple in Pauline theology is likewise something that becomes complete only when salvation history comes to a close. As for the statement in the Apocalypse that there will be no temple in the heavenly Jerusalem (Apoc 21:22), it seems to mean only that there will be no temple other than Christ in whom the saints will continually worship the Father. It does not deny that the saints themselves, assembled in praise, will constitute an ekklesia.

For many of the Fathers, the term "church" applies more properly to those who are gathered with Christ in heavenly glory than to those who are still living the diaspora existence of pilgrims here on earth. Hilary, for example, sees the Church as a communion of saints that reaches its perfection at the end-time. Thus he can refer to the Church, "whether in the sense of that which exists now or of that consisting of saints which will be hereafter."[68] We have already seen how Augustine, followed by the early Councils of Toledo, adopts the same point of view. Throughout the middle ages the notion of the *ecclesia triumphans* remained prominent.

In the twentieth century, these eschatological conceptions of the Church have once more come into favor. Vatican II states unequivocally that the Church "will attain here for perfection only in the glory of heaven."[69] On the Protestant side, Karl Barth speaks freely of the *ecclesia triumphans*,[70] and Edmund Schlink asserts that in the last judgment, Christ will save, perfect, and glorify the Church.[71] At the Evanston Assembly the World Council, in its majority report, spoke of the life of the whole Church as being militant on earth and triumphant in heaven. The Orthodox delegates at Evanston, while they protested that the unity of the Church is not merely eschatological, did not call into question the notion of the eschatological Church.

The dispute between those who define the Church as an essentially this-worldly entity and those who regard it as primarily celestial is partly, no doubt, a matter of terminology. All parties agree that some aspects of the Church, as we now know it, will pass away. These are, in brief, the elements that pertain to the Church as a community on the way to salvation and as an institution designed to lead man to that goal. The heavenly Church—in the minds of those who accept the concept—can hardly be called a means of grace; it will not have the functions of preaching the word, teaching doctrine, sanctifying the faithful, or issuing pastoral directives. Anyone who defines the Church essentially in terms of these institutional features will have to say, under pain of inconsistency, that the Church will be abolished at the eschaton.

It must, however, be asked whether the Church ought to be defined primarily or essentially in terms of these functions. Such an understanding of the Church, I should say, seems overly restrictive; it seems to misplace the accent, even as regards the Church on earth. Scripture and tradition, for the most part, depict the Church primarily as a community of salvation; they present its structural features in subordination to its communal aspects. If the Church is seen primarily as a people, a community of grace, we shall have to say that it by no means ceases to exist at the end of time; rather, it then becomes more Church than it ever was.

The modern tendency to look upon the Church essentially as an institution or as a means of grace stems, apparently, from late medieval and early modern dualistic thinking. The theology of this period tends unduly to juridicize society and to individualize salvation. In order to correct this twofold exaggeration, it seems important to emphasize the community aspect of man's religious relationship to God, both here and hereafter.

In a brief but important article, Rahner calls attention to the way in which modern spiritualizing piety has neglected the abiding importance of the humanity of Christ for the spiritual life of Christians. In this modern view, he points out, little importance is attributed to the glorified humanity of Christ, in particular as regards the life of the blessed. In the average theological treatise on the Last Things, Rahner observes, there is hardly a word about the Word as incarnate. "Is not rather everything swallowed up by the *visio beatifica,* the beatific vision, the direct relationship to the very essence of God which is indeed determined historically by a past vent—namely the event of Christ— but which is not *now* mediated by Jesus Christ?"[72] In opposition to this trend Rahner rightly asserts that the humanity of Jesus is the permanent gateway through which everything created must pass to come to God, for the personal Absolute can be found only in Him in whom dwells the fullness of the Godhead. If our religious acts are to reach God, they must have an incarnational structure mirroring God's own mediating activity.

If we consider now that the Church is the body of Christ, and that together with its head it makes up the whole Christ, we shall be led to affirm not only the incarnational but also the ecclesial character of our ultimate salvation. Blessedness will be seen as God's gift to the entire community, and to individuals in their capacity as members of the community of God's people. They will find God not simply in himself, but in Christ and in one another. All will mutually share the joy they experience, and will rejoice in each others' joy.

Will there be sacramental life in heaven? Generally this is denied. We are told that the economy of the sacraments will cease, for we shall have clear and open access to the reality which the sacraments obscurely represent. We shall not need the sacraments, it is said, for they are means of grace, and in heaven the goal itself, divine life, will be irrevocably ours.

There is a sense, to be sure, in which sacraments will cease. The eschatological tension[74] signified by the sacraments as we know them will be resolved. There will no longer be that discrepancy between *sacramentum* and *res,* between sign and saving reality, which renders the sacraments as we know them ambiguous. On earth we can never be sure that the saving reality is present where the sacrament is externally posited, or that grace is absent where the visible rite is not performed. Of the Church on earth the axiom, "Outside the Church no salvation," cannot be defended except with severe reservations. In heaven, however, the axiom will be rigorously true. The Church will include all sharers in divine life, and no one else. The life of grace, moreover, will not be merely internal. Everything in Scripture and in modern theological anthropology leads us to suspect the man's experience of God will be symbolically experesed through tangible and social signs, for otherwise our life in heaven would not be integrally human. What use would the risen body have? How would there be a true community of salvation? How would the life of glory penetrate all the dimensions of man's being?

We have every reason, therefore, to surmise that the saints will celebrate God's presence to them in expressive signs—signs that denote the presence, not the absence, of that which they betoken. Thanks to these signs, the saints will be bound together in mutual friendship. In heaven it will remain true, as it is on earth, that love toward God and toward our fellow men is inseparably intertwined (cf. 1 Jn 4:20). No doubt our earthly loves will be profoundly changed and transfigured. The self-centeredness, exclusivity, and particularity of our affections will be purged away. We shall experience a truly universal charity, not vague and abstract but intensely personal and concrete. Our family will no longer be limited to those who are bound to us by ties of flesh and blood (cf. Mk 12:18-27). In the universal community of the saints we shall find the splendor of God's goodness brilliantly reflected, and all these reflections will enrich and reinforce the immediacy of our experience of God. Thus with respect to the communion of the saints, and not simply with respect to the humanity of Christ, one may assert, in Rahner's words, that "eschatology does not mean the final disappearance of the symbol in favor of a naked intimacy of God with regard to the creature."[75] Our final salvation will be not merely Christic but also ecclesial.

In the light of these considerations, Küng's affirmations regarding the transistory character of the ekklesia seem unwarranted. By what right it is asserted that the ekklesia is "essentially of the present," "provisional," and "definitely the work of man"? Even on earth, it would seem, the Church is essentially the gift of God; it is a dynamic reality pointing beyond its present form. The eschatological character of the Church assures us that through the power of God it will remain, not simply until the end of history, but as a permanent feature of the consummated Kingdom.

3. RELATIONSHIP BETWEEN EARTHLY AND
HEAVENLY CHURCH

(a) BEING AND BECOMING

IF it be granted that the Church is not destined to pass out of existence at the parousia, it is important to inquire how the earthly
Church—the church known to us from experience—is related to the
heavenly Church, for the full coming of which we hope and pray. As
noted above, there is an unfortunate tendency in much of the theology
since the high middle ages to split the Church into two entities, each
complete in itself—a wayfaring Church that exists within history and
a glorious Church that will exist only after history as we know it has
come to a close. Far sounder is the earlier tradition, represented by
Augustine and revived in the twentieth century, according to which
there is only one Church, existing in two forms. The earthly Church
is the heavenly Church insofar as the latter is already present in mystery and sacrament on earth.

The relationship between the two phases of the Church can be variously conceived. According to one pattern of thought the Church is
militant on earth, triumphant in heaven. The military metaphor underlying this terminology is perhaps misleading. In imagining the Church
on earth as God's army arrayed against surrounding foes, we too easily
forget the presence of sin and evil in the Church and, on the other
hand, we too easily overlook the presence of goodness and sanctity beyond the borders of the Church. This metaphor also makes us miscon-
ceive the character of heavenly glory. The Church in eternity will
celebrate not so much its own victory as the victory of Christ in which
it shares thanks to him and despite its own unworthiness.

The relationship between the earthly and heavenly conditions of the
Church is frequently depicted according to the dialectic of promise and
fulfillment. This schematization is valuable insofar as the Church of
glory will be a consummation and blossoming of that which already
exists seminally on earth. The Church is the anticipation, the prolepsis
of the final kingdom. As these terms imply, the Church is something
more than a promise. A promise can be a mere matter of words, accepted in faith. But in the Church of the New Testament we have not
only a promise but a pledge, a down payment. And that which is paid
is a first installment, the firstfruits of that which is to come.

It is significant for ecclesiology that in Scripture the Holy Spirit,
rather than the Church itself, is designated as the pledge and the
firstfruits of salvation. These statements, scattered throughout the New
Testament, are most significant for ecclesiology. They represent a
claim that the Church belongs to the Messianic Age. In the words of
Ignatius Ziade, Maronite Archbishop of Beirut, spoken at Vatican
Council II:

> What are the last times in which we live but times in which the
> risen Christ is present in the world through his Spirit? These
> times begin with the resurrection of Christ when the new Adam
> becomes 'a lifegiving spirit.' These times, ontologically, are the
> 'last' because all things have been given by the Father and nothing
> substantially new is to be looked for. Basically, but nevertheless
> in reality, the kingdom of God is present among us; these times
> are the 'last' because the true newness, that is the Holy Spirit,
> has already come.[76]

The eschatological nature of the Church must be seen in terms of
its connection with Christ and the Holy Spirit. According to Christian
faith, Jesus Christ is the one in whom God has spoken his last word,
his irrevocable word of love. Independently of Christ, a man might
still legitimately wonder whether God's final word to man would be
one of just condemnation or one of grace and forgiveness.[77] In Jesus
this question is resolved. God fully communicates himself to mankind.
The event of Jesus Christ is therefore the eschatological event of mercy,
and the sending of the Holy Spirit, the Spirit of the risen Jesus, seals
the permanence of God's action for us in his incarnate Son. The
Church is the place where the abiding presence of the grace of Christ,
communicated to his brethren through the Holy Spirit, becomes historically manifest. The perpetuity of the Church, assured through the
unfailing assistance of the Holy Spirit, makes the Church a permanent
sign of the definitive character of God's self-gift in his Word made
flesh. Without this guaranteed perpetuity, the Church would not be a
fitting sign of God's eschatological redemptive deed in Christ. The
Church, therefore, is eschatological because Christ and the Holy Spirit
are eschatological.

Frequently the Church is designated as a sign of the eschatological
Kingdom. A sign it is, but the term "sign" is too weak. A sign of
its nature may point, and generally does point, to something absent.
The Church, however, is a sign of something present—present in a
real though hidden way. The Church signifies the grace of the Kingdom as already given, at least inchoatively, here on earth. In other
words, the Church is the "sacrament" of the Kingdom of God. A
sacrament is a sign of that which is present in mystery; it communicates not only the knowledge but the reality of that for which it stands.

The mystery of the grace of Christ transforming the hearts of men
is at work in the Church, but not exclusively in the Church. The
Church, through its faith and love, is a sign of God's loving offer of
salvation, not to Christians only, but to all men. It signifies the advent
of the Kingdom, not only inside the Church, nor only outside it, but
wherever this is occurring. The fact that the Church has the faith,
hope and charity to be a sign presupposes that it is a place where God
is causing his Kingdom to be in some special way, present. The eschatological Kingdom will therefore be the consummation of what is al-

ready present in the Church through its life of faith. But the final
Kingdom is more than a fulfillment of the Church alone; it assuages
that "eager longing" for redemption which, according to St. Paul,
animates all creation (Rom 8:18-23). Bonhoeffer is therefore correct
when he remarks: "The concept of the kingdom of God does indeed
embrace not only the consummation of the church but also the problems of the 'new world,' that is, the eschatology of civilization and of
nature."[78]

(b) Mission

IN the last few paragraphs we have been concerned with the eschatological dimension of the Church's being, and we have found it to
consist in the total dynamic orientation of the Church toward the Kingdom of God, which is mysteriously at work within it. From this standpoint we may easily proceed to discuss the Church's mission. If the
Church is the Kingdom of God inchoatively present in a sacramental
way, the activity of the Church must be, on the one hand, to express
this anticipatory presence of the promised Kingdom, and, on the other,
to prepare for the definitive advent of that Kingdom. The various
functions of the Church should be seen in an eschatological perspective.

The Church is, in the first place, a witnessing community. It has
the responsibility to announce the Kingdom that God has inaugurated
in Christ—the Kingdom that has come and is yet to come in a more
manifest way. The testimony of the Church is entirely determined by
its relationship to the eschaton that has initially burst into the world
through God's saving action in Jesus Christ. The Church celebrates that
Kingdom as being really inaugurated in Christ, and at the same time
it penitently bears witness to the eschatological distance between the
beginnngs already present and the fulfillment that is yet to come. It
does not over-optimistically confuse the beginnings of the new age
with the future consummation, but sustains itself with unflagging hope
in the power of God's love to complete what he has begun in the
glorification of Jesus.

Besides bearing witness to the non-believing world, the Church
must, secondly, make itself a credible sign of the content of its own
message, and thus foster faith in God's word. The Church therefore
has a mission to itself; it issues an unceasing call for self-renewal and
reform. If Christians are conformed to this world and seek their glory
from men, their words will be no more than a "clanging cymbol"
(1 Cor 13:1). But if the Church becomes a place where the values of
the Kingdom of God are evidently dominant, Christians will "shine as
lights in the world" (Phil 2:14), and men who feel drawn to the
Kingdom will wish to share in the Church's faith and life. The
Church must therefore seek to become a plausible anticipation of the
coming Kingdom, an earthly reflection of the new Jerusalem. To some

extent it will always be such a sign, thanks to the incessant outpouring of the Spirit of Christ, but it never succeeds in being, as fully as it should be, the sacrament of Jesus Christ.

A third aspect of the mission of the Church relates more to worship. The Church is a community of persons convinced that God has already inaugurated his Kingdom in the career of Jesus and in the sending of the Spirit of Jesus. Christians are alert, therefore, for the signs of this Kingdom of grace and love, peace and justice, brotherhood and mercy. They praise God for his gifts not only in the past but in the present, not only in the believing community but also in the larger human community. Alert to read the signs of the times, they celebrate what God is doing in their midst.

Fourthly, the Church has an active role with respect to the coming reign of God. It regards itself as an instrument in God's hands—as an agent for the extension of his lordship. In some periods of the past, when men have closely identified the Church as an organized community with the earthly realization of God's Kingdom, mission has been rather narrowly conceived as a effort to win new recruits for the Church itself. The Church will always rejoice when men wish to join it in witness and in worship, but to swell the ranks of its own members is not its primary mission. Its mission must be viewed in relationship to the Kingdom of God in all its dimensions. The Church will therefore seek to build up everywhere those ideas and institutions that further the values of the Kingdom. Christians will collaborate not reluctantly but joyfuly with men of good will who, even without being formally Christians, share something of the same vision. These men in their own way are bound to the eschatological goal of the Church—perhaps indeed more intensely so than some professed Christians.

Finally—and this is the point where the mission of the Church becomes most evidently eschatological—the Church strains forward in prayer and in hope to the final Kingdom, and seeks by every means to hasten the day when God will be all in all. From the beginnings, this theme has been prominent in the prayer of the Church. The Lord's prayer is itself an eschatological prayer—a prayer to the Father to make his Kingdom come.[79] In several passages going back to the earliest period, the New Testament has preserved for us the Aramaic invocation, "Marana tha" ("Come, Lord") (1 Cor 16:22; cf. Apoc 22:20)—a fervent petition for the parousia. The prayer of the *Didache*, quoted in Part I of this paper, powerfully expresses the same eschatological yearning. Although we now conceive of the parousia in a more complex framework, we must strive not to lose this eagerness for the future completion of God's gifts to his Church.

To what extent, if at all, does the Church believe that by its own efforts it can hasten the advent of the final consummation? On this point there is room for several schools of thought. A solid line of

theological reflection, with a firm biblical basis, assures us that it is
not for us "to know times or seasons which the Father has fixed by his
own authority" (Acts 1:7; cf. Mk 13:22). Even granting this, however, it may be conceded that God in his providence has determined
that certain events must come to pass on earth prior to the end of
history. One such precondition to be fulfilled, according to the apparent teaching of the New Testament itself, is the preaching of the gospel to all nations.[80] Some theologians, going beyond the letter of this
text, feel warranted in saying that the final Kingdom will not come,
through God's powerful intervention, until human effort "has gone to
its very limits and so is burst open by salvation from above by developing its own powers."[81]

These speculations concerning the relationship between human effort
and the ultimate Kingdom are important if we are to grasp the intrinsic connection between salvation history and eschatology. "According to Christian eschatology, the decisions taken in salvation-history will
be enacted in ever clearer forms and signs; they will fashion their
own embodiments and expressions in the most profound depths of
existence within the history of the world, even though the final judgment, which will make a clear distinction between the wheat and the
cockle within these objectifications, belongs to God alone."[82] A theology that refuses to assign any importance to man's efforts within
history, on the ground that this would curtail the sovereignty of God,
labors under a false antagonism between the human and the divine.
As we know from the Incarnation, God carries out his saving purposes
through the instrumentality of human cooperation. To be sure, man
cannot by his own unaided efforts presume to build the Kingdom of
God; but there is nothing to prevent God from building his own Kingdom, in part, through the cooperation of those who open their hearts
to him. Since Paul does not hesitate to speak of Christians as "God's
fellow workers" (1 Cor 3:9, Gk text), and since all God's work is
presumably directed to the final consummation, it may be surmised
that human effort, undertaken in God's service, will play a part in the
preparation for the parousia.

This conclusion does not imply that the Church will enjoy a terrestrial future of glory and success. The apocalyptic sections of the
synoptic gospels imply quite the contrary. It seems altogether likely
that the Church will be ever more severely tried by apostasy from
within and persecution from without. But we are assured that a
remnant will persevere to the end. This faithful remnant who resist
the blandishments of the man of sin (1 Thess 2:1-12) will in some
sense make possible the advent of the final Kingdom.

Will the heavenly city, and the glorious Church constituted by the
society of the saints, be literally a new creation? It will not be the
annihilation of all that presently exists, for the new creation has already begun, even here on earth, thanks to the outpouring of the Holy

Spirit. "If any one is in Christ, he is a new creation; the old has passed away, behold, the new has come" (2 Cor 5:17). All that is deformed by sin will be purged away by what, in biblical terms, may be called the powerful wrath of God. But the transforming love of God will bring to fruition everything that proceeds from the Spirit of Christ. As the Pastoral Constitution declares: "After we have obeyed the Lord, and in His Spirit nurtured on earth the values of human dignity, brotherhood and freedom, and indeed all the good fruits of our nature and enterprise, we will find them again, but freed of stain, burnished and transfigured."[83] While the aspect of judgment, therefore, must be kept steadily in view, this should not be allowed to obscure the dimension of fulfillment. The heavenly Church will carry to completion all the sound and holy elements in the Church as it lives and labors on this earth. In ways that we cannot accurately foresee, the Church will experience the loving but purifying approach of the Lord. To the extent that it is a community of faith and love, it will pass, by a smooth transition, into the glorious city prepared for it.

4. PASTORAL SIGNIFICANCE

THE foregoing speculations about the end-time may seem tenuous and far-fetched. Certainly one must speak with great hesitation about the final consummation, fully realizing that all human concepts fall far short of the gift for which we yearn. Nevertheless it is important, I believe, to maintain a lively eschatological awareness. While we cannot directly verify our statements about the absolute future, we can verify their effects upon man's experience here and now. The eschatological vision of the Church, in my judgment, is productive of many good effects. The recovery of this dimension of ecclesiology seems to me to correspond to five major needs of our time.

In the first place, we have a keen sense of the worldliness of the world—what some have called its godlessness. We are acutely sensitive to the discrepancy between the divine and the human, and we cannot help but feel saddened at the extent to which human sin and mediocrity have obscured the divine mission of the Church. The prevalant atmosphere of distrust with regard to all human institutions is rapidly permeating the Church itself. In this situation it becomes increasingly important to remind ourselves that the Church, while it contains the seeds of its future glory, is still under way. It still labors under external trials and persecutions and is internally weakened by the frailty and infidelity of its own members. If we are not to fall prey to despondency, we have to keep alive in our hearts the image of what the Church is called to become and what, by the power of God, it will ultimately be. We have to keep in mind that the sufferings of this time are not worthy to be compared with the glory that is to be revealed in the Church of the final consummation (cf. Rom 8:18).

Secondly, men of our day have an acute sense of historical relativity. They are conscious that human institutions, in order to function properly, must undergo a constant process of adaptation. In the
political sphere it has come to be axiomatic that no secular government
can claim to be immune from criticism as though its exalted origins
could protect it against being overthrown. In most parts of the world
primitive sacral institutions have been displaced by responsible con-
stitutional forms of government. In the Roman Catholic tradition, however, the Church has hitherto been deemed exempt from any radical
restructuring on the ground that its fundamental order was divinely
instituted by Christ himself.[84] We must be careful not to exaggerate the sphere of immutability. Many loyal believers are today
pressing for change and innovation for the sake of the Church
itself. Must the Church, they ask, lag behind the times in order to be
true to its own nature? Is there any evidence that the existing structures
of the Church were in fact instituted by Christ and imposed by him
upon all future generations? Must the self-identity of the Church be
conceived of as a matter of exemption from institutional change?

The eschatological view of the Church, by situating the fullness at
the end of history, liberates one from the tyranny of the past. It
regards the past and the present as preludes to a reality yet to come.
To propose a reformation of Church structures, in this perspective, is
by no means rash and impious. On the contrary it may be the only
way of obeying the divine imperative. The new creation of the parousia
is dynamically at work within our history, summoning us to transcend
the orders inherited from the past. The eschatological vision, by
focussing one's faith on the absolute future, generates a certain critical
liberty with regard to the value of ecclesiastical structures, even those
that have served well over many centuries This outlook is therefore
favorable to the current demands for institutional reform within the
Church. It harmonizes with our modern sense of responsibility for
shaping the institutions of the societies to which we belong.

Thirdly, Christians are still suffering from the effects of a prolonged
period of religious individualism. While the Church was willingly accepted as a means of salvation, it was not sufficiently appreciated as
a community of salvation. In fact, salvation was commonly understood
in purely individualistic terms, as a transaction between the isolated
soul and its God. In this perspective the Church was valued as a
necessary shelter from the dangers of the world or as a necessary
mechanism for ascending to the divine, but scarcely as a home where
one would wish to dwell. The modern insistence on the Church's
provisionality has done much to weaken men's ecclesiastical loyalties
and to make them feel estranged from the Church. The eschatological
vision of the Church, on the other hand, encourages a more positive
relationship between the individual Christian and the Church. If the
Church is seen primarily as a community of grace, and only secondarily

as a means or institution, people can relate to it in a more humanly satisfying way. In a time of general alienation from large and powerful institutions, these considerations seem especially pertinent.

Fourthly, we live in an era of ecumenism. Many Christians are in search of an ecclesiology that, without weakening their loyalty to their own communion, enables them to be open to all the sound Christian values that may be present in other traditions. Nothing was more crippling to this search than the idea, prevalent until recently, that the Church in some one existing form must represent the norm by which all other ecclesial communities are to be measured and judged. The new eschatologism, by grounding ecclesiology in the promised fulfillment, relativizes every historical realization of the Church, including that which obtains in one's own confession. While a person may legitimately and laudably situate himself within some one Christian family, he does not have to act as though his own communion possesses the fullness of the gifts of Christ, or as though the others could have nothing positive to contribute. On the contrary, every denominational church is seen as being still on the way to a perfection that lies beyond anything that can be accomplished within history. By undercutting confessional pride, this attitude removes a major barrier to ecumenical progress.

Finally we are living in an age that is seeking to overcome the dichotomy between the Church and the world. We are weary of the power struggles between Church and State that have loomed so large in Christian history and anxious to bridge the gap between an increasingly secular world and an increasingly sacral Church. Men are in search of a fraternal relationship between the Church and secular society under the signs of mutual concern and mutual respect. The eschatological outlook assures us that the present opposition between Church and world is merely provisional, and that all men, whether in the Church or outside it, are fellow wayfarers in progress toward the same destiny. The Christian can find tokens of God's final Kingdom not only in the Church but in the world, even in that world which has not yet heard or accepted the proclamation of the gospel. All men and all societies, insofar as they respond to the call of grace, whether historically mediated through the Church or not, are on the way to that heavenly city in which the Church foresees its own fulfillment. This conviction arouses a deep sense of kinship between Christians and groups that articulate their faith without mention of Jesus Christ. By its recognition that the new creation will be the ultimate future of the whole world, insofar as it stands under God's redemptive will, eschatological ecclesiology is in the widest sense ecumenical. Its horizons are as wide as the whole inhabited world (oikoumene) and indeed as wide as the cosmos itself. Only from the standpoint of the absolute future can one achieve this deep and all-embracing catholicity.

NOTES

¹ E. Lamirande, "Le temps de l'Eglise: notes en marge de s. Augustin et d'Oscar Cullmann," *Revue de l'université d'Ottawa* 32 (1962) 25*-44*, 73*-87*, p. 26. [This article is reprinted in Lamirande's *Etudes sur l'ecclésiologie de s. Augustin* (éd. de l'université l'Ottawa, 1969), pp. 149-81.]

² J. Jeremias, *New Testament Theology: The Proclamation of Jesus* (Trans. John Bowden) (New York: Scribner's, 1971), p. 170.

²ᵃ For a summary of Riesenfeld's unpublished lecture on this subject see Benedikt Schwank, "Daniel—Jesus—Paulus," *Erbe und Auftrag* 47 (1971) 506-8. I am indebted to Prof. Riesenfeld for kindly supplying me with this reference.

³ For an analysis of the ecclesiology of Eph 4:13-16 see Louis Bouyer, *L'Eglise de Dieu* (Paris: Cerf, 1970), pp. 324-28.

⁴ Elizabeth Fiorenza, "The Eschatology and Composition of the Apocalypse," *Catholic Biblical Quarterly* 30 (1968) 537-69, p. 567.

⁵ For a summary along the main lines of this paragraph see Rudolf Schnackenburg, "Kirche und Parusie," in H. Vorgrimler (ed.), *Gott in Welt*, vol. 1 (Freiburg: Herder, 1964), pp. 551-78.

⁶ *Didache*, no. 9; tr. James A. Kleist in *Ancient Christian Writers*, vol. 6 (Westminster, Md.: Newman, 1948), p. 20.

⁷ *Didache*, no. 10; *ibid.*, p. 21.

⁸ Hermes, *Le Pasteur*, ed. by Robert Joly. Sources chrétiennes 53 (Paris: Cerf, 1958), introduction, p. 35.

⁹ See references in Lamirande, *art. cit.*, p. 36*.

¹⁰ D. Ritschl, *Memory and Hope* (New York: Macmillan, 1967), pp. 115-39; R. Ruether, *The Radical Kingdom* (New York: Harper & Row, 1970), pp. 15-16.

¹¹ Wilhelm Kamlah, quoted in Lamirande, *art. cit.*, p. 43*.

¹² Ernst Bloch, *Man On His Own* (New York: Herder & Herder, 1970) pp. 129-30.

¹³ Lamirande, *art. cit.*, p. 86*.

¹⁴ H. R. Niebuhr, *The Kingdom of God in America* (New York: Harper Torchbook ed., 1959), pp. 19-22.

¹⁵ See Y. Congar, *L'ecclésiologie du haut moyen âge* (Paris: Cerf, 1968), pp. 107-198, 125-27.

¹⁶ Denzinger-Schönmetzer, *Enchiridion symbolorum* (32nd ed., Freiburg: Herder, 1963), no. 493. For other affirmations that the Church will reign forever with Christ see Toledo XI (A.D. 675, *DS* 540) and Toledo XVI (A.D. 693, *DS* 575).

¹⁷ H. U. von Balthasar. *A Theological Anthropology* (New York: Sheed & Ward, 1967), p. 38.

¹⁸ Y. Congar, "Eglise et cité de Dieu chez quelques auteurs cistérciens..." in *Mélanges offertes à Etienne Gilson* (Paris: Vrin, 1959), 137-202, pp. 180-81.

¹⁹ See Y. Congar, *L'Eglise de s. Augustin à l'époque moderne* (Paris: Cerf, 1970), pp. 141, 164-65. In these pages the first usage of the term *ecclesia militans* seems to be attributed both to Petrus Cantor (p. 141) and to John of Salisbury (p. 164).

²⁰ Y. Congar, *Lay People in the Church* (tr. Donald Attwater) (Westminster, Md.: Newman, 1957), p. 39.

²¹ *DS* 1000-1002.

²² Ruether, *The Radical Kingdom*, p. 76.

²³ See Jürgen Moltmann, *Theology of Hope* (tr. J. W. Leitch) (London: S.C.M., 1967), p. 38.

24 So writes J. R. Nelson, *The Realm of Redemption* (London: Epworth, 1951), p. 214.

25 R. Bultmann, *The Presence of Eternity* (New York: Harper, 1957), pp. 151-52.

26 *Ibid.*, p. 154.

27 R. Bultmann, "New Testament and Mythology," in H. W. Bartsch (ed.), *Kerygma and Myth* (New York: Harper Torchbooks, 1961), p. 43.

28 R. Bultmann, "Reply to His Critics," *ibid.*, p. 210.

29 *Ibid.*

30 K. Barth, *The Church and the Churches* (London: James Clarke, 1937), p. 33.

31 *Church Dogmatics* IV/1 (tr. G. W. Bromiley) (New York: Scribner's, 1956), pp. 643, 725-27.

32 J. R. Nelson, *The Realm of Redemption*, p. 231.

33 *Church Dogmatics* IV/3.1 (tr. G. W. Bromiley) (Edinburgh: T. & T. Clark, 1961), p. 321.

34 *Church Dogmatics*, IV/1, p. 669.

35 Cullmann, *Christ and Time* (Philadelphia: Westminster Press, 1950), p. 147.

36 For the texts of these addresses see E. Schlink, *The Coming Christ and the Coming Church* (Edinburgh: Oliver & Boyd, 1967), pp. 245-55, 256-68.

37 Text reprinted in Lukas Vischer (ed.), *A Documentary History of the Faith and Order Movement 1927-1963* (St. Louis: Bethany, 1963), p. 90.

38 *Ibid.*, p. 134.

39 *Ibid.*, p. 138.

40 *Ibid.*, p. 143.

41 For an account of these developments see G. Martelet, "L'Eglise et le Temporel," in G. Baraúna (ed.), *L'Eglise de Vatican II*, vol. 2 (Paris: Cerf, 1967), p. 521; also Barnabas Ahern, "The Eschatological Dimensions of the Church," in J. H. Miller (ed.), *Vatican II: An Interfaith Appraisal* (Notre Dame: Univ. Press, 1966), p. 294.

42 P. Molinari, *Saints: Their Place in the Church* (New York: Sheed & Ward, 1965), p. 172.

43 *Lumen gentium*, art. 9, in W. M. Abbott (ed.), *The Documents of Vatican II* (New York: America Press, 1966), p. 26. References to this edition will henceforth be included in the text, thus: *LG* 9, p. 26.

44 *Sacrosanctum concilium*, abbreviated *SC*.

45 *Unitatis redintegratio*, abbreviated *UR*.

46 *Ad gentes*, abbreviated *AG*.

47 *Gaudium et spes*, abbreviated *GS*.

48 B. Ahern, *art. cit.*, pp. 296-97.

49 Text in W. K. Leahy and A. T. Massimini, *Third Session Council Speeches of Vatican II* (New York: Paulist Press, 1966), pp. 141-45, p. 142.

50 H. Küng, *The Church* (tr. R. and R. Ockenden) (New York: Sheed & Ward, 1968), p. 81.

51 *Ibid.*, p. 87.

52 *Theological Investigations*, vol. 6 (tr. K.-H. and B. Kruger) (Baltimore: Helicon, 1969), pp. 295-312.

53 *Ibid.*, p. 298.

54 *God the Future of Man* (New York: Sheed & Ward, 1968), p. 125.

55 *Thology of the World* (New York: Herder & Herder, paperback ed., 1971), pp. 93-94.

56 *Theology and the Kingdom of God* (Philadelphia: Westminster Press, 1969), p. 75.

57 *Theology of Hope*, p. 325.

58 *Ibid.*, p. 326.

59 K. Rahner, "The Hermeneutics of Eschatological Assertions," *Theological Investigations*, vol. 4 (Trans. by Kevin Smyth) (Baltimore: Helicon, 1966), pp. 323-46, especially pp. 334-37. See also E. Schillebeeckx, "The Interpretation of Eschatology," in *Concilium* 41 (Glen Rock, N.J.: Paulist Press, 1969), pp. 42-46.

60 Rahner, *ibid.*, p. 336.

61 *Ibid.*, p. 337.

62 R. Otto, *The Idea of the Holy* (Trans. by J. W. Harvey) (New York: Oxford Univ. Press, 1958), p. 34.

63 Plato, *Phaedo*, 214; in *The Dialogues of Plato* (Trans. by Benjamin Jowett) (New York: Random House, 1937), vol. 1, p. 498. Kenneth Burke points out that the Platonic myth dialectically transcends the partiality of sensory images and the imperfect ideas derived from them and thus represents a "forward looking partisanship" moving toward the real and ultimate universal ground; *A Rhetoric of Motives* (New York: Braziller, 1955), pp. 200-203.

64 W. Pannenberg, *Theology and the Kingdom of God*, p. 77.

65 *Ibid.*, p. 76.

66 H. Küng, *The Church*, p. 92.

67 *Ibid.*, p. 93.

68 *Tract. in Ps.* 132, 6; as quoted in J. N. D. Kelly, *Early Christian Doctrines* (second edition, New York: Harper & Row, 1960), p. 410.

69 *Lumen gentium*, no. 48, p. 78.

70 *Church Dogmatics*, vol. IV/1, p. 669.

71 E. Schlink, *The Coming Christ and the Coming Church*, p. 116.

72 K. Rahner, "The Eternal Significance of the Humanity of Jesus for our Relationship with God," *Theological Investigations*, vol. 3 (Trans. by K. H. and B. Kruger) (Baltimore: Helicon, 1967), pp. 37-38.

73 *Ibid.*, p. 44.

74 J. Moltmann, *Theology of Hope*, p. 326, uses this term.

75 K. Rahner, "The Theology of the Symbol," *Theological Investigations*, vol. 4 (Trans. by K. Smyth) Baltimore: Helicon, 1966) p. 244.

76 I. Ziade, "Eschatology: Pastoral and Ecumenical Aspects," in W. K. Leahy and A. T. Massimini (eds.), *Third Session Council Speeches of Vatican II*, p. 10.

77 This is a point frequently made by Karl Rahner; see for instance his *Inspiration in the Bible* (Trans. by C. Henkey and M. Palmer) (New York: Herder & Herder, rev. ed., 1964), pp. 42-43; also his *The Church and the Sacraments* (New York: Herder & Herder, 1963), pp. 14-19 and Avery Dulles, "The Meaning of Revelation" in *The Dynamic in Christian Thought*, Vol. I, ed. Joseph Papin, (Villanova University Press, 1970), pp. 52-80.

78 D. Bonhoeffer, *The Communion of Saints* (New York: Harper & Row, 1964), p. 199.

79 See R. E. Brown, *New Testament Essays* (Milwaukee: Bruce, 1965), chap. 12, "The Pater Noster as an Eschatological Prayer," pp. 217-53.

80 Mk 13:9-10. See Vatican II, *Ad gentes* 9, note 34, p. 596; also O. Cullmann, *Christ and Time*, pp. 160, 163.

81 K. Rahner, "Christ and the 'New Man,'" *Theological Investigations*, vol. 5, p. 149.

[82] Rahner, "History of the World and Salvation History," *ibid.*, p. 112.

[84] Nothing here said contradicts the belief that Christ—either in his earthly or his glorified life—instituted certain offices that would continue to be necessary and functional throughout the history of the Church. This claim was of course made for the Petrine office by Vatican Council I.

Eschaton and Worldly Mission in the Mind and Heart of Jesus

Frederick E. Crowe

I AM conscious of taking on a difficult job when I offer to talk to you about the eschaton in the mind and heart of Jesus and to relate it to his mission on earth. Every word in the title raises a host of problems. To make it worse, the problems do not stand still; there will be different problems for different persons, or different problems for the same person depending on whether he is investigating as a historian or praying as a believer. Maybe then the best beginning would be to sort out some of the problems and indicate the questions I mean to deal with and the limits of the study I propose to make.

For historians concerned with the documents, which in this case are mainly the four gospels of the New Testament, mention of the mind and heart of Jesus will suggest that I am trying to do once more what every scholar now recognizes to be a futile task, discover and delineate the features of the historical Jesus. This was the effort of the liberal theologians of the 1800's and proved abortive. After Martin Kähler showed in 1892 that the gospel records are not biographies of Jesus but expressions of the faith of the evangelists,[1] and Albert Schweitzer followed with a classic work showing the nugatory results of the quest of the historical Jesus,[2] New Testament experts reconciled themselves to the fact that we do not know what Jesus said and did in the sense those words bear for historians today. Notice, we do not even know what he said and did, and here I propose to go farther than that: to penetrate beyond his words and actions to his mind and heart. It sounds like fundamentalism or maybe just fantasy.

Besides historians there are believers, and sometimes historical science and faith meet in the same person. I am sure that this is verified here, that those in my audience who are historians are also believers. As believers we may not forget that in talking about Jesus we are talking of one whom our fathers taught us to worship as Lord and Savior, the only name given to us by which we may be saved. And this further complicates the problem. When the words and deeds of Jesus disappeared, the loss was not just that of a bit of history, even of very sacred history, it was the loss of him who is our way, our truth, and our life. With Mary we have to say: "They have taken away my Lord, and I do not know where they have laid him." We no longer have the simple rule of conduct we once had, of looking up the gospels to see how the Lord acted, and transposing his pattern of life to our situation.

Of course, a thorough-going historian will tell us that a fully accurate biography of Jesus would not solve that problem anyway. He would say that the same historical cast of mind which has taught us so much about the gospels has also taught us a great deal about the relativity of language, ethics, culture, and all things human. In a sense then it does not matter so much that we do not know the words and deeds of Jesus; even if we did know his way of acting and his doctrine, we might find it so permeated with time-conditioned ideas and standards as to render it obsolete now as a model. We are a new generation, and we have to take seriously the question asked by Dietrich Bonhoeffer from his Berlin prison: "What is Christianity, and indeed what is Christ, for us today?"[3] We cannot repeat, parrot-like, the words and actions of anyone, not even those of Christ the Lord, when they belong in a different situation, occurred in response to different demands, and were guided by different cultural values from ours.

All this comes home to us in a special way and with peculiar force in the very area that is the concern of this Villanova Institute, the eschaton. For the mind and heart of Jesus, so far as we are able to conjecture it from careful, educated historical guesses, had quite a different view and estimate of the world and the eschaton from that we take for granted today. Nearly a century ago now, Johannes Weiss disturbed the liberal theology of his time with a book that showed how overwhelmingly the mind and heart of the Lord were oriented to the future kingdom and not, as the liberals believed, to the present kingdom of righteousness in the interior of every man's heart.[4] But, if Weiss is correct, then Jesus seems to live in another world than ours. Once more, it was Albert Schweitzer who made this thesis popular and gave us a classic passage to sum up the new view:

> The study of the Life of Jesus has had a curious history. It set out in quest of the historical Jesus, believing that when it had found Him it could bring Him straight into our time as a Teacher and Saviour. It loosed the bands by which He had been riveted for centuries to the stony rocks of ecclesiastical doctrine, and rejoiced to see life and movement coming into the figure once more, and the historical Jesus advancing, as it seemed, to meet it. But He does not stay; He passes by our time and returns to His own.[5]

The difference Schweitzer found so alienating was especially in this very area of eschatological thinking. The mind of Jesus, he thought, was exclusively set on the coming Kingdom, with the expectation that the day was near at hand. And we too, without the aid of Schweitzer, have noticed that the gospels do not present him as concerned with culture and art, science and civilization, sports or politics, the use of leisure, or the women's lib movement. His mission in the world seems to have been rather to save man from this wicked world than to promote the world's values. And this, especially since Vatican II and the Pastoral Constitution on the Church in the Modern World, makes the Lord seem less and less relevant to our age.

Add to this list of shattering blows the final irreverence that much of modern scholarship does not accept the word of Jesus as infallible. Schweitzer himself regarded Jesus as simply mistaken in his hopes, forcing the wheel of history to bring up his destiny as Son of Man, only to have it roll forward and break him in the process.[6] On the very day that I am writing this paragraph I find it said of a recent book that the author's

> treatment of Jesus's moral authority appears to rest on an almost fundamentalist idea of Our Lord's teaching as "direct from God", so to say, without seeing that Jesus's teaching, like everything else about the humanity of him whom as a Christian one believes to be the place and point of special divine activity in human history, can only rightly be understood in terms of the times, the background, and the conditions in which Jesus lived and spoke during "the days of his flesh". Nowadays oracular infallibility will not do, even in the incarnate Lord.[7]

In dealing with this complex problem I wish to take account of the fact that I am speaking to those who combine scholarship with faith, and I would do justice to both areas of life. I consider that I owe it to you as scholars to delimit my study and pursue it with accepted standards of critical research and honest regard for the facts and probabilities, but I consider that I owe it to you as believers to state my dogmatic position that you may know on what basis I carry out my study, to what I am committed and in what degree my mind is free. To this end the briefest possible statement would be that I wish to take modern criticism seriously, but I mean also to retain the faith of my forefathers. However that is an enterprise that many today find almost self-contradictory, and so I must take a moment to explain my position.

First then I wish to take the modern criticism and mentality seriously. I accept the force of Bonhoeffer's question as applying to us with peculiar urgency. They have indeed taken away my Lord and we must search for him again. I accept the fact that the gospels are not biographies, that we really do not know exactly what the Lord said and did in the way we would like to know. I accept as quite probable the view that Jesus did not claim to be Messiah or Son of God, that possibly he did not even claim to be Son of Man, that he did not particularly concern himself with the features of the true Messiah or with purifying the Jewish idea of the Messiah. To put the main point in the succinct phrase current today: The Proclaimer became the Proclaimed. That is, Jesus proclaimed the kingdom; we, on the other hand, proclaim Jesus. In all this I am not eliminating history with the gnostics, but merely acknowledging with the realists developments in the content of our faith and great areas of ignorance about its origins.

Further, I accept the fact that we cannot live in the same mental world as our forefathers did. It was easy for them—in fact, it was easy for us in childhood—to live with the "powers and principalities" of Paul all around them in the atmosphere. Copernicus had somehow not got through to popular piety. God was still "up there" above the clouds, and guardian angels hovered nearby in the air. The other world, though invisible, was close at hand—literally close at hand, in the spatial sense. So we had image to pit against image; against the world that is so much with us, displaying its tempting wares, we could set another world, that was almost as vividly present, to counteract temptation. We may still find it useful to picture such a world when we pray, and we may still find it helpful to our piety to read the gospels as if it were 972 instead of 1972; many of the "Jesus people" seem to do so and, if they insist on withdrawing from the stream of culture, I have no wish to disturb their peace of mind. But I am saying that we must know what we are doing; and, if we wish to live with a good conscience and inspire credibility in the academic sphere, we have to realize that the mental world of our forefathers has vanished, and along with it the picture-story world of the gospels.

Also I think I see the point of those philosophers who talk about man as the creator of his values. In a world where all things change and develop, the human good also develops. In a human world where meaning is constitutive of man and his institutions, developing meaning puts new values before one. In men who are not definable by genus and specific difference except at the level of the lowest common denominator, the level of mere potency, the significant element is in what is added, the differentiations that make one a Newman instead of a moron. It belongs to the liberty of man to make himself what he can be; it belongs to the intelligence of man to discover the possibilities of his becoming and to work out the means to realize them. In all this we recognize a factor that we can call the creation of values, and it is conceivable and probable that Jesus in his human life on earth was an instance of such creativity. But this means that in the quite different world of the 1970's the values that Jesus worked out for himself may not be exactly the values that we must by God's will work out for ourselves.

All this I can say with a peaceful conscience because I do not find that the results of modern historical investigation of the gospels really threaten my understanding of our faith in Jesus Christ, the Son of God. The faith of my fathers remains intact, and my understanding of it is in fact enriched by the critical work of the last two centuries. The ground of my peace is not just that critical history is itself very fallible and therefore not to be swallowed whole or made the criterion of what we may believe about Christ. It is rather that our articles of faith and the doctrinal explanations approved by the church, rightly understood, do not in fact conflict with history. The key word here is 'understand'—I said that the findings of history do not conflict with my *understanding* of our faith. This sounds quite a lot like some esoteric knowledge granted to me by special divine privilege, so I want to say at once that the fundamental understanding of our faith that I am talking about was given seven centuries ago by Thomas Aquinas, for whom I feel no need to apologize.

I would ask you here to remember that understanding as such is hypothetical. What I am putting forward is a hypothesis. Whether it can ever be verified is another question. But a theologian's job must begin with the sort of task I am attempting. He comes to the faith of his forefathers and to the source-documents much as a medical doctor might come to the scriptural accounts of an illness. The medical doctor brings with him a "science" of medicine, a whole set of concepts which is a powerful instrument of explanation. Nevertheless, when he studies the symptoms related by a Luke, his particular role is to ask, Might it be such and such a disease that we find described here? He is not competent to perform the exercise of textual and other criticism needed to determine the real state of affairs. He does not even know whether the man X, described as having such and such an affliction, ever existed. Similarly, the theologian brings to the gospel accounts of Jesus and to the faith of his forefathers, a set of concepts that enables him to ask, that gives him the duty of asking, Could this be the way it happened? His job is to supply a principle of possible explanation. He does not try therefore to say what actually happened or to write a biography of Jesus; but perhaps he supplies a necessary preliminary to asking the question of fact and, if the facts can never be determined, he at least has the intellectual peace that comes from grasping and conceiving a possible explanation.

What I wish to do then in this paper is address myself to the Thomist understanding of Christ's human knowledge, and (going beyond St. Thomas now) to show on that basis by what process the eschaton in the mind of Jesus might be linked with his observation and growing understanding of earthly realities. Secondly, I will try to provide a similar and parallel account of the eschaton in the heart of Jesus and to show by what process it might be linked with his discovery and acceptance of earthly values. Thirdly and finally, I will indicate how these two accounts could be brought to bear on the question of his earthly mission.

I. ESCHATON AND FINITE KNOWLEDGE IN THE
MIND OF JESUS

I BEGIN with Catholic dogma and doctrine on Christ and his human knowledge. It has a very long and very involved history, but we can cover it in short order with the seven-league boots of a systematic theologian. Nicea affirmed in 325 that the Son is God in the same sense as the Father is God.[8] We should neither maximize nor minimize this; the Nicene fathers did not say anything that went beyond the thrust of the New Testament, but they did say more than the New Testament says. Scripture, as St. Thomas remarks, often contains the articles of our faith "spread out . . . expressed in various ways, and sometimes lacking in clarity."[9] We need what the creeds give: a boiling down, a crystallizing, a clarification. And the resulting clarification at Nicea at once released other questions till then unformulated. With his divinity clearly affirmed, attention had to turn to his human state. It was established 126 years later at Chalcedon that he was also man like ourselves; as he is God in the same sense as the Father is God, so he is man in the same sense in which we are men. What follows from that in regard to human endowments? The question was answered after another 230 years in regard to the particular question of the human will: the God-Man has a human will such as we have.

The particular question of the human knowledge of Jesus never received the attention in the patristic councils that his will did. Different ages have different preoccupations; our preoccupation today would be more with Christ's mind than with his will, I should think, but we do not have councils running round defining dogmas the way an earlier age did. However, the conclusion was clear from Chalcedon: there is a human cognitional activity and knowledge in Christ. The further ramifications of that conclusion were worked out clearly only in St. Thomas' time, and then only slowly. But towards the end of his life, he had begun to get things straightened out. There was in the human mind of Christ a knowledge that is there by divine gift; most important under this heading is the vision of God, immediate knowledge of the divine essence. There was also in the mind of Christ what St. Thomas called acquired knowledge, knowledge based on experience and on ideas formed according to the cognitional process normal in a human being.

It was not this experiential knowledge that the scholastics studied most diligently. It was rather the divinely given knowledge and especially the vision of God that we term beatific. The question most to the fore dealt with the extent of this knowledge. Faced with Mark 13:32, "But about that day . . . no one knows, not even . . . the Son; only the Father," they could not avoid the question. But with their strong sense of Christ as their teacher, as him on whose word our faith depends, they were extremely reluctant to admit any area of ignorance even into his human mind.[10] Thus, St. Thomas expressly asks the question whether there was ignorance in Christ and answers no.[11]

We are now beyond the borders of Catholic dogma and there is no point pursuing the question further in that direction. For our Protestant brothers the question, I would say, has ceased to be of interest; they long ago abandoned the scholastic doctrine of Christ's immediate vision of God and have devoted themselves to his "acquired" knowledge; our introduction of the present question in medieval language must seem to them strangely artificial, academic, remote, old-fashioned—a relic of a bygone age with which they need not concern themselves.

For Catholics the problem is more complex. We do not wish lightly to abandon a doctrine our fathers worked out rather carefully and on good grounds. At the same time we must be aware of the age we live in and awake to the need of critical examination of our history. We know that the dogma of Nicea gave an emphasis to the divinity of Christ that has made it difficult for us to think of him as Man; the very difficulty we have in speaking of "Jesus" rather than of "Christ" or "the Lord" is an indication of the deep influence conciliar dogma has had on our psyche and piety. But, even if we do not abandon our dogmas or the conclusions that seem to follow directly from the dogmas, we still have to retrace the path by which we came, to see in every case what the intention of the church was, to discern the core affirmation and not be mesmerized by the particular language used, to discover and validate the grounds on which the church based her dogma or her view.

What I am saying is that the addition of history to dogma gives us a new problematic. We may not simply quote the words our fathers used to express their faith and consider the matter settled. We must rather observe the situation in each case and take account of the differences in expression as the situation changes from age to age. A very pertinent illustration occurs in the difference between Mark and John. The patristic and scholastic age based its Christology largely on John's gospel and found Mark's gospel, where ignorance is attributed to Jesus, an embarrassment. But a later age bases its account of the human Jesus more on Mark and finds John's gospel an embarrassment, for in John all knowledge belongs to Jesus and he does not need to ask questions of anyone.

Now it is possible to reconcile Mark and John by means of distinctions, but it is more important from the historical point of view to discover the context in which each evangelist wrote, and thus to arrive at a concrete understanding which makes the distinctions valid. Thus, Mark thinks of Jesus as the strong, the mighty Son of God, wresting victory from the forces of Satan; he does not think of him as the God-Man in the sense of Chalcedon, with human nature and divine nature; he would be utterly mystified by such terminology, and so he does not put the question we put: If he is God, how come he doesn't

know the date of the great judgment? Mark does not even expressly
see him entering the world from heaven, so he escapes a multitude of
problems. John, however, does explicitly think of him as entering this
world from heaven; moreover, he thinks of him as being one with
the Father, as having all that the Father has, including the Father's
knowledge. Hence, he attributes to him the widest possible knowledge of events on earth, past, present, and future. But John did not
have the Chalcedonian distinction of natures in the back of his mind
as he wrote; he did not therefore ask, Is this knowledge human or
divine? And not thinking of the question, he does not take the pre-
cautions that a modern theologian must take. He speaks as if Jesus
the Man had a ready supply of divine knowledge available; but this
I take to be his way of expressing the divinity of Christ, it is his
Christology. I do not see it as necessarily an account, a biographical
narrative, of events in the human life of Jesus.

But what becomes now of our "proofs" of the immediate vision of
God in Jesus? For we based them largely on texts from John, and
John, as we now understand him, does not appear to support our
thesis. It seems to me we must boldly assert that "proofs" always lag
behind a Catholic sense of the truth, that there is a global way of
conceiving a truth and an implicit way of affirming it long before we
formulate propositions that require proof, that in fact it is often heresy
which does the clarifying work needed to pass from such global and
implicit states of belief to the defined and explicit state. For example,
the Arian heresy clarified the question on the divinity of the Son of
God, and the genius of Athanasius discovered the proof that clinched
the matter: the same things are said of the Son as are said of the
Father, except the name of Father.[12] But, before this, proofs from
scripture were inadequate, just as the conception of the divinity of
Christ was global and undefined.

Similarly, I suspect there is a Catholic sense of the vision of God in
Jesus' mind. We apprehend it globally, not without reference to
particular texts, but we base it more on the general thrust of the
texts than on the exegesis of this or that particular text; in the latter
we are apt to go badly astray. If I try to articulate that faith here, I
am aware of trying to do a work parallel to that of Arius and Athanasius, as well as that of their predecessors in a long line. But I would
attempt it in some such form as this: What Jesus knows as a religious
teacher, he knows on his own, without asking anyone, without having
someone to vouch for him, without even needing, as the prophets
needed, to have the word of the Lord come to him. Possibly the here-
tical formulation we need to bring out our faith could be found in
just those words: he knows as a prophet does, surely the greatest of
the prophets but still only a prophet, to whom the word of the Lord
came in a special way. But I am not sure how a modern Athanasius
would destroy that heresy.

At any rate I mean to retain the dogmas of my faith, and I wish to retain also the accepted doctrines until the need to abandon them is proved. When the humanity and divinity of Christ created difficulties about his unity, the church's method was not the easy way out of denying one nature or the other, or of affirming some kind of society of two; it was rather the extremely difficult, and still ongoing, but enormously fruitful way of living with the problem and struggling to conceive anew and less inadequately the constitution of the God-Man. I think that there is a parallel here in regard to the vision of God, and that we should live with the difficulty and see whether the result-ing struggle does not result in a new and fruitful penetration of the mystery of revelation.

What then is the difficulty, and how did it arise? The difficulty is that the doctrine of the vision of God seems to give Jesus a complete blueprint of creation in which he can read all that was or is or will be, and this is difficult to harmonize with the synoptic evangelists and other writers, who have Jesus learning in various ways, ignorant of the last day, asking what seem like real questions, and being surprised at the discoveries he makes. Further it seems to remove Jesus from us as a model, for he becomes a kind of automaton, subject to a fate predetermined and preformulated, and not at all a man who had to make decisions, sometimes playing it a bit by ear, and learning by the things he suffered.

But how did such a view of the vision of God arise? It arose from a "picture-thinking" concept of the immediate knowledge we believe Jesus to have had of God. We think of Jesus seeing the Father "face to face"; we add the Augustinian (and Thomist) doctrine of all creation being contained *in Verbo,* in the Word the Father utters; and now we have all we need for the "picture-thinking" view of Jesus' higher knowledge. Let us put this notion in all its naiveté. The no-tion is that Jesus could gaze upon the other world as we look upon this one. As we see hills and trees, towns and homes and animals and men, so there is another world of objects spread out before the mind's eye in Jesus; he saw his Father in majesty, the Holy Spirit was somehow visible though he has no long white beard to manifest him-self, the armies of angels were hovering there, or forming fours and right-wheeling in great precision. Moreover, he also sees this world of ours in all its spatio-temporal totality; the whole of human his-tory and its events are somehow exposed to view; the future is visible at a glance, and no questions remain to be asked. In our piety towards our dead we think of them "looking down" upon us from the home of the blessed; but Jesus could see all this while he lived on earth, by reference to some kind of blueprint which perhaps we do not very clearly image in our minds.

Such a view is perfectly natural in the sense that it is the normal view to adopt as a first approximation. It corresponds to the biblical phrase, face to face; it is a spontaneous conception of intellectual knowledge based on the mode of ocular vision with which we are so familiar and by which we are so naturally influence in our cognitional theory; it has been given a kind of sanction by the theologians through their use of the term "vision of God."

But suppose that is not what the immediate knowledge of God is. Suppose that the phrase, face to face, is not a premise from which conclusions may be drawn in the manner of logic, but simply a metaphor which has to be translated into more technical language before conclusions are possible. Suppose, more positively, that immediate knowledge of God is not a knowledge of particular items at all, but more a global view; suppose that this "view" is more an understanding that a concept; suppose that, as understanding, it is characterized more by the power and range of activity it gives the subject than it is by the list of objects on which it bears; suppose that even with such immediate knowledge of God there remains a real, prolonged, and difficult process to empirical understanding and knowledge of the created universe, of the course of human history, and especially of distant and obscure items like the date of the last day; suppose also that St. Thomas had not integrated the vision of God with the learning process proper to men on earth,[13]—suppose all this, I say, and see how much remains of the problem, whether it is not possible to accept both history and doctrine and still live in intellectual peace.

My own view is that on the suppositions stated the problem of reconciling the vision Jesus had with the normal learning process found in man, largely vanishes. We can accept the thrust and intention of the traditional doctrine we received from our fathers, and still agree with Mark the evangelist and with modern history, that Jesus was a Man who thought things out, asked questions, was surprised by the answers, learned day by day the details of his mission, and did not know the date of the last judgment. I wish to explore this possibility, but I hope it is clear that my main objective is not to prove a doctrine but to render an intelligible account of it, in particular so to explain it as to effect the desired reconciliation of vision and learning process in Jesus. That means two sub-sections in this part of my paper: explaining the vision of God, and relating the vision of God to knowledge of this finite world.

1. THE VISION OF GOD—A THOMIST UNDERSTANDING

WHEN we speak of the vision of God, we are speaking of mystery. The traditional way of dealing with mystery is by analogies, and I have three: our spontaneous notion of being, the experience of the mystics, and our own profoundest knowledge in daily life. The first is probably the dullest, but it is also the most effective theologically, and I am going to spend some time on it, beginning with the

Thomist view of intellectual light and developing St. Thomas's view
with the help of Lonergan's ideas on the notion of being.

The fruitful approach to the Thomist doctrine of "light" is by
contrast with the doctrine of first principles.[14] We are familiar, through
our training in logic, with the idea of a premise, or set of premises,
from which conclusions can be derived. We come to realize that the
premises themselves, most of them, are already conclusion from higher
premises, and so we come to the idea of first principles which are at the
basis of all organized knowledge, such apparently utterly basic premises
as: A thing cannot be and not be. The good is to be done. Etc. And,
if we make logic the source of cognitional process, the creative agent,
then we stop with these first principles as the ultimate basis of knowledge.

For St. Thomas they are not ultimate at all. Behind them lies the
native endowment and power of intellect, which St. Thomas often
designates as a "light." It is the source of all principles, even first
principles; it makes them intelligible, it uses them as instruments for
further intellectual process. It is an active power, operative and self-
sufficient in the whole range of knowledge pertaining to natural reason. It is a participation, a created off-print, of God's intelligence;
but just here we have to correct Augustine: when he speaks of judgment by reference to the eternal reasons, we have to understand this,
not as a matter of looking at truths inscribed in the divine mind, but
as a matter of having in our own minds an active power which is able,
of itself, to pass judgment and attain truth. There is a sense then in
which it is quite true to say that we have all knowledge in our minds
from the beginning, for we have a light in which first terms and first
principles and all knowledge based on them can become known.

Still, that is not the whole story. We are well enough aware of
the pain of the learning process to realize that the natural light of
intellect does not give us actual knowledge of particular objects. There
are then two sources of our knowledge, one intrinsic to mind (its own
light) but the other extrinsic, the *sensibilia* by which particular objects
and areas of science are brought under the illumination of intellectual
light. Just as corporeal light is not itself a determined color (in the
Thomist conception) but is able nevertheless to make all colors visible,
so intellectual light is not particular knowledge but is able to bring all
particular knowledge to actuation. The relation then of intellectual
light to specific ideas is that of undetermined cause to determined
effect, the relation of a general power ranging over its field to particular products of that power.

This Thomist doctrine is transformed by Lonergan into a doctrine
of the spontaneously operative notion of being,[15] or the pure notion
of being:

The pure notion of being is the detached, disinterested, unrestricted desire to know. It is prior to understanding and affirming, but it heads to them for it is the ground of intelligent inquiry and critical reflection. Moreover, this heading towards knowing is itself a notion, for it heads not unconsciously, as the seed to the plant, nor sensitively, as hunger for food, but intelligently and reasonably, as the radical *noêsis* towards every *noêma*, the basic *pensée pensante* towards every *pensée pensée*, the initiating *intentio intendens* towards every *intentio intenta*.[16]

This notion of being is present in all conscious cognitional activity of man. It is there as "a dynamic orientation to a totally unknown."[17] It is all-pervasive: "It underpins all cognitional contents. It penetrates them all. It constitutes them as cognitional."[18] It is the principle of all inquiry and reflection, the criterion of all judgment.

It is conscious, and manifests itself vividly in questions, in the need and urge to know, in the malaise of an unsatisfied intellect. But it is not conscious in the manner in which a red light or an alarm-bell enters the field of consciousness. It is not obtrusive; it is not ordinarily adverted to; even philosophers may never notice it; those who do, have great difficulty formulating their notion of it; those who do formulate their notion, have great difficulty conveying it to others.[19]

It is this light of intellect or notion of being that Lonergan uses as an analogy for what Christ understood through his immediate vision of God and for the way this understanding relates to the knowledge Christ acquired and used in daily life. Christ's understanding of the divine mysteries was inexpressible; it corresponds to the words heard by St. Paul—"so secret that human lips may not repeat them" (2 Cor 12:4). Yet his communication of the divine mysteries to others was carried out in the common language whose meaning he shared with them. There had therefore to be a translation from one understanding and knowledge to the other. Now the natural light which is our native endowment, Lonergan's notion of being, is also in its own way inexpressible; yet in another way it is expressed in our daily lives, in all we know, and in the very desire we have to know God. Christ's knowledge is similarly inexpressible, much more radically so, yet it becomes manifest in his life. There is a difference in that we operate in pursuit of the goal, with a desire to see God, where Christ operated from the attained goal, communicating what he had to others. But there is a similarity in that the vision of God gave him no actual knowledge that was expressible. He had to win this slowly; he labored to express what was first given in an inexpressible form; he labored, as it were, to fill a vacuum.

There seems to be here an analogy which we can use to understand the presence in Christ of the vision of God, to understand its influence, ever active but not obtrusive, and to understand its relation to the experiential knowledge gained in daily living. How this may work out in the concrete will occupy us later.

My second analogy is the experience of the mystics. I presume that what they were given Christ was given in greater measure. If the difference from Christ is qualitative, we would proceed in two steps, from our experience to that of the mystics, from theirs to Christ's. If the difference is just quantitative, we seem at first glance to lack any basis for analogy; the mystics are almost as far removed from us as Christ is. But even then there is one factor that makes their experience useful to us as an analogy: they have talked extensively about it, where Christ did not do so. He was not able to do so in the vocabulary of his time; he did not think of doing so, given the particular interests of his time; he would be quite surprised if we put questions to him in the language of St. Teresa of Avila or St. John of the Cross, surprised and somewhat at a loss to know what we meant. So the mystics serve to lead us to him, whether their difference from him be qualitative or quantitative.

What I find relevant now in the mystical experience, is the inexpressible character of their knowledge, and the great efforts they make to express to us what is beyond words. Poulain's documentation and analysis are useful here. It is said of a certain Blessed Hermann Joseph: "... the Lord revealed to him the whole beauty and glory of the firmament.... But afterwards ... the Prior could get nothing more out of him than that he had received such unspeakable rapture ... that it was beyond human understanding."[20] Poulain also quotes Teresa of Avila: "... we enjoy a favour without knowing what it is";[21] and says himself "... as the soul experiences difficulty in understanding her state, so she finds it very hard to describe it."[22] And John of the Cross says that as the knowledge in the mystic state is "general and obscure ..." with "the intellect unable to conceive *distinctly* ... so the will also loves generally and *indistinctly*."[23]

Poulain therefore refers to the need the mystics have to invent images in order to express what they have experienced, and we have some remarkable comments of Teresa on her efforts to find an image that does even remotest justice to her vision—I think of the four ways of watering a garden, which she used to describe states of prayer.[24] He relates also that theologians are apt to ask the mystics what images give rise to their experiences, but the mystics themselves are astounded by such a question, since their state is quite beyond images.[25] Again, he speaks of a prayer of silence, not of the suppression of all activity,[26] but a prayer in which: "All sounds are hushed. The soul is wholly immersed in an act of possession which seems to endure without any variation."[27]

I think we have in such accounts a very powerful instrument for understanding the mind and heart of Jesus. There is an a priori element in that view, the presumption I mentioned that whatever the mystics had Christ had in greater degree, but that seems reasonable to suppose. There is often a state of rapture in the mystics which we cannot easily verify in Christ, but this may well be an effect in the early stages; there may be more tranquility accompanying the later habitual possession of the mystic gifts, the sort of tranquility we seem to find more normally in Christ.

A third analogy is found in our own ordinary faith experience. What I mean is, the most fundamental ideas we have remain preconceptual; they are not expressed in words, though they shape our lives and guide our thinking and judging and deciding. To illustrate this, we might think of our inability to say anything appropriate on the great occasions of life—disaster and death, or love and success and triumph. There is an understanding by which we react appropriately but silently. Or we might think of our proverbs, which express the profoundest wisdom of common sense, but are almost always expressed in metaphorical language, where more is meant and understood than is uttered. That is, lacking the word of rational discourse, we fall back on the preconceptual means of the artist.

This seems to me especially true of what we hold by faith. I recall here what I said earlier about the profoundest truths of our faith resting not so much on particular texts of scripture as on a global view, a "sense" of rightness that we cannot easily put into words, though we can recognize faulty formulations (and thus heresy is always easier to spot and judge than orthodoxy is to formulate). To illustrate this, we must think of the way we find our own "expressions" of faith in our dreams.[28] That is, public language is still lacking and so each one finds his own private language to express to himself what is held by all of us without words. Or think of the way we vaguely sense the thrust of a biblical parable, say, the parables of crisis, even though the imagery of the gospels may have little power in the present context and we struggle to find another (just here dreams may have their role and give each believer his private set of parables).

2. VISION OF GOD AND KNOWLEDGE OF THE FINITE

THE structure of my idea on the eschaton and worldly mission in the mind of Jesus is as follows: I start with the notion of the vision of God as an act of understanding, an act of understanding which is global and does not include as explicit items the objects of either this world or the other but only the divine essence; I wish to proceed from that to the formation in Jesus' mind of particular items of knowledge concerned with his life on earth and his mission. In this way I hope to provide some hint of the way the Lord Jesus could know and know with authority, could be our teacher in a way the prophets could never be, and yet have to think deeply to find his message and express it to others.

The first part of my exposition—conceiving the vision of God as a global act of understanding—has been long and difficult, but I think it was essential. There is no use rejecting the vision of God in Jesus until we know with accuracy what it means, and there is no easy way to find that out. But we have still a long way to go in working out how this "eschaton" in the mind of Jesus can be related to finite knowledge; I turn now to the second task.

A fundamental condition of the search is expressed negatively: there are no words or ideas in the mind of Jesus as an immediate result of the vision of God. You have accepted, I hope, the premise that there are no images; the vision of God is not an ocular act, a gazing upon a field of visible objects. But we must go farther and say there are no words or ideas either; that is, if we wish to conceive the state of Jesus' mind prior to his human experience as a baby, we must erase every concept we meet in scripture or tradition or catechism or any other source. In this respect, his mind was like the *tabula rasa,* the clean slate, the scholastic theologians talk of.

Let me spell this out in tedious detail. The object of the immediate knowledge Jesus had through the vision of God did not contain the word "God" or the words "divine essence," nor did it contain the word "Father," or the word "Son," or the word "Spirit," still less did it contain the word "Three." It did not contain the word "Creator' or the word "Judge" or the word "Almighty" or the word "Eternal" or any of the words, "Rock," "Shepherd," "Shield," and the others which are applied to God in what we call the Old Testament. Much less did this knowledge he had contain words or ideas for this world, or his mission in this world, or the familiar things of everyday life at Nazareth. It did not contain the words, "papa" or "mama" or "temple" or "scripture" or "knife" or "fork" or anything of the sort.

I would apply this with special emphasis to an area where I think much modern theology is on the wrong track, the self-knowledge Jesus had or the knowledge he had through what some theologians consider to be his self-consciousness. What I am saying then is that the immediate knowledge Jesus had of God did not include the word "I." I believe the efforts made to build a theology of his knowledge of God on his self-consciousness are ill-advised. I cannot go into that now; for the moment I am content to say that the ordinary child does not know the word "I" but has to learn to use it. I am told that this occurs at about four years of age, and I know that the mere use of the word at the age of four leaves us a long, long way from understanding the reality of the self. There is no privileged position to be given therefore to the "I" in the hierarchy of things understood; on the contrary, it is one of the last things we come to understand. I see no reason for asserting anything different about Jesus.[29]

Moreover, I do not see any religious reason for supposing that the Lord Jesus went around trying to understand himself, or searching the scriptures for passages that pertained to him. The scriptures were not part of the object of his immediate knowledge of God either; the ordinary sinner does not think of messianic passages as applicable to himself, and I should think that the saints are even less inclined to that kind of narcissism. I would think, then, that the Lord Jesus, if he came eventually to think of the Servant passages in connection with his own life, would first think of them in the way we might think of them, not as a divine prophecy uttered several centuries earlier and pointing to "me," singling "me" out, but rather as a guide to God's thinking about all his children and therefore to be taken seriously by "me" too.

To hammer at this point once more, I would insist that Jesus did not have ideas of the future ready at hand whenever he wished to consult them. He did not have the betrayal by Judas given with the vision of God. He did not have the success or failure of the morrow's mission already affirmed in his mind before he began it. Further, he did not have the other world before his eyes as he walked to his death; there is no other world given in the vision of God, in the sense of an after-life continuous with this life and linked to it by the gate of death. Death, for Jesus as for us, was the dark exit beyond which nothing appeared.

We could put the main point in another way by saying that every day was to Jesus a fresh experience, an encounter with newness. The notion that, coming from the heavenly world, he brought with him a full view of both this one and the other, is to be exploded; his baby eyes opened on a world as new and strange as the one we meet is to us. His growing up was an experience in novelty; his becoming acquainted with the scriptures was an introduction to new religious ideas; his vocation was a call from God as startling and thrilling as that of any of the saints.

But maybe by now I have made that negative point with enough emphasis. At least, if I have not done so, further repetition is not likely to help. It is time to turn to the positive side: how does the vision of God that Jesus had relate to his thinking, to the way his mind worked to understand his world and his mission there, to the way he thought out his sermons and his teaching? I ask you to notice that my question is not simply how his mind worked on empirical data—it worked the way yours does, attending to data, forming schematic images, gaining an insight into the image, etc.; you can apply your own cognitional theory here. But I am asking how his vision of God affected that process and entered into it. In such a highly speculative enterprise we need all the guidance we can get, so I propose to start rather remotely with two clues and some backing in the prestige of St. Thomas.

The first is the parallel which I see between the way God is All yet becomes Man, and the way Jesus might know the All and yet have to go through a process to know this or that particular item of knowledge. The divine Being, then, is the All, the infinite ocean of all substance; and yet we cannot say that God is a tree, or a horse, or, prior to a certain event two thousand years ago, a Man. If he would *be* a tree, or a horse, or a man, he must *become* tree or horse or man. He did in fact will to become Man, and this becoming was an event; something happened that could be truly called a *fieri,* and in that sense a process. What I am suggesting is that, with all due account being taken of the differences, a parallel can be conceived to help us understand, or at least accept as possible, a process in the mind of the Lord Jesus. If he has immediate knowledge of God, he knows the All, and that All is the infinite ocean of being. Nevertheless, this does not automatically give him knowledge of a tree, or a horse, or a man, particularly not of *this* tree, or *this* horse, or *this* man. That is, knowledge of the All, though it contains knowledge of everything "in globo," does not contain it as individuated. For that, you need a process.

Secondly, we have a clue in Thomism to serve as guide in thinking out what this process might be like. St. Thomas, with his emphasis on the universal and the abstract in human knowing, thought that the knowledge the saints derive from the vision of God is not so much knowledge of this or that particular object as it is of general reasons, causes, explanations, the *species et genera rerum, et rationes earum.*[30] Even if we lean more towards the particular and concrete today, we can still use St. Thomas as a guide. I would myself supplement his idea with Lonergan's "scissors-action" of heuristic method: there is a lower blade that rises from data and an upper blade that moves downward from general ideas.[31] I conceive therefore the mind of Jesus to operate according to this scissors-action, with the upper blade supplied by his understanding of God and the most general preconceptual ideas that derive from that understanding, ideas on man and life and the universe and duty, and the lower blade supplied by the thousands and thousands of items of data that met his eye and ear and taste and smell and touch during his life on earth.

But now we come to the point where many of us, and the systematic theologian especially, are likely to be deficient. If we are to follow the scissors-action that operated between the data the Lord Jesus observed and the vision he had of God, we need as accurate a knowledge as possible of the data. This means having in our memories an image of the hills and lakes and rivers he saw, the towns and villages, the homes and synagogues. We should be familiar with the artefacts he knew and used, the pots and pans, the tables and chairs, the hammers and saws, etc. We should know the customs of the land and the time—in weddings, in taxation, in education, in agriculture, and the rest. We should even think in the language he used, pray the prayers he prayed, and hear the scriptures he heard, giving the same sense to the words that he would give.

That at least is the ideal, and I begin my task very far indeed from the ideal. In that situation mistakes are likely. Still, I am not particularly anxious; if I do not know what kind of axe the Lord Jesus used, I can presume from the fact that the experts use my English word 'axe' to translate the original, that there is some similarity between the Lord's axe and the one I use. Again, if errors occur here, they are not apt to be pernicious—not nearly as dangerous, in my view, as errors about that I-consciousness of the Lord. And yet I feel it as a painful lack that I am so handicapped in thinking out the Lord's thinking; in my poverty I ask for the alms of your superior knowledge. If I share with you what can be said on the more abstract level, you may be willing to share with me what you know of the concrete data of the Holy Land.

There is an in-between area that is not the field of either systematic theologian or historian of the concrete, and it is here I really feel most painfully the lack of guidance. I mean the lack of a history of introspection, and its emergence among the biblical people in particular. When did the dream first become differentiated as a category, understood in contradistinction to waking experience? When did the notion of a question come to formulation and receive a name? I presume that for some thousands of years the human race may have asked questions by gesture or word or intonation, without knowing they were asking questions or having a word for it. When did the word "if" come into usage, and even when they began to use it, as they have done in the scriptures, did they have the category we call supposition clearly differentiated?

I will not delay on the ordinary experiences and intellectual growth of childhood. In my hypothesis the child Jesus would look, wide-eyed, upon his world the way any child does. There is on the face of the infant of a few months a look that distinguishes him already, in my opinion, from the kitten or pup; the kitten may look upon a ball of yarn with great interest, but his interest is pragmatic: he wants to play with it; a child can apparently just look, lost in wonder: "Children's faces looking up Holding wonder like a cup." So the child Jesus would look on the slanting beam of sunlight coming in the door, on the knife his Mother was using to cut the bread or cheese (a knife which he would naturally try to get hold of and examine), on the stranger whom Joseph brought to dinner; so he would listen to the strange noises these grown-ups were making as they moved about their strange business. He would come to distinguish some of these strange noises, would fix in his memory the Aramaic equivalents of "Mama" and "Papa" and learn that one was linked with this person who fed him and changed his diapers, learn that the other was linked with this man who seemed so big and strong. Etc. etc., etc. Why should we go through what is largely fanciful and full of anachronisms? The main point for me is this: that the child Jesus, and the boy, and the young man, looked and wondered, and thought and came to understand, and did so with the ordinary ideas and concepts that belong to daily life in Palestine; he may have done so more quickly, more surely, under the influence of his vision, but without any direct influence on the actual content of the ideas formed—the content was empirically based.

When we come to religious ideas we should not think that the situation is totally different, as if the immediate knowledge of God supplied him with "religious" ideas where it was disdainful of mere secular ideas. In my view it is almost equally distant from the one and the other. We have to ask ourselves in what sense the word "God" is a religious word and how it comes to have a religious meaning for the child. There is nothing special in the three letters; they can be turned around to mean something else altogether. There is nothing special in the sound which makes it rhyme with who knows how many other words. What experience gives it a religious meaning, and by what signs are we led as children to link its use with that experience? My hypothesis says the experience which gives it meaning is the experience of coming to the limits of the human, of arriving at horizons, boundaries, of looking farther and coming up against sheer mystery—not just the mystery of what is over the next hill when we explore it as boys, but the mystery of what is beyond the grave, as when we watch them bury our grandmother. And the sign, my hypothesis says, which leads me to link the sound "God" to such an experience is found in the sudden illumination, tranquil or piercing, with which I recognize, for example in seeing my father and mother at prayer, that those who for me were the acme of human power, the almighty beings of my world, the eternal ones who were before I came and would be as far into the future as my mind could reach—the illumination with which I recognize they are not "God" but worship One who is.

We do, however, have to recognize differences when we try to apply this to the boy Jesus, but it is important to locate the differences and determine their influence. As I see it, there is no initial difference in the stock of particular words and ideas. There is an enormous difference in the illuminating power of the interior resources available. The scholastic would indicate this in terms of objects: the object of vision is the divine essence, the intellect of the infant has no formed object but is pure potency to any and all objects of human intellect. We cannot omit the objective but I find it more helpful to put the emphasis on the subjective and to speak of desire attained and desire still reaching out, or of a light that contains all that is visible within itself and a dark light that illuminates objects but is itself invisible. When I turn to objects I would say that in one case there is global apprehension of the All and in the other there is the pure desire to know All though nothing is yet understood or known. We may recall here how close the All and Nothing are in the vocabulary of the mystics, and I venture the guess that they are so close because in neither case is there anything like a particular word or idea.

The difference then is in inner resources and not in finite objects known. St. Thomas held that even in us all knowledge is somehow given with the native light of intellect, and it seems to follow that the differences in the boy Jesus would rather accelerate his learning process than eliminate it. He would recognize so much more quickly, in the sight of Mary and Joseph at prayer, their conscious subordination of themselves to Someone higher; he would identify that Someone so much more easily with the object of his interior experience. But, with all this granted, and giving due reverence to the Son of God, I think he would come to use the word "God" in somewhat the same way you and I came to use it. And if he learned to use the word "God" as we did, much more would he learn to use all the other words that formed part of his human vocabulary.

II. ESCHATON AND FINITE VALUES IN THE HEART OF JESUS

MY title commits me to speak about the eschaton in the mind and heart of Jesus. To speak of "mind" is to direct our thoughts to ideas and knowledge, but to speak of "heart" is to direct our thoughts to values. The "eschaton" in the heart of Jesus would refer to the ultimate value that engaged his heart in a fulfilling way. Our problem then in this section is to study that value in an analysis that will enable us to relate it to his earthly mission. We will be dealing, in other words, with the hierarchy of values in the human heart of Jesus, with the place given there to God and man, to a transcendent world and to this transient one. Eventually we will have to ask about the relation of his values to his daily life and conduct and thus come to their influence on his vocation and work in the world, his earthly mission.

My general procedure in this section will remain the same: that is, I will assume a hypothetical view as explanatory principle; I will expose it first in abstract generality and then speculate how on this basis we may relate the eschaton to finite values of human life on earth. The main effort then is to contribute an idea, leaving the work of verification and judgment to another time or to other persons. But in all fairness I ought to warn you that the support for my hypothesis and speculation is flimsy, more so than when I talked of the human knowledge of Jesus. In that case there was, if not a dogma, at least a long tradition of thought in the church; but there does not seem to be a parallel tradition on the question of the heart of Jesus and the values that engaged it. That statement is likely to provoke instant opposition from those who think that, if Jesus taught us anything at all, it was a set of true values. I may be inviting some opposition later on, but some is quite unnecessary, and I would like to eliminate the latter by explaining the sense in which I meant my statement.

I do not mean then that there is no evidence in the New Testament of a Christian hierarchy of values. There is a very definite hierarchy of this-worldly and other-worldly values, which are so sharply contrasted as to result in outright opposition. Paul and James agree on this, the one asserting that the wisdom of the flesh is enmity to God and the other that to be the friend of this world is to be the enemy of God. The doctrine of the beatitudes spells out the idea, and the doctrine of the perfect obedience of Jesus to the will of his Father, even when his own will spontaneously recoils, gives it a concrete focus.

Neither do I mean that this idea lacks a tradition. What is more characteristic of Christian spirituality than the imitation of Christ and the efforts of the saints, one after another, to discover his way, that is, his set of values, and make it their rule of life? I naturally remember here the Spiritual Exercises of St. Ignatius, the founder of my own religious order, where you have the exercise on the Two Standards setting forth the sharp contrast and conflict between the values of Jesus and those of the world, and the Principle and Foundation relativizing all worldly values in the principle of indifference. Even the theology manuals take up the question in their own way with theses on the sanctity of Jesus and his confirmation in grace. And the councils went so far as to define dogmatically that there is a human will in Christ, showing an interest here that they never showed in his intellect.

What do I mean then when I say that we have little in the way of tradition to help us in the present question? I mean that the *process* by which Jesus formed his set of values never came into question. Why should it? If you imagine a mind with a view into the other world, with the clearest picture of the joys of heaven and the torments of hell, then you have no need of any process of value-formation. The situation is clear at a glance. At least the great distance, the infinite qualitative difference, between this world's values and those of the other world is clear. You may work out more subtly the steps by which you are led to choose the better or the worse, the ways Satan has of ensnaring men's hearts, but this is not really an objective determination of the values themselves.

Now, however, our understanding of the Thomist concept of the vision of God has removed this easy supposition in which values are determined independently of us and may be taken for granted. Further, modern philosophy forces upon us the consideration that man is to a large extent the creator of his own values. The two facts conspire to raise a new question about the process in the heart of Jesus. We have to ask how he formed his heart, what forces were at work, to what extent he accepted the values of his time and culture and to what extent he forged new values of his own. We have to penetrate to the basic value which held his heart and see how that can be made operative for us today. Otherwise we drift without rudder or anchor; we judge Jesus by what is superficial in his conduct and, if that seems little relevant today, we have no way of locking our hearts into something more permanent and reliable. It is fairly clear, for example, that Jesus took little interest in the arts and sciences, the culture and civilization, even of his local world, much less of the great world of the Mediterranean. The church, however, takes a great interest in arts and science, culture and civilization. What are we to make of this? Is Jesus not our model? Or is he our model when we so will it, and not our model when we decide otherwise? You see that, unless we undertake a careful analysis of the process by which we formed his values and distinguish the universally valid from what was particular to his time or his vocation, we are without trustworthy guidelines in the Christian way of life.

Let me digress for a minute from the route of objective theology. The difficulty, as I have put it, is not just academic. I do not apologize for that. We are personally involved here, and to a high degree. When we speculated on the knowledge of Christ, we were not quite so immediately involved; there is surely a line of inflence from what we hold on Christ's human knowledge to what we recognize as a personal call to ourselves, but the line is long and indirect. Not so here. What we judge Christ to have set before himself as his value, that we ourselves must take as our value, if we are to be Christian. So it has been tacitly assumed. We could speak theoretically of a simple objective study of Christ's values, with its relevance to life for us held as a second question arising in distinction from the first. But in fact we have to discover agreement between Christ's values and ours, either by converting ourselves to what we find in him, or by finding in him (setting out to find in him) what we have already adopted as our set of values. I have to recognize openly and confess to you what you know for yourselves, that my mental power even to conceive the values Christ held is drugged by the opium of many a counter-attraction that appeals to me, and my power to assert these to be his values is treacherously influenced by those I have already taken as my own.

That little digression was necessary if we are to keep our perspective, I think. But now back to business. We will look at the New Testament set of values and subsequent tradition in a very general way and then see whether, with the help of modern thinkers and categories, we can speculate usefully on whatthe process of value-formation was in Jesus. We remember always that we have no direct access to what he said and did, the data that might reveal this process; we have direct access only to what the New Testament writers said, and we cannot assume that they understood their Lord perfectly.

In general then the early New Testament writings show a marked orientation to the other world. The earliest document we have is Paul's first letter to the Thessalonians and it sets the tone at once in its description of the conversion undergone by the Thessalonians; they turned from idols, Paul says, to serve the living and true God "and to wait expectantly for the appearance from heaven of his Son Jesus" (1 Thess 1:10). That phrase, "to wait expectantly," is especially significant. It is the key to what has been called the interim ethic of Paul: we are not to make much of marriage, sorrow, joy, buying, wealth, and the rest, because: "The time we live in will not last long. . . . For the whole frame of this world is passing away" (1 Cor 7:29-31).

As time goes on, however, and Jesus does not appear, it seems to be borne in upon the Christians of the young church that the coming of Jesus may be delayed, and delayed a very long time indeed; they had better settle in then for a longer stay than they had expected. With this realization two trends develop. One is more material and concerns the use of this world's goods, the formation of institutions, and the like. This trend comes out quite clearly in the pastoral letters to Timothy and Titus, where institutions are forming and you have explicit reference to the use of marriage, foods, etc.: ". . . God created them to be enjoyed with thanksgiving by believers who have inward knowledge of the truth" (1 Tim 4:3). The other trend, more spiritual in character, is towards an understanding of our condition in the world as one of partially realized eschatology; that is, there is a sense that we are already living in enjoyment of the final state, in communion with God and his Son Jesus through their Spirit who dwells in us. This is particularly evident in John's writings: "Everyone who believes that Jesus is the Christ is a child of God . . . every child of God is victor over the godless world" (1 John 5:1,4). We have already arrived, you might say; indeed, this is almost explicitly said: ". . . even in this world we are as he is" (1 John 4:17).

I don't wish to exaggerate, and I know that the sketch I have given is terribly "simpliste." There is community of ideas on a broad basis in the New Testament, and what is new is not wholly new. The element of "waiting expectantly" is there from beginning to end, not only in 1 Thessalonians but far on in the pastorals, as well as in 2 Peter and in John. On the other side, the element of present communion with God and his Son in the gift of the Spirit is also found from beginning to end of the New Testament writings. So is the element of the right use of this world's goods: when Paul is telling his Thessalonians to endure patiently to the expected end, he is also telling them to get busy about their daily occupations, and not to hang around waiting for someone else to feed them (1 Thess 4:11-12; 2 Thess 3:10-11). And, of course, everywhere there is inculcated love for neighbor, a love that shows itself in concern and deeds and not merely in words. Nevertheless, despite the strong continuity, I think there is a fairly steady trend in the direction indicated.

What subsequent history did was accentuate the polarization without, however, adverting to it clearly or dealing with it intellectually. I hesitate to expand that point, for anything I say will be hopelessly

superficial, but even a superficial view gives markers of great significance. One marker is the effective triumph of the position represented
by Clement of Alexandria over that represented by Tertullian. Tertullian thought that Jerusalem, the church, should have nothing to do
with Athens, the world of culture and especially of philosophy;
Clement of Alexandria held the exactly opposite opinion and his view
prevailed; despite spasmodic outbreaks of Tertullianism, I do not think
that there has been any turning back on the part of the church from
the direction vindicated by Clement. But another marker is the per-
sistence in the church, notably in her liturgy, of Tertullianist senti-
ments: collect after collect in the Roman missal urges us to despise
the things of this world, *mundana despicere,* and to set our heart on
heavenly things, *amare caelestia.* In other words, we have developed
that ambivalent attitude I mentioned earlier: we go on collecting art
treasures and cultivating philosophy and the sciences, while at the
same time we profess our faith in our Lord who, it seems, couldn't care
less about such matters. I do not think we have taken up this question
as a church and settled for ourselves what we really believe.

Neither the New Testament, then, nor subsequent tradition has
solved the problem of a Christian way of linking the values of this
world to transcendent value—"Christian" being understood here in
the sense of deriving from Christ's own values. Much less has either
one of them investigated the question that will occupy us now, of the
process by which Jesus formed his values. We may be able to get more
help from modern thinkers and their categories, and in this hope I turn
to Ernst Troeltsch. He does not clearly distinguish exegesis from
speculation but his views have impressed me and they will serve to
introduce the hypothetical ideas I wish to contribute.

What Troeltsch tries to give, I think, is a general perspective. He
sees the preaching of Jesus as emphasizing the great judgment of the
coming of the kingdom of God, and the formation of a community
based on the hope of the kingdom. Jesus does not speculate on the
nature of the kingdom; it means the rule of God on earth to be
followed by the end of the world and judgment. His demand is for
preparation; fundamentally, it is for the sanctification of the individual for the sake of God, with an ethic emphasizing purity of intention and reverence for all moral commands. He is marked by the
religious idea of the presence of God and by the thought of the
infinite value of the soul, to be attained through self-renunciation for
the sake of God. Here the gospel is very radical, not ascetic, but
severe. It does not allow doubt on the possibility of practice. Still there
is a character of joy, gentleness, readiness to forgive. It is not an
asceticism that is a provision for the future, but only a severity that
makes almost superhuman demands.

Troeltsch follows this with a section on the sociological characteristics
of the gospel ethic, a topic most germane to his study. There is an un-

qualified individualism based on call to fellowship with God and the infinite value of the self. But this very individualism also contains a strong idea of fellowship with one another, basis on the fact that those being purified for the sake of God meet in him. In a further section Troeltsch takes up the gospel ethic and general social values and finds no interest there in social problems which belong to this world and perish with it. There is no thought of the state; it is the rule of God that interests Jesus, not the rule of the Jewish people. Nor is there an economic policy; we are to live for the day, share with others, work for a living. There is a more detailed teaching on the family, which Jesus uses for symbols of God's highest attributes, and the idea of the family is a fundamental feature of his feeling for human life. But sex will not exist in the kingdom, and one may have to renounce family for the kingdom. The message of Jesus then is not a program of social reform but a summons to prepare for the coming of the kingdom. Even the kingdom is not a new social order founded by God. It creates a new order on earth, but not one concerned with the state, or society, or family.[32]

Against this background we can introduce the real question: how Jesus formed his mind on values and organized them hierarchically in his heart. Here again I call upon Troeltsch, in a work dating from the last days of his life, a set of lectures that he never in fact delivered, death intervening before he could do so.[33] Three of these lectures fall under the general title of "Ethics and the Philosophy of History," and the second of the three is called "The Ethics of the Cultural Values." It is towards the end of this lecture, almost in passing, that Troeltsch voices his views on the origin of systems of ethics and introduces the question in regard to Jesus.

The context of this passage is as follows. In a previous chapter Troeltsch has dealt with The Morality of the Personality and of the Conscience, which he sees as purely formal, as lying outside history, as leading to the timelessly valid. But that supplies just one thread in the fabric of ethical consciousness; a quite different one is introduced under the heading of goods and ends, ethical values. These are entirely historical creations: family, state, law, economic control of nature, science, art, and religion. These realms are not at first matters of ethics, but belong to specific and independent sciences; for example, the family is the subject of sciences of the sexual life and its sociological forms of organization. Only in the last place do these sciences look for the character which these realms *should* assume and thus merge into ethics.

How does a system of values come into being? A number of attempts to construct such a system proceed from a simple beginning to a simple goal. This is easier for a morality of consciousness, but harder for an ethics of cultural values. New and original attempts were made in the 19th century, but in the end they must admit defeat:

> All these attempts at a deduction of the system of values, be they
> based on the nature of Reason, or on that of the Community, or
> on the World-process, or on the religious goal, are helpless in the
> face of the fullness and vigour, and also of the tensions and cross-
> purposes, of cultural values in real life.[34]

Still cultural values have to be welded into a homogeneous whole;
however this is done, not theoretically, but unconsciously—the system
is evolved as a pure fact. In moments of crisis and in periods of greater
maturity a conscious synthesis becomes necessary. It will be an a
posteriori construction. It must assimilate the bases of its own de
facto existence, and only then refine and evolve itself. It does this by
determining the direction, by bringing out the central value and or-
ganizing the rest around it.

This last for Troeltsch is a personal act. It is also a personal act
to link this system with the morality of consciousness. There is no a
priori system available for this:

> Statesmen, reformers, poets, prophets, are usually active agents
> in this work. In spite of all their most elaborate reflections they
> can at bottom adduce for themselves no other plea than that of
> Jesus: "He who is of the truth heareth My voice."[35]

Faith ultimately decides and justifies the decision.

I have been greatly impressed by the passages from Troeltsch but,
now that we are moving from a system of values to its subjective foundations, I am going to shift my study from him to Lonergan. Possibly we could find further precious clues in Troeltsch and, in fact,
I think there is much to ponder on the relationship of Lonergan's ethical views to his, in the way they both see the formal and material
elements of moral consciousness, and in the way they see the person
as source, through inner experience or conversion, of the values he
finds in the objectively existing universe. But, as you perhaps know,
my own mind has been formed profoundly—irremediably, some would
say—by long study of Lonergan and I find it so much more con-
venient to search for clues in his writings.

As it happens, the most useful passages I have discovered are found
in a paper which Lonergan delivered here at Villanova University in
your symposium of one year ago, though the same passages occur in
the now published *Method in Theology* and I will therefore quote
thm from that work. The passages deal with the relationship of love,
faith, and belief. Lonergan accepts the distinction between faith and
belief, calls faith "the knowledge born of religious love,"[36] and makes
belief refer to the word of religion, "the judgments of fact and the
judgments of value that the religion proposes."[37]

There are three terms then to be explained: love, faith, and belief.
The first is best understood in terms of the state of being-in-love. The
state is dynamic. Being-in-love:

takes over. It is the first principle. From it flow one's desires and fears, one's joys and sorrows, one's discernment of value, one's decisions and deeds.[38]

That much is generic. But there are different kinds of being-in-love of which being-in-love with God is one:

It is God's love flooding our hearts.... It grounds the conviction of St. Paul that "there is nothing in death or life ... nothing in all creation that can separate us from the love of God in Christ Jesus our Lord" (Rom 8, 38f.).[39]

Being-in-love with God

is the basic fulfilment of our conscious intentionality. That fulfilment brings a deep-set joy that can remain despite humiliation, failure....That fulfilment brings a radical peace...bears fruit in a love of one's neighbor that strives mightily to bring about the kingdom of God on this earth. On the other hand, the absence of that fulfilment opens the way to the trivialization of human life in the pursuit of fun, to the harshness of human life arising from the ruthless exercise of power, to despair about human welfare springing from the conviction that the universe is absurd.[40]

Secondly, faith is the knowledge born of this religious love. It corresponds to Paschal's reasons of the heart which reason does not know. It is an intentional[41] response to values. It is not the factual knowledge reached by experiencing, understanding and verifying, but "another kind of knowledge reach through the discernment of value and the judgments of value of a person in love." When the love is religious love, "there is added an apprehension of transcendent value" consisting "in the experienced fulfilment of our unrestricted thrust to self-transcendence, in our actuated orientation towards the mystery of love and awe."[42] And, thirdly, there is religious belief arising out of faith:

Among the values that faith discerns is the value of believing the word of religion, of accepting the judgments of fact and the judgments of value that the religion proposes.[43]

I have quoted Lonergan at some length on the relationship of love, faith, and belief, not because I expect to use all the details of this relationship in putting forward an hypothesis on the mind and heart of Christ, but simply for one aspect of his discussion, the harmony that prevails between mind and heart in his exposition. I do not in fact think that in Christ, or in anyone who "sees" God, the first knowledge is born of love; rather, I take it that the first understanding is already knowledge and from it love proceeds on the model of Love in the Holy Trinity. But the harmony is the same. The difference is that in Christ the immediate knowledge of God is the principle of his love and obedience, whereas in us the love of God and our obedience to him form the principle of our faith.[44]

What we are dealing with then is a unitary consciousness formed by the harmony of mind and heart. It is a unitary consciousness that is fundamental, that pertains to one's being, that makes one what one is. It is a basic consciousness that is operative, that overflows into one's conduct and one's life. In this the parallel is close between the consciousness of Jesus and our own. On that basis I presume to quote again from Lonergan's paper in a passage where he links transcendent value with other values:

> As other apprehensions of value, so too faith has a relative as well as an absolute aspect. It places all other values in the light and the shadow of transcendent value. In the shadow, for transcendent value is supreme and incomparable. In the light, for transcendent value links itself to all other values to transform, magnify, glorify them. Without faith the originating value is man and the terminal value is the good man brings about. But in the light of faith originating value is divine light and love, while terminal value is the whole universe. So the human good becomes absorbed in an all-encompassing good.[45]

In this context of the link between transcendent and other values my own question now emerges: how is this link established in the consciousness of Jesus? What was the process in his heart by which other values were created and placed in the light and shadow of transcendent value? I assume that the link in values is derivative from a prior link in judgments, and then my question becomes, How did he effect the transition from a judgment on transcendent value to one on temporal value, or from a judgment on temporal value to one on transcendent value? As always, we keep in mind that we do not attribute these terms to him; we do not even attribute distinct acts of judgment to his mind; we do not attribute any clear advertence on his part to what was going on in his mind. If there was a process, it was spontaneous and unreflected; if he objectified it in any way, it would probably be by means of dreams, myths, images and the like.

With all this in mind I should say that the process now in question parallels the transition from his vision of the All to knowledge of particular items of the concrete universe, that is, knowing what-is leads spontaneously, through the negating power of the mind, to conceiving what-is-not. Conceiving what-is-not leads through the creative power of the mind to conceiving what-is-not-yet-but-may-be. Conceiving what-is-not-yet-but-may-be leads through reflection on personal responsibility to the idea of what-is-not-yet-but-may-and-ought-to-be-through-my-intervention. At this point the practical judgment emerges, the notion of particular value has been implicitly introduced, and we have the path outlined from apprehension of transcendent value to apprehension of human, cultural, religious values, the sort of thing Troeltsch talks about.

We can specify the course of this transition a little more concretely. The gospel commandment tells us to love God above all things and our neighbor as ourselves. The appearance in the horizon of Christ's consciousness of the-good-to-be-done is on biblical grounds to be set in the context of love for others. But this too has its abstract and philosophic counterpart, investigated these days by pioneering branches of philosophy. The good for us is the human good, and the human good is inextricably bound up with our relations to others. Just as the self appears and is conceived simultaneously with and in correlation with the other, so the need we see and the good we conceive in response to need is defined by our knowledge and love of others. A helpful parallel here is found in our doctrine of God's creative thinking. God's goodness is *diffusivum sui*, it overflows spontaneously to be shared by others; similarly, Christ's response to the goodness of God leads directly to his concern for his fellowman.[46]

We can also clarify the process in Jesus by contrast with our own. We ourselves experience a "conversion" of heart, maybe repeated conversions, as we move from lower to higher values in the course of a lifetime. Religious conversion is the shift from all values of the human universe to the transcendent value that God is. Normally we think of the order and direction as that I have indicated: from earthly to heavenly, from human to divine. We meditate on the ephemeral character of life on earth: "Your life, what is it? You are no more than a mist, seen for a little while and then dispersing" (James 4:14). We come from consideration of these limits to what is without limit, the boundless being and goodness of God. Whether in actual fact our hearts follow this order of development is another question; it may be that God brings us to a sense of the ephemeral through first giving us a dim anticipation of the eternal. However, when we come to reflect on the relationship, we almost necessarily see it in terms of a shift from lower to higher, simply because we can understand and are moved by the lower in a way proportionate to human nature, whereas we cannot understand the higher but live in faith, seeing through a glass darkly.

Jesus too would establish in his heart a relationship between the earthly and the transcendent, but I think there would be a reversal of the order and of the emphasis. The direction would not be so much a conversion from lower to higher as an emerging appreciation of lower means to a higher end. Thomas Aquinas saw conversion as a change in the end one sets before oneself, with the possibility remaining of choosing various means to the one end by which we are drawn. The heart of Jesus would not undergo the radical change that is conversion to another end of life, but it would experience ever new appreciations of ways and means. He would come to see the way of the suffering Servant of Isaiah as that way in which God means his chosen representatives to go. He would learn obedience by the things he suffered; that is, obedience would become a value to him as derivative from the value which is the goodness of God and the rightness of God's will.

In this way it would be easy in principle to account for the particular choices he made during life and the successive stages in his realization of the Father's will. I say, in principle, for always in actual fact we are handicapped by inaccurate knowledge of what he said and did, and what the circumstances were in which he said and did it. In principle, then, he could come to appreciate the value of being unattached to the world's wealth; it could become part of his set of values, and this in a process that would resemble the process the saints experienced, a Francis of Assisi or an Ignatius of Loyola. He could come to appreciate the value of having disciples who would extend in space and time the message he could not personally bring to everyone. Etc., etc., etc. At this point, we come to our last section, the worldly mission of Jesus.

III. THE WORLDLY MISSION OF JESUS

EARLY in my paper I quoted Bonhoeffer's question, "What is Christianity, and indeed, what is Christ, for today?" That question has been nagging at me since I first read it I don't know how many years ago. In some very fundamental but not very well-defined sense (that global apprehension I keep talking about) every Christian knows what Christ means for him today and every day. We die. We want desperately to live. Jesus lives after death and because of him we too will live. So he means everything to us. No amount of realized eschatology, or new secularity, or resolution in the face of our being-toward-death, has given me the power to cope as I move towards the dark exit. Only my faith in the risen Lord is any real help here.

But theologians may not stop at faith. We would be simple cop-outs if we did. For our faith is handicapped when its meaning is undefined. The urgency of Bonhoeffer's question remains—not the urgent need of a new apologetic for our faith, but the urgency of articulating more fully and defining the meaning of what Christ is for us today, and answering the questions that arise. For they do arise. "Jesus lives after death"—the very word "after" raises a question. It was "after" Good Friday for the apostles, for Mary and those who stood by the cross on Calvary. But was it "after" for Jesus himself, and what would "after" mean for him? He "lives" but that word too raises a question on the mode of life he enjoys. A senseless question, St. Paul said as he went ahead and tried to answer it. We too have to try to answer it. We are never going to overcome the darkness of faith by any of our theology, but we have to look for the dawn and we would not be what God made us if we did not try to do so.

So it is with the question we come to now of the worldly mission of Christ. It is not enough to say that the eschaton in the mind and heart of Jesus is the understanding, the knowledge, and the love of God. This could be said of the angels, it could be said of the blessed in heaven, it could be said of some non-existent human race who never lived on earth but were created in the eschatological state. We were not so created; we are born into this world, and the Son of God was incarnate in this world. What has this world to do with the eschaton? How do we relate the understanding, knowledge, and love of God that Jesus had to this very human world of arts and science, of culture and civilization, a world that after all God created to be enjoyed with thanksgiving by believers who have inward knowledge of the truth?

I have spent a long time and taken you through some very dull thinking in order to set up an answer to that question, but I saw no alternative if we are to have anything but a superficial answer. The options were to regard Jesus merely as a prophet to whom the word of the Lord came, or as one who had in his own inner resources that out of which the word of the Lord is spoken. If we opt for the second we are dealing with a participation in the divine understanding of mystery out of which God himself speaks when he chooses. Such an eschatological understanding is not readily related to the finite words and ideas of ordinary human activity, but we had to think out that relation in some plausible explanation if we were to talk usefully of his worldly mission. Now, however, the bulk of the work is done and our task in this final section considerably lightened.

First of all, we are not going to expect Jesus to have available from the start innate ideas and ready-made blueprints of his work. As he did not have the word "God" or the word "I" written on his mind, neither did he have the words "mission," "redemption," "Savior," etc. When he first heard those words he did not know their meaning, but had to learn it as we did. When he learned their meaning, he did not at once apply them to himself, as we do not. As he learned obedience by the things he suffered, so he learned by slow degrees what his vocation was.

Secondly, I would expect this learning to follow the pattern of the scissors-action we spoke of earlier. We may have models for this nearer at hand. It is said of Ignatius of Loyola that he had an experience soon after his conversion, in which he saw his future work laid out for him.[47] The strange thing is that he still had to discover the details of his work year by year and day be day, with much prayer and reflection. Yet I do not think we need distrust the tradition on that early experience of his. It is just that a great deal of thinking has to intervene between the general idea, the *species et genera rerum, et rationes earum,* which may have been given him, and the particular, concrete form the idea takes, which was not given him.

It seems to me that in a similar way the Lord Jesus went on specifying his mission step by step. By way of illustration I continue my effort to make an educated guess and speculate that an important step could have been taken at the age of twelve. I am not about to decide whether Luke was recording historical fact or constructing a story with a point, when he wrote about the child Jesus in the temple, but I have the liberty of any believer to suppose it could have happened the way he describes it. And then how would I reconstruct the Lord's thinking? I would say that at the age of twelve profound bodily and psychic changes are taking place in a boy. A new world is opening before him, and new possibilities of life. We all know how boys at a certain age despise girls, and then rather suddenly find them extremely attractive, begin to carry their books home from school, etc., etc. It's an old story and a familiar one! I see no reason to suppose that the boy Jesus didn't have experiences and feelings that correspond in large measure to our own, due weight being given to different environmental and cultural factors. But also at this very time new questions of a religious nature are coming to formulation in his mind: what is the purpose of life? what is man on earth for? what should he do with the sixty or seventy years that may remain to him? He has read or heard the scriptures, he knows about the boy Samuel being called by God in the temple. As he and his people come up to Jerusalem reciting and singing the gradual psalms, he finds a new meaning in the holy city, in the courts of the Lord, in dwelling in the house of the Lord.

So two new worlds open at once before him and, because it is not clear that their paths point in the same direction, he is faced with a decision. There is the world of the humanly good, of trades and skills, of marriage and family, of village life with its uneventful course and religious satisfaction. There is also the world of the temple, of the sort of life Samuel was called to. It is not hard to imagine the lines forming, with a strong impulse towards one and a quiet but persistent call to the other; it is possible to imagine the resolution of the conflict in the direction of the second, of his staying in the temple, convinced that his Father was calling him to a special vocation. It is possible even to conceive that he learned, after some days, and on the return of his parents, that he was not called just yet to remain in the temple as Samuel was, that a further process of maturation awaited him and must precede his definitive response in a specific way. But I wish to emphasize that the option was real: he could choose variously —there was no blueprint in heaven to look at.

In all this there would be operative the scissors-action of his knowledge of God on the one blade, a knowledge itself wholly unspecified as to categories but one from which vague and very general categories were gradually forming, and his boyhood experiences on the other blade, his memory of what Mary and Joseph said, of what he heard in the synagogues, of what he experienced at prayer. Speculation on various other steps of his career might be similarly carried out—what happened at his baptism, what went through his mind on encountering opposition from the leaders of his people, how he formed his views on going up to Jerusalem at the end of his public life, and in this way we could work out how he conceived his worldly mission in general.

I am not concerned so much to determine what his particular vocation and mission was in its details, as to insist that he had to work it out, and to understand *how* he may have worked it out and why he seems to have done so with such indifference to earthly values. So I underline again the fact that he learned what his mission was. What I said about his knowledge, that the empirical part of it came to his mind with startling newness, and what I said about his values, that he discovered and accepted those that were not transcendent, has also to be understood of his decisions. He did not have an action kit provided by the triune God as he left the courts of heaven for his mission on earth. We have continually to remind ourselves that he did not leave the courts of heaven as Man, that he had never been there as Man.

So we have to try to understand how he worked out his mission on earth. My own contribution to this task has to be made in abstract, general terms, and so I would say that he would find in the fulfilment of his own human nature (for which terms he would have biblical images, or unformulated ideas or perhaps vague conceptions) the notion of what man is and what man is to be. At some point in time he would learn, for this too would be a discovery, that other men did not have the vision he had, or the clarity of his apprehension of divine value. At this point he would more clearly perceive his mission to be one of service, and perceive himself to be "the Man for others," though, if Cadbury is right,[48] this modern phase is a bit anachronistic.

We can reduce the abstractness if we return to Troeltsch and adopt his more biblical terms. He specified the notion Jesus had of God as a notion of a holy Will, and more particularly as a holy Will directed to his creation and his people, a Will issuing a divine claim on the obedience and service of Jesus.[49] In some such biblical terms, I think, would Jesus become conscious of his responsibility; in biblical terms again would he become conscious of his solidarity with his people and his responsibility to work for and with them; in biblical terms would he come to realize the shortness of life, the limits set by a divine plan to the time of human response to God, and in some such context would he conceive the sense of urgency he shows, the exhortation to seize the *kairos,* and what we call the "crisis" parables.

But how do we explain his attitude towards the values of humanism? towards progress? towards abolition of injustice, and the like?

For in our time we have come to take a certain positive attitude towards
these and to associate such an attitude with our Christian faith. Lonergan, for example, finds that "faith is linked with human progress and
it has to meet the challenge of human decline." Faith and progress
thus help one another: "Faith places human efforts in a friendly universe . . . Inversely, progress realizes the potentialities of man and
nature. . . ."[50] And this seems thoroughly Christian and yet not to
reflect the immediate interests of Jesus himself.

We should not be "simpliste" about Jesus, however. We can say
that he recognized human values within a certain range. As far as we
can judge from the gospels, he knew and practiced the customs of
human courtesy (Luke 7:44-46). He apparently had a sense of the
value of the well-spoken word, of the well-chosen illustration. He
seems to have recognized the value of human trades and settled occupations. He seems to have studied the politics of the situation and not
to have needlessly antagonized the men in power. He perhaps learned
to sing (Matthew 26:30) and took the ordinary means, that of asking
the doctors, to learn the traditions of his people (Luke 2:46).

But the degree of interest in any human value is a function of the
particular situation. It is one thing to learn and respect and observe
the ordinary rules of courtesy, and quite another to make them your
life-study, either academically or practically. Christ was not called to
write such a book as Emily Post wrote. And when I say that he was
not "called" to do this, I mean to indicate a very central factor in the
"circumstances" that help locate a value in one's hierarchy. God calls
each one of us individually. General rules may provide the institutions within which we function, and guides to the validity of the interpretation we give his call. But there is a surplus element that does
not fit into the general rules. Colwell, speaking of our efforts to
categorize Christ, says we are like a man applying a measure to Christ,
who always finds him sticking out all around the edges.[51] It is the
same with an individual vocation. The individual person's call from
God has elements that stick out over the edges of general rules. And
Christ is an individual person with his own individual human nature.
Perhaps in another era he might have been a university professor lecturing on the history of courtesy, instead of being a carpenter building
chairs and tables in Nazareth; and in that university context he might
have pondered his mission to the world. But his vocation was to be
a carpenter and then, putting his carpentry behind him, to proceed
directly to the main concern of life, without ever denying the value
of carpentry in God's scheme.

So we have to exercise the ordinary rules of good judgment when we
examine his life and doctrine for his views on cultural values. We
look in vain for nuggets of wisdom on the value of an education, on
the exercise of the franchise, on the beauties of music and painting,
on the importance of mathematics, on experimental farms and fish

hatcheries for the improvement of basic industries, on the need and
value of football for growing boys, on the precious gems of the Latin
and Greek classics, and so on through an interminable list of the items
we might draw up to classify the set of values of our own or of a bygone age. His silence, I would say, is the silence of disinterest without
being the silence of condemnation. We are not faced with a choice of
black or white. To make poetry your career, to love poetry, to have
undeveloped power of appreciation of poetry, to condemn poetry—
these are four of many possibilities and we may not say that, if Jesus
is not in the first category, he must be in the fourth. His disinterest, I
suggest, was not programmatic, but just tactical or maybe involuntary
and an accident of history.

It may seem harder to explain his disinterest in starting schools
and hospitals, campaigning against slavery or for the development of
underprivileged peoples and the emancipation of women. For here
there is question of justice and charity. But a moment's reflection may
show these ideas too to be anachronisms. The idea of a hospital is a
slow growth in itself; even when you have the idea, its practicability
is a function of the availability of ways and means. Progress and the
improvement of the human lot in general are still more remote and
even slower to emerge. To make a very long story a little bit shorter,
human thinking has a history of thousands of years; it needs thousands
of years just because of the material substratum involved, just to give
impressions time to form, images time to reach schematization, questions time to emerge, ideas time to ramify, etc. To expect all this to
happen in a moment or even in a lifetime of thirty years, just because
a man has the vision of God, is really nonsense.

I began this paper with a reference to Jesus as our Lord and Savior,
as the way, the truth, and the life our model. I return to that idea now
and ask what, at the end of this study, can be said of the ideas and
values of Jesus as guides for our minds and hearts. I hope that at least
I have helped you eliminate a mistaken conception of the traditional
doctrine on the vision of God. I hope we are now ready to talk of
his encountering the world as fresh and new, of his learning day by
day the values his people cherished, of revising them and moving beyond them in the creation of new values. I hope we are ready to grant
the time-conditioned character of his mind and heart in regard to
finite objects and even in regard to his language about the Infinite
and his choice of ways and means to orient ourselves towards the
Infinite. And therefore we may not simply attempt to quote him
when there is question of the development of the third world, or condemnation of Fidel Castro, or dialogue with hippies and "Jesus freaks."
These are *our* questions to be solved by *our own* intelligence working
in the light of faith.

But I have been just as concerned to eliminate mistaken views at
the other end of the doctrinal spectrum. I have come down on the

side of the traditional doctrine of the vision of God in Jesus; I thereby make him once again our Teacher, and take a stand against radical
secularity. What he teaches us is transcendent. He saw God, he knew
God, he loved God. He also loved God's creation and by that fact is
at one with the best in modern secularity. But our notion of creation
is expanded through him; he himself is the first creation of God and
what he experienced in himself he knew to be God's ultimate purpose
in creation. That is what makes nonsense of radical secularity. The
good of man is to be divine, but humanity is not divinity. Man is not
made for bread alone but for every word that proceeds from God, and
this word is more than bread for the hungry, music for the musical,
culture for the masses, the whole range of what we regard as the human
and civilized and cultural good. It is more, not quantitatively, but
with an infinite qualitative difference. And this is what we learn daily
from Jesus as from one who knows and needed not that any man should
tell him on even that the word of the Lord should come to him to reveal it.

In my world then of subways and movie houses and ringing tele-
phones and electric typewriters I do not ask the gospel record how the
Lord Jesus handled it all; that is my own problem. But what I learn
from the Lord Jesus is that I must handle it because he has relativized
it.[52] It is not the All; there is always more. When I have learned
from him that there is "more," the "less" can never again be the
same. The "more" becomes my goal, not just as the distant end of a
journey but as a fulness of mind and heart that accompanies me on the
way. And Jesus is the way, not by reason of dress or state in life or
particular vocation or prayer-language, but by reason of his life and
passion and death, and the relationship to God which gave him his
fulness of mind and heart, relativized all things earthly, and kept him
united to God even as he went through the dark exit.

My last word is that what he means to me seems to come out most
plainly in my experience of my own deficiencies and differences from
him rather than in my positive approach to his state of mind and heart
and his way. I mean, for example, that as I struggled to write this
paper amid the ringing of phones, and the piling up of correspondence
to be attended to, and the working out of the thousand and one little
crises that find their way in a steady stream to the doors of administra-
tors, I came to realize far better the calm strength of mind that was
his through his vision of God. I could understand a little how his
vision remained even when the crowds pressed upon him and neurotic
heirs urged him to settle their lawsuits—remained and enabled him
to concentrate on the purpose of life and the urgency of the *kairos,*
while still relativizing the finite elements in which the *kairos* found
its context. Similarly, it is in the weakness of seeking distractions from
boredom and in the cheapness of so many of my heart's choices and
the triviality of so much of my pastime, that I discern and dimly appre-

ciate the heart of him who belonged to his Father, was one with his Father, and did always the things that were acceptable to his Father.

Of putting words on paper and making books there is no end. The fathers of the church distinguished theology, the science of God, and economy, the science of his work on earth for our salvation. Then, tired of all their endless words, they developed the notion of negative theology, an approach to God through what we do not know and cannot say about him. Maybe, after all these words on Jesus, we need a "negative economy" to bring us closer to his mind and heart through recognizing how he is different, and discovering in the fickleness and instability of our minds and hearts the horizon beyond which our Leader beckons us.

NOTES

[1] Martin Kähler. *The So-Called Historical Jesus and the Historic, Biblical Christ* (Translated by Carl E. Braaten. Philadelphia: Fortress Press, 1964). This Seminar Edition translates the first and second essays in the 1896 edition of the original German book.

[2] Albert Schweitzer. *The Quest of the Historical Jesus. A Critical Study of Its Progress from Reimarus to Wrede* (Translated by W. Montgomery. London: Adam and Charles Black, 1910). The German original appeared in 1906; a new English edition was published by Macmillan (New York) in 1968.

[3] Dietrich Bonhoeffer. *Letters and Papers from Prison* (London: Fontana Books, 1953), p. 91: "The thing that keeps coming back to me is, what *is* Christianity, and indeed what *is* Christ, for us to-day?" There are many editions of Bonhoeffer's Letters, so the most helpful reference is to say that this question is in his letter of April 30th, 1944.

[4] Johannes Weiss. *Jesus' Proclamation of the Kingdom of God* (Translated by R. H. Hiers and D. L. Holland. Philadelphia: Fortress Press, 1971). The German original appeared in 1892.

[5] *Op. cit.*, p. 397.

[6] *Op. cit.*, pp. 368-69, where we read the following: "The Baptist appears, and cries: 'Repent, for the Kingdom of Heaven is at hand.' Soon after that comes Jesus, and in the knowledge that He is the coming Son of Man lays hold of the wheel of the world to set it moving on that last revolution which is to bring all ordinary history to a close. It refuses to turn, and He throws Himself upon it. Then it does turn; and crushes Him. Instead of bringing in the eschatological conditions, He has destroyed them."—J. Moltmann, *The Theology of Hope*, London, 1967, informs us (p. 39, n. 1) that this passage was deleted from later German editions of Schweitzer's book.

[7] From an anonymous review of a book by J. N. D. Anderson *(Morality, Law and Grace)* in *The Times Literary Supplement* (London), March 24, 1972, p. 342.

[8] In the Nicene phrase, the Son is *homoousios* or consubstantial with the Father. But this was turned into the plain English I have used by G. L. Prestige, *God in Patristic Thought* (London: S. P. C. K., 1952), p. 213.

[9] *Summa theologiae*, II-II, q. 1, a. 9 ad 1m: "diffuse...et variis modis, et in quibusdam obscure."

[10] The scholastic supposition—a perfectly valid one, in due course formulated—was that anything Christ said as Man to men, he said out of the only knowledge he had at his human disposal, the knowledge in his human mind. There is a widespread and almost ineradicable error among those who believe in the divinity of Christ, that he had at his disposal, when he opened his lips to speak, the fulness of divine knowledge. But the divinity no more put divine knowledge at his human disposal than the divine Infinity gave him a bodily weight of an infinite number of pounds, or the divine Eternity made him an infinite number of years old.

[11] *Summa theologiae,* III, q. 15, a. 3; see also q. 10, a. 2, where the question is whether the soul of Christ knew all things *in Verbo*—the answer is yes.

[12] Athanasius. *Oratio III contra Arianos,* #4; *De synodis,* #49. See Bernard Lonergan, *De Deo Trino,* vol. I (Rome: Gregorian University Press, 1964), pp. 23, 48, 54, 85, 131, 140-41, 142-43, 202.

[13] This failure to integrate is the more likely since only late in life did St. Thomas reverse his former position and admit experiential knowledge in Christ: see *Summa theologiae,* III, q. 9, a. 4 c.: "... Et ideo, quamvis aliter alibi scripserim, dicendum est in Christo scientiam acquisitam fuisse."

[14] These three paragraphs summarize a section of my article, "Universal Norms and the Concrete 'Operabile' in St. Thomas Aquinas," *Sciences ecclésiastiques* 7 (1955) 115-49; see especially pp. 121-29.

[15] Bernard Lonergan, *Insight: A Study of Human Understanding* (London: Longmans, Green and Co., 1957), p. 352.

[16] *Ibid.,* p. 642. The Index (*s.v.,* Being—pure notion) wrongly gives the reference, p. 641.

[17] *Ibid.,* p. 349.

[18] *Ibid.,* p. 356.

[19] If I am right, this point will be important for understanding how Christ could lead a fairly normal life while still enjoying the vision of God. It would therefore be good to get hold of it, and I suggest the following analogy as useful: we are continually conscious of ourselves in all our psychological activity, yet we do not necessarily advert to ourselves or think about ourselves, for we are preoccupied with the object of our activity; in a similar way we do not advert to the notion of being even though it is present, consciously present, and continually operative.

[20] A. Poulain. *The Graces of Interior Prayer. A Treatise on Mystical Theology* (Translated by Leonora L. Yorke Smith. London: Kegan Paul, Trench, Trubner & Co., 1928), p. 278. The French original appeared in 1901; it has been re-edited and reprinted many times.

[21] *Ibid.,* p. 119.

[22] *Ibid.,* p. 120.

[23] *Ibid.,* p. 121.

[24] *The Life of St. Teresa of Jesus ... Written by Herself* (Translated by David Lewis. London: Thomas Baker, 1904); see ch. XI, #9 (p. 78): "I shall have to make use of a comparison; I should like to avoid it.... But this language of spirituality is so difficult of utterance for those who are not learned, and such am I...." Teresa then proceeds to her comparison of watering a garden.

[25] Poulain, *op. cit.,* pp. 122-23.

[26] *Ibid.,* pp. 127-28.

[27] *Ibid.,* p. 131.

[28] Two recent books are useful for exploring the possibility that our

dreams express to us a religious understanding that is preconceptual (though I do not attribute that phrase to either author): John A. Sanford. *Dreams: God's Forgotten Language* (Philadelphia: J. B. Lippincott, Co., 1968). Morton T. Kelsey. *Dreams: The Dark Speech of the Spirit. A Christian Interpretation* (New York: Doubleday & Co., 1968).

[29] It would be unfair to list opponents, reject their position, but not allow them "equal time" to expose their views. Yet it is utterly impossible to discuss the debate in a footnote. All I can do is give the source of the views underlying my own presentation: Bernard Lonergan's *De constitutione Christi ontologica et psychologica* (Rome: Gregorian University Press, 1956); a later exposition is given in his *De Verbo Incarnato*, 1964, but it is unpublished and hard to obtain.

[30] *Summa theologiae*, I, q. 12, a. 8 ad 4m; see also q. 106, a. 1 ad 1m.

[31] *Insight ...*, pp. 312-13, 522-23, etc.

[32] Ernst Troeltsch. *The Social Teaching of the Christian Churches* (Harper Torchbooks, 1960), vol. I, pp. 39-69 (=ch. I, part 1).

[33] *Christian Thought: Its History and Application. Lectures Written for Delivery in England During March 1923* (University of London Press, 1923).

[34] *Ibid.*, p. 92.

[35] *Ibid.*, p. 98.

[36] Bernard Lonergan. *Method in Theology* (London: Darton, Longman & Todd, 1972), p. 115.

[37] *Ibid.*, p. 118.

[38] *Ibid.*, p. 105.

[39] *Ibid.*

[40] *Ibid.*

[41] "Intentional"—that is, directed towards an object (not "intentional" in the sense of "deliberate").

[42] *Method in Theology*, p. 115.

[43] *Ibid.*, p. 118.

[44] There is a problem here in relating the early Lonergan to the later Lonergan. The precise question regards the interrelation of mind and heart. Most of Lonergan's work in Christology was prior to 1965 when he spoke in terms of intellect and will and saw understanding in the mind of Christ as prior to love in the heart of Christ. But most of his work on values is subsequent to 1965; he does not speak now of intellect and will but of levels of consciousness and when he applies this to us in our human condition on earth he sees falling-in-love with God as prior to faith in the traditional sense. Would he now see this as the order that obtains in the blessed and in Jesus? I am inclined to think that he would not but, not wishing to clutter up this paper with questions that may be of much greater interest to me than to my audience, I am leaving argumentation to this footnote.

The general principle operative here is that the relationship of mind and heart is the opposite in our religious experience and faith life of what it is in the blessed and what it is conceived to be in God. That is, the order in God is Father, Son, and Holy Spirit; or, in the Thomist transformation of these biblical names, the order is Understanding, Word, and Love. And this I take to be the natural order of the rationally conscious universe, the order therefore that obtains in the blessed who understand with a fulness that elicits expressions of awe in a never ending series and results in an eternally repeated act of falling in love with God. It is also the order for "natural" man on earth who determines his responsibilities on the basis of what he knows to be the facts. But in the graced activity of our faith life the order seems to be the reverse, as Lonergan had noted some years ago in his *De constitutione Christi ontologica et psychologica*: Ordo naturalis "quodammodo invertitur cum Deus per gratias infusas magis voluntatem quam intellectum ... movere possit et soleat" (p. 99). That is, the Holy Spirit is given to enable us to believe in the Son who will lead us to the Father. This inverse order is paralleled in the field of the virtues: charity floods our hearts and enables us to speak the truth of what is revealed; this truth we then try to understand in the painful and inadequate achievements of theology.—I conclude from all this that in Jesus the immediate knowledge of God is the principle of his love and obedience, whereas in us the love of God and our obedience to him form the principle of our faith. And this, I think, would be Lonergan's position.

45 *Method in Theology*, p. 116.

46 When I wrote that line, I simply took its truth for granted. But it was a good lesson for me on how little we know about Jesus to read afterwards Henry J. Cadbury, *The Peril of Modernizing Jesus* (London: S. P. C. K., 1962) and discover another viewpoint: that Jesus did not think so much of my neighbor's need as of my own duty to act rightly; the altruism of the social gospel is not characteristic of his approach (see ch. 5: "Limitations of Jesus' Social Teaching," especially pp. 101-111). It is also a lesson in the slowness of communication that Cadbury's book, which I just discovered, was first published in 1937.

47 This was the vision he had beside the Cardoner river, during the year he was at Manresa. Ignatius does not himself in his "autobiography" say that he saw his future career in this vision, but the tradition seems to have begun among those who talked with him about his experience, with Nadal a main source; see Roger Cantin, "L'Illumination du Cardoner," *Sciences ecclesiastiques* 7 (1955) 23-56. The validity of the tradition is debated, with a goodly literature on the matter. Hugo Rahner is strong for the view that Ignatius saw the outlines of his Company, *The Spirituality of St. Ignatius Loyola: An Account of Its Historical Development* (Westminster, Md.: Newman Press), 1953, pp. 96-103. Paul Dudon is on the other side, *St. Ignatius of Loyola* (Milwaukee: Bruce), 1949, pp. 452-455.

48 See note 46 *supra* .

49 *The Social Teaching* ... (see note 32 *supra*), p. 53.

50 *Method in Theology* (see note 36 *supra*), p. 117.

51 Ernest C. Colwell. *New or Old? The Christian Struggle with Change and Tradition* (Philadelphia: The Westminster Press, 1970), p. 104.

52 Historians relativize one period of history by measuring it against the indefinitely great possibilities revealed by other periods, but Jesus relativizes radically and ultimately by measuring all history against the Eternal.

A Processive View of the Eschaton as Community of Love

Eulalio Baltazar

THERE are two parts to my talk, the first part being a discussion of
tion here is how to conceive it in a processive way. How do we
from the processive point of view.

There are many forms of process thinking. The one I adopt here
is inspired by the thought of Teilhard de Chardin.[1]

I. PROCESS THINKING AND THE ESCHATON

THE eschaton as a theological category is the Parousia. Our question here is how to conceive it in a processive way. How do we
reinterpret the classic and traditional view of the eschaton based on
classic metaphysics as an other-worldly region devoid of temporality?
But of course, the more basic question is why reinterpret this classic
view at all? Well, for those who find security and comfort in the
traditional view, reinterpretation is unnecessary. But for those who
cannot see how a departure from temporality can be a perfection of
the temporal and how a flight from earth can be a fulfillment of the
earth, a reinterpretation of the eschaton is necessary. Ultimately the
way one conceives of the eschaton depends on one's view of the destiny
of the earth. There is a theological tradition that sees the destruction
of the earth, and another which sees its consummation and fulfillment
instead. The former view tends to see the eschaton as other-worldly
and totally transcendent; the latter inclines to a more this-worldly and
immanentist position. Thus the problem as to how to conceive the
eschaton resolves itself into the more general question as to the relation between transcendence and immanence. The advantage of the
transcendentalist view of the eschaton is its ability to present the radical
and qualitative difference between this world and the eschaton. It is
able to make room for the theological fact of God's *judgment* on this

world, for this world is sinful and corrupt. It therefore needs to be radically changed. But the transcendentalist view in the minds of many is dehumanizing, because it makes human fulfillment and liberation an abandonment of earth and of time. It is unable to justify commitment to social change, to fighting for justice against exploitation and manipulation of the poor and the oppressed. It produces a perpetual tension and schizophrenia in Christians who because of their jobs must devote themselves to the things of earth and yet because of their transcendentalist view cannot totally give themselves to the pursuit of excellence in their work. Some immanentists attempt to correct these supposed shortcomings of the transcendentalist position but in the process are unable to take account of God's judgment upon the world. Other immanenists in their passion for secularity have identified the Kingdom of God with the secular city[2] and in projecting the nature of the eschatological future have envisioned it according to the present quantitative values of the secular world, namely, in terms of material and economic prosperity for all. Thus the qualitative difference of the eschaton from the secular world has been ignored. The question then is how to show both the transcendent and immanent nature of the eschaton. To show transcendence as the possession of timelessness will not do, for then it is impossible to show how the timeless can be immanent in the temporal and be perfective of the temporal. On the other hand, to identify the eschaton with temporality will not do either, for the transcendent nature of the eschaton cannot then be explained. How can the eschaton be in time and yet somehow transcend temporality?

Teilhard de Chardin has located the maturation of the world at the Omega point. But having said this he leaves many questions unanswered. How does one relate grace to evolution? How can one show the radical and transcendent nature of the eschaton if the changes within the evolutionary process are a gradual rather than a radical and revolutionary kind? How relate the eternity of the eschaton to evolution? What happens to those who die? How are they a part of evolution? Teilhard has not answered these questions explicitly either because of the limitations of his methodology or because of a deficient philosophy.

What we need to do first is to get a clearer understanding of the nature of time. In the classic and metaphysical view of the eschaton, implicit in it was a view of time as negative, that is, as tending to non-being and death as it moves forward into the future. The reason for this is that the ancients did not have an awareness of the processive and evolutionary nature of time. Indeed, it is not to be denied that they saw development with respect to individual growths as in the case of a seed or fetus that grows to full maturity. But they did not have an inkling that there is a macrocosmic process of evolution such that the various species of life evolved. With the view of time as negative, it was logical for classic theology based on classic metaphysics to portray salvation as an escape from time.

Today, however, modern man sees time as positive, that is, as productive of novelty in such a way that there is more at the end than at the beginning of a given process. Conditioned by this view of time, modern theology has become more historical as opposed to the metaphysical. Redemption is thus portrayed existentially as a history of salvation. But this move does not necessarily make the eschaton immanent in the world. For a distinction is made between salvation history and evolution. Salvation history is outside the evolutionary process.[3] The reason for this is the necessity of preserving the gratuity of redemptive grace. Salvation is not something that can be achieved by the natural powers of this world, hence, not by evolution. Evolution, it is claimed, does not save; the grace of God saves. But if the history of salvation is distinct from evolution, the problem of making the eschaton immanent to a world in process remains.

In reality there is not much difference between the metaphysical view and the salvation history view. Both of them are other-worldly, that is, isolated from the world that science has discovered. Evolution does not figure at all in redemption. It is claimed that it has its own natural goal or end; its goal cannot be the eschaton which is achieved by the power of grace, not by natural selection. The result of either view is to put the Christian faith in isolation from the evolving world. Indeed we must save the gratuity of grace and also of the eschaton. But aren't we paying a great price—the isolation of theology from the world? What is needed is to show the immanence of the eschaton in evolutionary time.

The inability of traditional theology to make the eschaton immanent in evolutionary time is due in part to the Aristotelian heritage and to a scientistic view of evolution. The Aristotelian philosophy of nature sees nature as possessing natural powers to achieve its own natural end. Grace is thus superimposed on nature, instead of being constitutive of it; otherwise, we fall into the Pelegian heresy. Grace ends up being extrinsic to nature.[4]

I believe that one has to give up the concept of nature when thinking of grace, for grace is not so much related to nature but to the person, since grace as God's gift of love is properly addressed to that in man which can respond to love, hence to the personal in man, not to impersonal nature. If we use the category of the personal it is possible to make grace constitutive of man while at the same time maintaining its transcendence.[5]

The second difficulty in making grace immanent to evolution is due to the scientistic concept of evolution. From the scientific point of view, God cannot enter the picture in the evolutionary process as a co-principle of evolution, for he is beyond empirical verification. The scientist using scientific method can only explain evolution in terms of causes that are observable scientifically. Thus he concludes that evolution operates through natural selection or some other natural cause. The theologian makes a mistake if he takes this valid scientific concept of the causality of evolution and then concludes that only natural causes operate in the evolutionary process. With this concept, the theologian must necessarily exempt grace and the eschaton as fruit of the process of evolution, else the gratuity of grace and of the eschaton would be endangered.

What is needed is a philosophic reflection on the nature of the causality of the evolutionary process. From a philosophic point of view we come up with two opposed conclusions. The first is that the evolving universe is self-sufficient and self-transcendent and therefore does not heed God as co-cause; and the second is the affirmation precisely of God as co-cause of evolution. The first position is affirmed by Marxist ideology; the second, by Teilhard de Chardin.[6]

From the Teilhardian view, God is the Ground of the evolutionary process. Briefly, an analysis of the phenomenon of growth as transcendence reveals that anything which grows in our experience always needs a "ground" so to speak, that is, something other than that which grows. A seed that grows needs the soil, moisture, oxygen, sunlight, etc. as ground; the fetus needs the womb; the animal, its environment; the personal I needs a Thou for the maturation of personality in love. Thus, if we look at the macrocosmic process of evolution as a process of growth then we would have to conclude that it too needs a ground and we call this ground God.

In process thought, the theological category of creation is reinterpreted to mean that God evolves the world, the presupposition being that the world is still unfinished. Evolution then is God's creative action expressed in time. If our analysis is correct that God is the Ground of Evolution, then it follows that the goal is not achieved by the sole powers of the universe in process. The gratuity of grace and of the eschaton are thus safeguarded. It is possible therefore to make grace and the eschaton part of the evolutionary process. And it would be quite correct to say that evolution saves.

The question now, however, is that although we have achieved the immanence of the eschaton, we may have given up its transcendence. As immanent, the eschaton is within evolutionary time and therefore has a dimension of time. And being eschatological, it implies future time. But what does future time mean? Is it in the same line as historical time? Does the eschatological future mean, let us say, 6000 A.D.? If one were to conceive evolutionary time as simply a line that marches forward in which each moment of time is like a dot in a horizontal straight line, then there is no basis for transcendence, since each dot is of equal ontological value as any other. Going beyond a previous position does not necessarily mean transcendence. But neither is time to be conceived as a forward movement that quantitatively increases much

like a rolling snowball. There is increase and hence some sort of transcendence here, but this transcendence is neither radical nor qualitative
enough. Hence the year 6000 A.D. seen as the sum of a quantitative
increase of what came before does not express the radical and qualitative
difference of the eschaton, since this future merely represents the
region of transcendence of cultural evolution such as the growth of
cities, nations, cultures and civilization. Thus, the category of history
is unable to show the transcendent nature of the eschaton.

To grasp the radical change that takes place in the eschaton, the
Scriptures liken it to the transformation that takes place when a grain
of wheat is planted and then germinates.[7] Resurrection is a dying of
the seed in order that it be reborn into a new life which is a new time
dimension. In the biblical example of growth, the time that it takes
for the seed to expand and increase in size short of germination is of
a different time dimension from that of the time after germination.
From this example, we are thus able to differentiate historical time
as the time before transformation, and eschatological time as the time
after transformation. Furthermore, we are able to see that just as the
oak is qualitatively different in form from the acorn, so eschatological
time produces qualitatively different forms from those evolved in historical time; however, there is evolutionary continuity between the
two time dimensions. Therefore, eschatological time should not be
termed suprahistorical or supernatural if these terms mean radical discontinuity between the two orders or dimensions.

For the metaphysical minded, the issue is not immanence but transcendence. The notion of judgment taken in its full implication seems
to mean revolutionary change, not evolution. Hence, the eschaton is
not achieved by evolution. The basic question here is the distinction
between evolutionary and revolutionary change. If we conceive evolution as just quantitative increase in which the form remains the same as
a seed increasing in size but all the while keepings its form as seed,
then a more radical form of change such as the transformation of the
seed into a plant would have to be termed revolutionary. But our point
precisely is that this more radical form of change is part of the evolutionary process. In other words, the principal category is that of evolution. Revolution is within the context of evolution, for evolution ad-
mits of two kinds of change: quantitative and qualitative. One is
gradual and the other radical. It is false to equate evolution with
gradual change and then to oppose it to revolution as radical change;
for in the actual situation, all the most radical changes we know like
earthquakes, the extinction of species, cultural, political and economic
revolutions are all within the context of an overall macrocosmic process
of evolution. For example, the very radical change from matter to
life or from unconscious matter to conscious matter which in any frame
of meaning would be termed revolutionary change is yet part of one
continuous macrocosmic process of evolution. What is essential to the

concept of evolutionary process is not gradual change but continuity. Now, the concept of revolution seems to imply discontinuity, while evolution implies continuity. But the terms continuity and discontinuity are relative terms. In order to contrast two types of change, for example, the increase in size of a snowball and the germination of a seed, we speak of the former as continuous and the latter as discontinuous change. But what appears as discontinuous to common sense is really continuous when seen in a broader context. Thus the common sense view finds it difficult to see the continuity between rational life and irrational life, for to common sense what is irrational cannot possibly produce what is rational. But the actual process of evolution goes by a different logic, namely that for a thing to become itself, it has to become other than itself. Thus, the acorn has to become a non-acorn, that is an oak; the infant has to become a non-infant, that is, an adult in order to become themselves. Common sense plays tricks on us if we demand that in order to accept the tradition to rational consciousness from lower forms of life, we have to find there a diminished form of rational consciousness. This would be like prescribing that to find the early form of the oak, we must condition ourselves to look for a miniature oak form. If at the lower level we already had life, then what need the evolution of life? Or if we already had consciousness, then what need the evolution of consciousness? But if we accept evolution realistically, it follows that if we find consciousness at a later stage, then we have to look at the earlier stage as state of nonconsciousness to be able to see continuity. It is thus possible to accept that unconscious matter evolved to consciousness or that nonliving matter evolved toward living matter. Similarly when we try to conceive the nature of the eschaton, we must be prepared to use the logic of paradox. It would be false to project the future in terms of the forms we see now. Thus, as St. Paul has said, no eye has seen nor ear heard nor is it within the wildest imaginations of man to attain even some glimmer of what God has prepared for those who love him. We cannot even ask a proper question about it, for whatever questions we ask are necessarily based on present forms and experiences which must be however denied as representative. To gain an understanding of the eschaton we must push beyond scientific rationality toward mysticism.

But at this point the metaphysical minded confronts the process thinker on the mystery of death. How does one understand death within the context of process? For is not death a judgment, that is, a radical break from the things of this world, from temporality and history. If present human existence is to be identified with history and temporality, should not the place beyond be properly termed superhistorical, hence, metaphysical? The superhistorical or the beyond history it seems can only be conceived as timeless, for if it were also temporal then it would mean that one is still subject to the vicissitudes of time, to its sufferings and injustices. The concept of heaven as parousia implies freedom from injustice, sufferings, and death which are the fate of all those imprisoned in time. Thus, it would seem that a processive view of the eschaton cannot present the above-mentioned qualities of the eschaton, since a continuation of the present into the life beyond death would hardly be considered heaven. But that is precisely what an evolutionary approach seems to imply if evolution means continuity, rather than discontinuity.

By way of contrast, the traditional metaphysical view of death is presented as a union with and a participation in the life of God. Since the life of God is traditionally viewed as timeless and eternal, dying must have to be presented as a departure from time into timelessness. In so doing, it had to have an anthropology in accord with its eschatology. Thus, man was presented dualistically as composed of body and soul, that is, as composed of a material part and a spiritual part, both of which are substantial principles (id quo) of one concrete substance (in quod). According to this metaphysical anthropology, it is precisely because there is a spiritual substance in man that is independent of matter, namely, the human soul, that makes it possible for man as opposed to animals and plants which also have souls, to participate in the timeless life of God. Implicit throughout metaphysical philosophy and theology is the presupposition that the spiritual is related to the timeless, while the material is related to temporal. Only man among living things has a spiritual soul; animals and plants have material souls. By material here is meant not that the souls of animals and plants are corporeal but that their operations are so immersed in matter that they may be called material. For example, vegetative activities found in both plants and animals such as digestion and reproduction necessarily require bodies. Likewise, purely sense activities of animals show that animal souls are material because the objects of sense like color, sound, weight, smell, taste are measurable according to hue, intensity, saturation, loudness, pitch, and so on. By way of contrast, the intellectual operations of man such as conception, judgment, reasoning and willing are considered immaterial activities because an idea or a concept abstracted from the material conditions of the phantasm with the help of the agent intellect is immaterial. By an immaterial concept is meant that the idea or concept let us say, "man" abstracts from the sense particularities of concrete men, like their height, weight, color, and so on. As abstract the concept can be predicted of all individuals that pertain to the class concept man. The concept is thus called a universal and its universality depends on its immateriality. The brain, of course, is needed in all these so-called immaterial activities, but its necessity is purely that of a necessary condition, rather than a cause of these immaterial operations, much like a translucent window that lets the sunshine in but is not itself the cause of the light in the room; rather it is the necessary condition for the

light coming in which is caused by the sun. So, too, the brain is just
a condition; the efficient cause of the concept is the intellect. Besides
this philosophical proof of the immateriality and spirituality of the
human soul is a theological proof, namely, the traditional position
that the human soul was created directly by God and infused into the
body either at the moment of conception which is the prevailing view
or at a later stage according to St. Thomas. The fact then that the
soul came directly from God rather than having been evolved as was
the case with animals and plant souls means that it is spiritual in
nature.

So much for metaphysical anthropology. Now, how does this anthropology relate to eschatology? In accordance with this metaphysical
view, at death, there is a separation of body and soul. The body cor-
rupts and goes back to earth; the soul departs to heaven and because
it is spiritual it is able to participate in the timeless eternity of God.

Metaphysical theology is perfectly logical. Because the timeless is
better than the temporal, then its theodicy or doctrine of God has
to present God's eternity as a timelessness; traditional anthropology
must also emphasize man as other worldly, putting more value to the
spiritual which is immaterial and atemporal than to the bodily which
is material and temporal; and finally, traditional eschatology following
on these metaphysical views of God and man presented death as a departure from this world of temporality and contigency into heaven
eternal.

The basic objection to an other-worldly anthropology is that expressed by Robert Johann:

> One of the difficulties with a spiritualist anthropology is its
> tendency to make man a stranger in the world. For some thinkers,
> to hold that man is spirit, albeit *embodied spirit,* is to hold that
> he has access to another world besides this one, another world that
> is his true home. As spiritual, man may be *in* the world but is really
> not *of* it. He is only 'passing through.'[8]

The result of this dualism is a compartmentalization in man's life:
an outer life of the body lived in time, and an inner life of the soul
lived in eternity.

Another difficulty arising from the separation of body and soul
after death is the question of personality. Personality, in the traditional metaphysical view, is a relation resulting from the union of
body and soul. After the separation at death, what happens to it? No
adequate explanation has been given.

From a more theological point of view, metaphysical dualism does
not seem to square with Credal Faith which emphasizes not so much
the separation of the soul as the resurrection of the body. Now, how
does a metaphysical theology that sees heaven and God's life as timeless bring the human body into heaven without at the same time de-

stroying its nature precisely as material, that is, as temporal and historical. And above all, from a Scriptural point of view, metaphysical
dualism of body and soul is anti-Scriptural, for in the Scriptures man
is always seen as a whole. The dichotomy is not between body and
soul but between the whole man as either sinful or fleshly (sarx),
or as a man of God (ruach).

Leaving the criticism of metaphysical anthropology aside, we can
also bring forth a criticism against a metaphysical theodicy which
presents God's eternity as timeless.

Contrary to the belief of many that the timelessness of God's eternity is Scriptural is the true one that it is "a divine time which overflows, holds together, and envelops all other times. . . ."[9]

This view of God's eternity as temporal was also the view of primitive Christianity before Platonic philosophy was used as a framework
for the theological systematization of Scripture. Thus as Oscar Cullmann reminds us:

> Primitive Christianity knows nothing of a timeless God. The
> "eternal" God is he who was in the beginning, is now, and will
> be in all the future, "who is, who was; and who will be" (Rev 1:4).
> Accordingly, his eternity can and must be expressed . . . in terms
> of endless time.[10]

There was justification for a metaphysical theology in the past,
since, to convert the Greeks the Gospel had to be expressed in Greek
categories. For Greek thought the timeless was the region of being.
Thus for Plato, man was his spiritual soul; his body was a prison.
God dwelt in the timeless beyond. And eschatology for Hellenism,
as Cullmann observes

> can consist only in the fact that we are transferred from existence
> in this world . . . bound to . . . time, into that Beyond which is re-
> moved from time and is already and always available. The Greek
> conception of blessedness is thus spatial; it is determined by the
> contrast between this world and the timeless Beyond; it is not
> a time conception determined by the opposition between Now and
> Then.[11]

Today with our historical and evolutionary outlook, a nonmeta-
physical theology might be more meaningful and certainly be in closer
conformity to the Scripture. As we have indicated earlier, God's life
is expressed biblically in terms of time rather than of timelessness;
man is conceived nondualistically, emphasizing the resurrection of the
body rather than the salvation of the soul. Similarly the eschaton is
seen as occurring in the eschatological future. But these are the Scriptural data. Our task is to formulate theologically these data so as to
form a coherent whole. We need to formulate a theological view of

God and man as process so that we can also present death as process.

The task of showing man as process, I have already attempted. As a matter of fact, the attempt was given in a talk here at Villanova on the occasion of the first Theology Symposium. In that talk[12] I tried to show that all of man evolved, that man is wholly temporal, having come from evolution and nowhere else. This evolutionary view is not contrary to the doctrine of creation since, as we have shown, evolution is not a wholly natural process. Evolution from the *philo-sophic point of view* as opposed to the scientific view needs a ground and we call this ground God. God's creative action of producing man is thus by way of evolution.

An analysis of man's uniquely human activity also shows that man is ordained to time and process rather than to the timeless. Thus, the uniquely human activity which differentiates man from the animals is not so much the ability to think in a conceptual way which is a very tenuous position, for animals too do think and learn, but man's ability to foresee. Of all the animals, man alone can foresee, plan, provide. In these activities, the future is a necessary dimension. Man alone among the animals is able to fear death because he can grasp it as a future event; man alone can be subject to anxiety and care because he grasps the future as uncertain and uncontrolled. The distinction between animals, and man is not atemporality but precisely temporality expressed as the greater ability of man to gather time through human consciousness. Animal consciousness can gather only so much of the past by memory, part of the present by sense perception, and the future is hardly achieved by consciousness if ever. Human consciousness by way of comparison is better able to gather the past by going back billions of years, better able to attain the present by conceptualization, and to foresee the future. Man is a prophetic and predictive animal. The ability to attain so-called "universal" concepts is not so much the ability to attain timelessness as the ability to attain past, present and future.[13] What distinguishes man from the infrahuman levels is his type of temporality we call historical. Infrahuman beings like animals, plants, and inorganic substances are not in historical time. The historical is a new dimension of time distinct from the cosmic time of inorganic substances and the biological time of plants and animals.

I have also shown how God's eternity may be expressed as the Fullness of Time.[14] Time as an evolving reality evolves from contingency to immanence. A non-evolutionary view of time is one that keeps on being contingent as it moves on into the future, never reaching a stage of fullness or maturation of time itself. But what does it mean for time to mature or attain fullness? To get an idea of the notion of the fullness of time, let us compare historical time and cosmic time. Historical time is the time subject to human consciousness and purposiveness; cosmic time is the time that governs atoms and molecules. Cosmic time is chaotic, without direction, short-lived, unstable; his-

torical time relatively speaking is purposive, more stable, immanent
to itself in self-consciousness. In man, past, present and future are
somehow gathered together. Through memory, man is able to gather
the past; through reflection man is able to coexist with the present,
and with foresight, imagination, hope and belief both past and present
are able to somehow coexist with the future. Thus, through human consciousness, time for the first time becomes transparent to itself, hence
immanent. Human temporality represents the maturation, hence, the
fullness of time of the infrahuman levels. Time, instead of flowing
out as in the case of cosmic and biological time is somehow preserved
in historical time. But historical time is not its own fullness and source
of maturation. There is need of a Ground which gives the future to
historical time and brings it to maturation. God's eternity, then, is
the fullness of time, as the ground or source of maturation, much as
the ground is the source of growth and maturation of plants or the
womb, the source of maturation of the fetus. God as the Fullness of
Time does not himself grow, just as the mother who gives maturation
to the child in her womb is not that which grows but that which gives
growth. The Fullness of Time does not imply the cessation of all
motion or activity. The image of time as a horizontal straight line
that comes to a stop once growth is reached is not a true image of
evolutionary time. Rather, when the fullness of time is reached such
that past, present and future in that line of growth are integrated or
gathered together this means the fullness of activity. Indeed, there is
more activity in the infant in the line of growth towards the adult
than the adult itself which has ceased to grow. But the activity of
the adult is a greater activity in another sense than that of the infant,
that is, in the line of human activity, for the adult has developed
powers, physical, intellectual, moral powers compared to the undeveloped powers of the infant. The activity is more integrated, more
purposive, more stable, more rational, and so on.

At death then, man attains to a participation in the eternity of God
which is the Fullness of Time. This participation does not mean the
cessation of all activity, but rather the commencement of the fullness
of activity since we are able to gather and take a hold of all of ourselves and are thus able to give the whole of ourselves to each and
every act of ours, compared to human activity in historical time in
which we can give only part of ourselves—our present and our past
which we can remember, but not much of our future.

Dying, in the context of process thought, is not a flight into timelessness but a passage into a new time dimension—the eschatological
time dimension which is a higher stage of time than historical time.
Just as historical time is qualitatively different from the biological time
of animals and plants or the cosmic time of atoms and electrons, so
is eschatological time qualitatively different from that of historical
time. And just as plants and animals have no conception whatsoever

what it is to be in historical time, what the activities would be in that time dimension, e.g., what rational activity is, what willing is, what fear of death is, what love is, what getting an education means, and so on, so we who are in historical time have no conception as to the activity in the after-life. All we can say is that it would be an immeasurably higher form of activity, something superhuman, but we are unable to form an idea of it since our categories by which we grasp meaning are all historical rather than eschatological.

But having stated that dying is a qualitative change from the historical time dimension to a higher one, the eschatological, the question still remains, namely, where are the dead? In the metaphysical view, we simply say that good souls go heaven, without asking further where heaven is since heaven being a timeless region cannot be located in point of time. But if after-life is a new time-dimension, then those who die must be located somewhere. But where? To say they are in eschatological time does not help our understanding very much. Are the dead somehow in this world then, since they are not in an other-worldly realm?

The question, "Where are the dead?" in order to be answered properly must first be qualified. There is the common sense view that stones, plants, animals and men share a common place we call world or universe. Thus, when we ask, where are the dead, we are asking, where are they within a common place we call world or universe. But this type of questioning is false and illusory. For place must be understood in an evolutionary and processive way, not in a static way. In other words, from a processive point of view, different places imply different time dimensions. In a static way, atoms, plants, animals and men are in a common place. But in a processive way, atoms, plants, animals and men have different places. Place is relative to one's space-time dimension in the evolutionary process. Thus, an atom, a plant, an animal are not in my place as a historical being, nor could I as a historical being be present at the time of cosmic evolution. In metaphysical philosophy and theology a being's nature is not determined by time, for time is merely an accident. But in process thought, one's nature, so to speak, is determined by one's place in evolutionary time. Thus an atom is precisely an atom because it occurred at the stage of cosmic evolution, and man is precisely man because he came into being at a particular stage of the evolutionary process. Within historical time, an atom, a plant, an animal are nowhere to be found. In the biological space-time dimension an animal, say a dog, will be able to grasp man as another animal, performing the activities of motion, having shape, color, etc., emitting sounds and so on. But it is unable to perceive man as an ex-animal, that is, as willing, thinking, and so on, for man as intellectual is in a different space-time contiuum.

To come back to our question: where are the dead? We answer that they are not in our historical time. Are they in this world? If by this world we mean the world grasped by our senses, no; but it does not mean that they are in an other-worldly place, anymore than the biological time dimension is outside the evolutionary process simply because it is not grasped by atoms and stones. To help us understand that the eschatological time-dimension is not other-worldly but is somehow part of this universe, let us imagine the universe to be a gigantic cube or dice. A cube has three dimensions: a line which is a one-dimensional figure, a surface which is two-dimensional, and the cube itself which is three dimensional. Now let us imagine that there are beings inhabiting each of these dimensions. In the line, there are beings whose activity is all one-dimensional: motion to and fro. These one-dimensional beings have no true idea what a two-dimensional being is, for in trying to imagine it in terms of a one-dimensional frame of reference they have distorted it. Again when they try to imagine what a two-dimensional place is, it is in terms of a one-dimensional place that they try to grasp it. When one of these one-dimensional beings asks the question: "Where are these two-dimensional beings?" he is implicitly presupposing, where are they within the one-dimensional world, for that is the only world he knows. Thus, when one of these one-dimensional beings dies and goes into the two-dimensional world, he is nowhere to be found among the living. He is suprasensible, so to speak, since he cannot be grasped in terms of one-dimensional mode of knowing and consciousness. Yet, the two-dimensional space-time dimension is part of the cube. It is not something apart from it. We in historical time are like one-dimensional beings who cannot imagine or perceive other dimensions in this universe. Our form of consciousness is able to operate within the historical time dimension. Yet, there are other time-dimensions to the universe which we are not aware of and for which a new qualitatively different form of consciousness is needed. We can get an inkling of them from man himself as the highest point of the evolutionary process so far. Extrasensory perception, prophetic powers, are some indications. There are depths in the unconscious region of man which represent the level of the superconscious, the region of the numinous which man has not yet attained. As Teilhard notes, the human brain as symbolizing human consciousness is tending towards the formation of a supra-brain that will enable us to be reborn to a new time dimension—the eschatological.

Those who have died are like two-dimensional beings who are nowhere to be found in the one-dimensional world and yet are very much in the universe seen as a multi-dimensional process. Two-dimensional beings represent a higher level of activity and participation in the three-dimensional world than one-dimensional activity. In fact, just as a surface is an infinite line, so two-dimensional activity represents the fullness and maturation of one-dimensional activity but of which, nevertheless, one-dimensional beings have no grasp.

Those who have died are still part of the evolutionary process, and are participating in it and doing more for its successful consummation than are men in historical time. The Communion of Saints does not mean praying to a saint in a timeless beyond who cannot understand what is going on in time, but praying to the saints who are in time and who know what is going on in time because they are precisely in a higher dimension of time much as men in historical time are able to know plants and animals and atoms who are in cosmic and biological times more than these know of themselves. As long as the final judgment has not come, all those who die are in evolutionary time. In a sense they are in heaven, for just as the surface is the infinite of the line and the cube the infinite of the surface so eschatological time is the "eternity" so to speak of historical time or historical time the eternity of biological time. But they too are still waiting for the final judgment, for the Fullness of Time.

Summarizing the first part of our talk, we tried to present a processive view of the eschaton as the fullness of time of historical time. It is qualitatively distinct from historical time. Along with the processive view of the eschaton we also presented briefly a processive view of man as structured for the future in terms of the highest activity of faith, hope and love; and we presented a processive view of God's eternity as the Fullness of Time. To attain this Fullness of Time we must labor within evolutionary time. There is no other road. In the second part of our paper, we will discuss love as the energy that powers our pilgrimage towards the eschaton as the Fullness of Love.

II. A PROCESSIVE VIEW OF ESCHATOLOGICAL LOVE

IN the first part of this paper we presented a processive view of the eschaton without, however, describing it as a society or rather as a community of love. There we simply tried to show that the eschaton is not an other-worldly realm divorced spatially and temporally from this world. On the contrary, we said that a processive view of the eschaton shows it to be related to this world evolutionarily as being the new time dimension which comes after the historical time dimension. In the course of presenting this processive view of the eschaton, we also had to present a processive view of man and of God, for a change cannot be introduced in one area of theology without a corresponding change in the other areas. We said that a processive view of the eschaton necessitates a processive view of man as a wholly temporal being, that is, as totally evolved and whose central and unique human activity is the gathering of time. Man's destiny is not in some timeless region, but in time. It is by the possession of time that one survives, and conversely, it is by the loss of all time that one ceases to exist. For this reason, evolution is nothing else but the development of organs and powers for the attainment of time. Evolution evolved toward human consciousness because through it time is more fully attained through memory, conceptual knowledge and foresight. Eschatological time, on the other hand, is attained in this life through the activities of faith, hope and love.

If the possession of time is the measure of the fullness of being and activity, then God, who in the processive view is the Fullness of Time, is also the fullness of being and activity, or, rather, he is the Ground of being and activity. The destiny of man and all levels of evolution is a participation in God's eternity as the Fullness of Time. Our participation in it is called eschatological time.

So much for a brief summary of the first part of our paper. Now, we would like to show that the essential characteristic of eschatological time is love in its fullness and that this love is totally evolved, as opposed to the other-wordly view of love as infused from above. We will show also how love is the ultimate energy for the building of the earth.

We have already established in the first part of our paper the possibility of the total immanence of love and also its gratuity. To recapitulate briefly, we noted that because God is the Ground of evolution, it follows that whatever goal evolution achieves is achieved not by the powers of evolution alone, but also with its Ground which is God. The goal of evolution is therefore not only immanent as being a product of the process of evolution, but also gratuitous and transcendent because it is achieved thanks to its Ground. It is thus possible to accept as the goal of evolution a community united by grace or love, without falling into the heresy of Pelagius. But to show the possibility of a love-community as the goal of evolution is not sufficient. We must show that evolution actually is tending towards this community of love. Of course, the Scriptures tell us that the eschaton is a state of peace, unity and harmony of all creation with their maker. It is not sufficient, however, to graft this theological truth to the evolutionary process without showing precisely how that goal is achieved by the dynamics and activity of the evolutionary process itself. Our task then is to show that evolution is the evolution of love and that its end product is the fullness of love.

Teilhard de Chardin helps us to see how evolution may be considered as the evolution of love. Thus, he says:

> Considered in its full biological reality, love—that is to say the affinity of being with being—is not peculiar to man. It is a general property of all life and as such it embraces, in its varieties and degrees, all the forms successively adopted by organised matter. In the mammals, so close to ourselves, it is easily recognised in its different modalities: sexual passion, parental instinct, social solidarity, etc. Farther off, that is to say lower down on the tree of life, analogies are more obscure until they became so faint as to be imperceptible.[15]

Thus, using the evolutionary perspective, Teilhard sees love as the general property of all life. But in order to see it at the lower levels, one has to see its various modalities. And farther down the evolutionary ladder, it is more difficult to find the presence of love. One can only conclude in a general way, as does Teilhard, that love is the affinity of being with being.

There are those who cannot admit the evolution of love. The reason for this is a static mind-set which demands that to verify the presence of a given reality in the past one must look for it in precisely the form in which it presents itself in the present. The Aristotelian principle of identity and noncontradiction valid for a static world which states that A is A and cannot be non-A is invalid in an evolving world. This logical and epistemological principle is the stumbling block to the possibility of ever seeing the evolution of love. We must start with the basic presupposition that a thing evolves, for to start with the Aristotelian principle of non-contradiction is to deny a prioristically this very presupposition. Let us start then with the hypothesis that a thing has evolved. To verify the truth of this hypothesis, one has to use the principle of paradox, namely, that to find the identity of A in the past is to look for a non-A form, for this is precisely the implication of evolution, that is, that there has been a qualitative change of form. There is an inchoate form and an evolved form. Now, the inchoate form cannot be the same as the evolved form, else there would be no evolution. Thus, as we mentioned in our first talk, the acorn is not the same in form as the oak. So it would be wrong methodologically to look for a miniature oak in the evolutionary past. Similarly, to look for love which presents itself today in 'hominised' form, we must be prepared to look for it in a 'nonhominised' form. It would be false methodology to demand that, at the level of the molecule, molecules have some form of miniature consciousness and will which can elicit a miniature or minimal degree of love. No, a molecule does not love the way a human being loves. But love at this lower level is expressed as the propensity of one molecule to unite with another. As Teilhard reminds us:

> If there were no internal propensity to unite, even at a prodigiously rudimentary level—indeed in the molecule itself—it would be physically impossible for love to appear higher up, with us, in 'hominised' form. By rights, to be certain of its presence in ourselves, we should assume its presence, at least in an inchoate form, in everything that is.[15]

Process thought is not being metaphorical but quite literal when it sees the inchoate forms of love at the lower stages of the evolutionary process. Molecular attraction, cell association and multiplication, and at the higher levels of life, sexual passion, reproduction and social soidarity are literaly the various forms and stages of love. Love is manifestly found in its hominised form as the interpersonal attraction of personal centers of consciousness. Hence, it is psychic and conscious. But it is difficult to see love at the lower levels because we cannot imagine inanimate and unconscious matter as being psychic or conscious and therefore as being able to love. Again, however, we have to learn to see how consciousness could have evolved from the lower levels. If evolution means transformation, then for consciousness to have undergone transformation, it must at first have been in a nonconscious state which is what matter is. From an evolutionary point of view, matter is frozen or solidified spirit, hence already possessed of an internal propensity to unite. This propensity manifested itself after billions of years as physical convergence or love.

The process of psychical convergence is a process of cephalization or cerebralization. In other words the particles converge to attain and form a nucleus, center or head. Thus, the atoms converge to attain and form the molecule as their center; molecules converge to form the cell as center; the various organs of an organism are united through a nervous system that is concentrated in the brain or head; human beings as personal centers of consciousness unite to form a family, a clan, a tribe, a town, city or nation—all with heads or leaders. But evolution transcends all these forms of convergence in order to attain a universal center of convergence or supreme head—the Omega point. The fullness of love is achieved only when humanity is united with and centered upon its Omega.

The Omega maintains the unanimity of the world's reflective particles. Hence its energy or dynamism is that of love. The Omega is both lovable and loving. Teilhard identifies this Omega with the cosmic Christ who draws all things to himself by the attractive power of love. Here, Teilhard echoes Christ's words: and I if I be lifted up will draw all things to myself. The eschaton, then, is a community of love which includes not only reflective particles but material creation as well, for as St. Paul says, material creation also is groaning to be redeemed. Process thought gives an explanation for the foregoing passage of St. Paul. Thus, since love which is the basis for redemption is found not only at the level of man, but also at the infrahuman level, then by virtue of the presence of love at the infrahuman levels, these levels too can be redeemed.

The Omega point as the source and fount of love radiates its love to the lowest levels of evolution. Teilhard sees this action as actually taking place today through the Eucharist. Thus he says:

> Christ—from whom and in whom we are formed, each with his own individuality and his own vocation—Christ reveals Himself in each reality around us, and shines like an ultimate determinant, like a centre, one might almost say like a universal element. As our humanity assimilates the material world, and as the Host

assimilates our humanity, the eucharistic transformation goes beyond and completes the transubstantiation of the bread on the altar. Step by step it irresistibly invades the universe. It is the fire that sweeps over the heath; the stroke that vibrates through the bronze. In a secondary and generalized sense, but in a true sense, the sacramental Species are formed by the totality of the world, and the duration of the creation is the time needed for its consecration. *In Christo vivimus movemur et sumus.*[17]

But the Omega cannot do this process of redemption alone. It needs man. Thus, the future of evolution depends upon the conscious direction of man, for man is evolution conscious of itself. Man's locus of operation within the evolutionary process is the noosphere. The noosphere is the realm of reflective consciousness, the dimension of history and civilizations, the sphere of society and culture. The future of the noosphere hinges for Teilhard on the growth of amorization, that is the free circulation of love energy in the world.

For Teilhard, present evolution is taking place in the souls of men and in their mutual union. The main instruments for the next evolutionary stage are not so much mechanistic and technological as psychological and moral.[18] This point brings us to the phenomenon of religious communities and their role in evolution. Religious communities represent the high point of unification of evolving reality at the present time because through the religious and moral principle of love man is able to unite himself with his Omega and with the infrahuman levels of evolution. Measured by love as the basis for organization, religious communities transcend civil societies based on material conditions for their unification, in terms of universality and depth of association.

Let us now take the prime example of a religious community, namely, the Church, and see its role in the evolutionary process. Jesus founded a Church of which he is the head. The one important commandment that binds the members is love. One law Jesus left—that his followers love one another as he has loved them. He himself set an example of love: Greater love than this no man has that a man lay down his life for his friend. In the evolutionary context, we might say that Jesus is the spearhead of that little flock that will lead the human community towards ultimate unity in Omega. In the words of revelation, he is the first born, the first fruit. And having gone ahead, he has left the Church to carry on his work of redemption which in evolutionary terms is creative union. The Church then is a force for unification. It is the source of love energy.

In the system of thought of Teilhard, the Church is the phylum of love, the Christified part of the universe, mediatrix between God and the world, the principal axis of redemption through love, the principle of progress and of reconciliation of tendencies and movements in the noosphere which are in themselves divergent.

For Teilhard to say that the Church is a phylum is much more than a metaphorical expression. A phylum in the biological sense is a zoological group or branch having its own power and specific law of autonomous development; it grows and expands through socialization. It is a living bundle.[19] What defines a phylum is the "particular direction in which it groups itself and evolves as it separates off from neighbouring forms."[20] Now just as at the level of the zoological, there are various groupings or phyla, so at the level of the noosphere or human consciousness. Civic societies and communities are organized on the basis of material factors such as race, biological kinship, economic considerations and so one. But the Church represents a qualitatively different principle of organization. As Teilhard notes, the Church is a "qualitative value which expresses itself—like all biological progress— by the appearance of a specifically new state of consciousness," namely, Christian love.[21] The Church is a new phylum because its principle of synthesis is new and qualitatively different from those of previous organizations, this principle being that of love. As Teilhard notes:

> It is a phenomenon of capital importance for the science of man that, over an appreciable region of the earth, a zone of thought has appeared and grown in which a genuine universal love has not only been conceived and preached, but has also been shown to be psychologically possible and operative in practice. It is all the more capital inasmuch as, far from decreasing, the movement seems to wish to gain still greater speed and intensity."[22]

In the vision of Teilhard, cosmogenesis evolves into biogenesis, biogenesis into noogenesis and noogenesis into Christogenesis. As he says: "If the world is convergent and if Christ occupies its centre, then the Christogenesis of St. Paul and St. John is nothing else and nothing less than the extension, both awaited and unhoped for, of that noogenesis in which cosmogenesis—as regard our experience—culminates. Christ invests himself organically with the very majesty of his creation."[23] In this scheme of evolution, the Christian faith is destined to save and even to take the place of evolution.[24] In Teilhard's evolutionary view, evolution has no exit, no possible issue outside the Christian axis.[25] As he explains:

> I have tried to show that we can hope for no progress on earth without the primacy and triumph of the *personal* at the summit of *mind*. And at the present moment Christianity is the *unique* current of thought, on the entire surface of the noosphere, which is sufficiently audacious and sufficiently progressive to lay hold of the world, at the level of effectual practice, in an embrace, at once already complete, yet capable of indefinite perfection, where faith and hope reach their fulfilment in love. *Alone,* unconditionally alone, in the world today, Christianity shows itself able to reconcile, in a single living act, the All and the Person. Alone, it can

bend our hearts not only to the service of that tremendous movement of the world which bears us along, but beyond, to embrace
that movement in love.[26]

From the foregoing passage, a question of capital importance arises.
Thus, if the Church is the phylum of love, the principal axis of evolution and without which evolution fails, what happens to the atheist,
the Marxist, the Buddhist, in short, the non-Christian? How about
those who neither know nor love Christ? It would seem that if what
Teilhard says is true, then one has to be a Christian somehow, that is,
be part of the phylum of love which is the Church to attain Omega
and hence redemption. Is the eschatological community then only
Christian?

For Teilhard, it is the totality of men that is the subject ultimately
capable of spiritual transfiguration and of forming together a single
body and a single soul in charity. But this is as far as Teilhard would
go. He does not explain explicitly how nonChristians could be part
of this totality which is the eschatological community. We could only
surmise that one of the reasons for his silence was the severe strictures
imposed by the Roman authorities on his system of thought. But it is
possible, I believe, to give an answer to the question of the salvation
of the nonChristian within Teilhard's own system of thought.

First of all, let us note that Vatican II theology has moved away
from the traditional Tridentine theological position with respect to the
salvation of nonChristians. Thus, not only does Vatican Theology grant
salvation to both the atheist and the nonChristian but also grants the
same salvation granted Christians.[27] Hence, it is not a "natural" salvation but a supernatural one, that is, one in the order of grace. Furthermore, Vatican II theology maintains that nonChristians are saved
precisely as nonChristians, that is, the atheist is saved not by becoming
implicitly or anonymously Christian but precisely by remaining an
atheist.[28]

Within the processive view we can explain the Vatican II position
by saying first of all that salvation is creative union with Omega.[29]
In Scriptural terms this union with Omega is expressed as a covenant
union. Now, we are proposing that the eschatological covenant should
not be called Christian; otherwise, atheists and other nonChristians
who are saved are in effect really krypto-or implicitly Christian, which
is not in accordance with the Vatican II view that atheists and other
nonChristians are saved precisely as atheists and nonChristians. The
Omega is wider than Christianity. It is not the sole goal of Christians,
but of all men. We are introducing here a distinction between the
covenant in Jesus to which Christians belong and the eschatological
covenant which is the covenant of the cosmic Christ, the word Christ
meaning simply savior, a term which is also applied to Krisna. With
this distinction which is based on a very traditional view that the

cosmic Christ is wider than Christianity, wider than the Scriptures, wider than the Christ of Christian theology and belief it is possible to say that the atheist and the nonChristian need not be implicitly Christian to be saved. In other words, he need not be a member formally or implicitly of the covenant in Jesus to be saved. He does not have to be baptized, be a formal member of the Church, accept a certain set of beliefs. This position seems to be confirmed by the Scriptures when they admit various covenants in which individuals could be saved. Thus, besides the covenant in Jesus and the eschatological covenant with the Lamb there is the Mosaic covenant, the covenant with David, the covenant with Noah, and the creation covenant. These covenants were decisive points in the sovereign administrations of grace and of promise, hence specifically redemptive in purpose.[30]

Given these various covenants, one need not be within the covenant of Jesus to be saved. One need only to belong to one of these or other covenants granting that there are other covenants not mentioned in the Scriptures. Now, for the atheist, a covenant that corresponds to that of the covenant in Noah seems to be the appropriate context of his salvation. In this type of covenant, no awareness of God is required, since it is a covenant made also to the infrahuman levels of creation. No awareness or intelligent understanding that there is a covenant or that one is making one is needed; no response is asked, no formal commandment is demanded as a condition for the bestowal of grace and redemption. All that is required is to cooperate in the continuation and preservation of life for the sake of the future of the new earth, in the case of man, and for the infrahuman levels, merely to continue to reproduce and thus preserve, prolong and create life.[31] Thus, it is possible for individuals to deny the possibility of an Omega or of an Absolute. All that is necessary, to use the words of Teilhard, is a fidelity to the things of earth. Faith in the world, changing it for the better in one's own little sphere is the basic faith needed. It need not be the more explicit faith as contained in the covenant of Moses or of Jesus. This faith in the world contains the power and saving energy of love because this faith unites one with the future of the earth. From the processive point of view, love of the things of earth is the common and essential constituent of all faith-covenants. Without the hellenic conditioning that makes us see faith as propositional truth, we can see that love of the things of earth is also the basic constituent of faith in the Scriptures. Thus we are told in the following passage:

> When the Son of Man comes in his glory, escorted by all the angels, then he will take his seat on his throne of glory. All the nations will be assembled before him and he will separate men from one another as a shepherd separates sheep from goats. He will place the sheep on his right hand and the goats on his left. Then the King will say to those on his right hand, "Come, you whom my Father has blessed, take for your heritage the kingdom

prepared for you since the foundation of the world. For I was hungry and you gave me food; I was thirsty and you gave me drink; I was a stranger and you made me welcome; naked and you clothed me, sick and you visited me, in prison and you came to see me." Then the virtuous will say to him in reply, "Lord, when did we see you a stranger and make you welcome; naked and clothed you; sick or in prison and go to see you?" And the King will answer, "I'll tell you solemnly, insofar as you did this to one of the least of these brothers of mine, you did it to me."[32]

Thus, it is not the assent to the truth of a set of theological propositions that is necessarily going to save one, but how human we have been. The one commandment of Christ is love. Love is expressed as love of the human, love of the world. As Teilhard de Chardin observes, "Up until now, love of one's neighbour has meant doing him no harm and binding up his wounds. From now on, without losing any of its compassion, charity will complete its work in lives dedicated to human progress. . . . Indeed, such a Christianity is still the true Gospel, for it represents the same force applied to lifting up humanity beyond the material in a love which is universal." Or again he says: Charity no longer demands that we merely bind up wounds; it urges us to build a better world here on earth and to be the first ranks of every campaign for the full development of mankind.[33] This better world is to be built in and through love. The ideal is expressed Scripturally as an eschatological community of love.

But the building of a better world in terms of a community of love must be properly understood. Love has to be seen as a dynamic force, not for preserving the status quo but for change. What is not often realized by many is that love in practice is ambivalent. To many it is the smooth and nonviolent side of love that is equated with the meaning of love. It is understood as a sentiment of good feeling, harmony and peace with one's neighbors; loving means the preservation and enhancement of what is. It means not creating a fuss; not stirring up trouble. Love is equated with passivity. The other side of love as destructive, harsh, violent, even ruthless is not seen. On the contrary, qualities of violence, destruction and ruthlessness are equated with hatred and evil. It is this other side of love, the shadow-side or dark side that I wish to bring out.

First of all the traditional definition of love as a passive virtue, equated with law and order, with preserving the status quo must be seen as derived from a static philosophic world view, and not from the Scriptures. Christian theology which became hellenized was reinterpreted in terms of the static hellenic world view. Thus God was seen as creating a finished universe. God created each species, endowed them with all the powers and potentialities to achieve their ends. In this view, all men need do is to preserve nature which was finished. Man must preserve things; try to keep them in their so-called pristine beauty, as perfect as when they first came forth from the hands of God. This static view is anti-evolutionary. It sees perfection in the beginning. To love things then is to preserve them. To preserve is to refuse to admit change, because change is seen as destructive of what a thing is. With the hellenic mind-set which saw the future as negative and as tending towards non-being, and truth as immutable, the Church took on the function of a curator of a museum. It identified itself with the forces that opposed change. Church leaders were chosen for their lack of imagination and absence of prophetic powers. They were the first systems analysts whose function it was to maximize law and order and authority and to maximize the status quo by threats of anathema for any slight change or variation. In short, lack of creativity and prophecy were maximized by rewarding them with positions of leadership. To love the Church was simply to obey. The viewpoint of timelessness was quite logical, for everything was finished; everything was systematized; everything had an answer in a static and finished universe. There was therefore no room for the visionary, the prophet. When Church leaders preached love they preached it as a purely private virtue. Love did not have a role in the building of the earth. Love did not pertain to the changing of social organizations and institutions that opposed and exploited people. Viewed as other-worldly, it was mostly expressed in terms of fidelity to ritual and ceremony, to the frequentation of the sacraments, and the amassing of indulgences.

To see the power of love as this-worldly and as a force for change, to see love as prophetic and visionary, one has to give up the static mind-set, for the universe is not finished but is in process of evolution. A thing is not what it is but what it will be. To love a thing then is not so much to keep it from changing, but precisely to change it for the better. There is obviously risk involved, but to take the other option of not risking at all is to lack faith and love; in fact to refuse to let a thing evolve is really a hatred of the thing, since to wish it not to change is to wish its death. An unchanging thing in an evolutionary world is a dead thing. Survival, the hope of life and being is in evolving. To love a thing then is to evolve it; to direct it toward its fullness in the future.

But to properly direct a thing to its future, one must have faith, hope and vision. In short, one must cultivate prophetic powers or depend on those who are truly prophetic. If the Church is the phylum of love which is the symbol and sacrament of the eschatological community of love, then the leaders of the Church must be chosen for their visionary and prophetic powers. Once this vision is outlined, the task of love as a spiritual force for change begins. Love takes on the function of judge of the present. As judge, love points out what must be changed in the present. Love is thus a revolutionary force, upsetting the present order and its mode of organization for the sake of a higher organization which results in higher being, higher actualization.

This dynamism of love may be illustrated in the case of the growth of the child to adulthood. To love a child is to guide it, direct it to become a responsible adult. First it means weaning the infant from the mother, upsetting the security of the infant, drawing it away from its small organized world with the mother as center to a wider world which is more real. Then for the child to grow up, it has to give up the things of a child, as St. Paul observed. Growing up is violent. It calls for the giving up, often at the cost of great pain, anxiety, and insecurity, of one's previous world or organization for a higher one in which one's being is more actualized. False love, on the other hand, is pampering and spoiling the child with the result that growth is stunted. What is true of a child is true of all growing realities. Growth is the process of maturation attained by the acquisition of a new center, a new convergent point or omega. We can see this process verified in the macrocosmic process of evolution itself. Thus, to attain a new level of being, the atomic world had to give up its atomic center and take on the molecule as a new and higher center; the molecule in its turn in order to attain the new dimension of life had to give up its own molecular center, restructuring its previous mode of organization so as to be centered on the cell; the cell in its turn had to multiply and unite, giving up its own individual center, and after millions of years, to be unified by a central nervous system centered on the brain, resulting in the new dimension of consciousness. Consciousness in its turn evolved by the acquisition of newer and higher centers of consciousness until fianlly it reached human consciousness as center, enabling it to reach the new dimension of history. The new dimension of history is characterized by the emergence of human communities which require for their growth, first the acquisition of centers of organization and secondly the surrender of these centers for a higher and more universal one. In the acquisition of new centers, history has shown a great amount of waste, violence and death. But it need not always be this way. The mode of transition from one center to another needs to evolve from violence to nonviolence. One way of minimizing force and violence is the realization by peoples that evolution advances as a whole or it advances not at all. As Teilhard notes, "The outcome of the world, the gates of the future, the entry into the super-human—these are not thrown open to a few of the privileged nor to one chosen people to the exclusion of all others. They will open to an advance of *all together,* in a direction in which *altogether* can join and find completion in a spiritual renovation of the earth. . . ."[34]

An obstacle to the acquisition of a new center is the refusal to love expressed in current terms as superpatriotism and racism. Patriotism in itself is a principle of unification, but it becomes an obstacle to unity when one takes the attitude that one is a citizen of a nation first before one is a citizen of the world and when one acts on the principle: my country right or wrong. Racism is likewise an obstacle to world consciousness. As Teilhard observes: "False and against nature is the racial ideal of one branch draining off for itself alone all the sap of the tree and rising over the death of other branches. To reach the sun nothing less is required than the combined growth of the entire foliage."[35]

In evolutionary terms, superpatriotism and racism are the forms which entropy takes at the level of the noosphere. Entropy in its widest sense is the loss of energy for creative union. It is the counterforce to love energy, and like love, it evolves and takes on various forms depending on the level of evolution. At the lowest level, entrophy takes the form of loss of physical energy, or radioactive decay resulting in the dissolution of material substances. At the level of the cell, entropy takes the form of the loss of organic life, hence biological death. And at the level of the noosphere, which is the level of personal centers of consciousness, entropy takes on the form of ignorance, prejudice, hate, which are forces of disunity sundering the brotherhood of man.

The lower levels of evolution have somehow transcended entropy by obeying the very law of their beings to unite and to converge. In the process, evolution attained the stage of reflective consciousness, thanks to the infrahuman levels. Man as evolution conscious of itself must now transcend the entropy peculiar to his evolutionary dimension. He must attain full freedom through reflective action and fully human choice.[36] He must learn to love. To love means to remove all sorts of basic inequalities. To love is to actively will the other to be what he is, that is, a person. A person is one that is inner directed and endowed with the fullness of freedom. To reduce a person to the status of a thing and commodity is not to love the person, but to hate him. A society which reduces many of its citizens to the status of things to be manipulated and exploited through its political and economic institutions is a force of entropy. It is a violent force, doing violence to the person. The force of love must abolish this force of entropy. If this force of entropy is backed by law and order defined by those in power, then love is not on the side of law and order. Love therefore requires the destruction of this law and order in order that a higher law and order be achieved. In this case, love becomes a sword of liberation.

Love is not on the side of rich and privileged nation states which through economic imperialism prevent third-world nations from attaining economic development and freedom, which, in short, put national interest over world interest. Nor is love on the side of rich and powerful individuals who have attained their status through the manipulation and exploitation of others. Ironically, however, when Christian leaders preach love to the world, it is almost always preached to the disinherited and the oppressed for the spirit of anger and rage which they harbor against the oppressors. The oppressed are advised that the church would support their cause much more readily if the spirit of love were manifest in it.[37] But as Reinhold Niebuhr observes: "What the church fails to realize is that its responsibility is chiefly for the moral and spiritual attitudes of the privileged rather than the disinherited; for it is the former who makes professions of Christian idealism."[38] The hypocritical protestations of love for the oppressed by the privileged is underscored by Niebuhr:

> If the portion of society that benefits from social inequality and which is endangered by a rising tide of social discontent attempts to counsel love, forgiveness, and patience to the discontented, it will convict itself of hypocrisy, except it is able first of all to reveal fruits of the Spirit, which it commends, in its own life. Even if it were to reveal some fruits, but too meager to justify a more trusting and a less vehement attitude on the part of the underprivileged, its moral ideals would be regarded as pretensions.[39]

Niebuhr concludes that "if the church wants to insinuate the spirit of love into the social struggle it ought to begin with the privileged groups, not only because it has greater responsibility for them, but because those who hold entrenched positions in the social struggle are obviously under the greater obligation to be imaginative in gauging the needs and discounting the limitations of those who suffer from social injustice."[40]

It is doubtful however whether Church leaders would take effective action against the rich as long as the economic existence of the churches depends upon the privileged. If there is a falling off in the number of vocations, if the young search for other means of exercising Christian love than through the institutional Church, it could be because the Church has by and large been a defender of the status quo instead of being a force for change and renewal.

The Church, to be an effective force in the building of the Body of Christ which is the Earth, must first acquire a dynamic and evolutionary consciousness. It must see itself as a phylum of love and as the focal center through which love energy radiates toward the human community and down to the infrahuman levels. It has to give up the static view which makes a radical distinction between its service to the world and its liturgical function. For science, as Teilhard notes, leads to adoration.[41] The world is naturally religious. From the processive point of view, evolution is nothing else but the liturgical procession of all created and evolving reality which started several billion years ago and which is at present tending with man at its head toward the eschatological love feast with Christ as High Priest, as sacrificial first fruit and first born and with all creation as co-offerers.

But to achieve that eschatological communal feast of love we must go back to the fields, that is, to the world, and labor for the building of a better earth. From the fruits of our labor we can then gather around the table for a sacred meal that is truly symbolic and effectively sacramental of the eschatological community of love.

NOTES

[1] For an outline of Teilhardian process thought, see my book, *Teilhard and the Supernatural* (Baltimore: Helicon Press, 1966), Part II, 77-209.

[2] For example Harvey Cox's earlier views in his book, *The Secular City* (New York: The Macmillan Company, 1965).

[3] Salvation history theologians approach theology from an existential philosophic perspective. Now existentialism studies only human temporality and brackets evolution, especially of the infrahuman levels, as irrelevant since it considers the latter as outside the realm of freedom since they are governed by the purely mechanistic laws of science, it claims. Existential philosophy is thus deficient as a frame of reference for the formulation of the total story of God's saving acts which, as St. Paul says, include not only the redemption of human temporality but of material creation as well.

[4] The theory of Karl Rahner which sees the supernatural from an existential perspective as *the supernatural existential* does not, in my opinion, make grace really immanent to nature. See my discussion of this point in *Teilhard and the Supernatural* (Helicon Press, 1966), pp. 51, 56-63.

[5] It would be going too far afield to discuss how precisely the category of the personal is able to show both the transcendence and the immanence of grace. For a thorough discussion of this question see *Teilhard and the Supernatural*, Ch. VIII Man and Grace.

[6] I have discussed at length in my book *God With Process* the philosophic position that God is the Ground of the evolutionary process. See Chapter III, pp. 91-104.

[7] See, e.g., 1 Cor 15:35-38.

[8] See his article, "Matter and Spirit," *America*, (July 10, 1965), p. 52.

[9] See the *Vocabulary of the Bible*, ed. J. J. von Allmen (London: Lutterworth Press, 1958), p. 424.

[10] See Oscar Cullmann, *Christ and Time*, trans. F. V. Filson (Philadelphia: Westminster, 1950), p. 63.

[11] *Ibid.*, p. 52.

[12] "The Evolution of the Human Soul," in *The Dynamic in Christian Thought*, I ed. Joseph Papin (Villanova: The Villanova University Press, 1970), pp. 223-253.

[13] *Ibid.*, pp. 234-235.

[14] See *God Within Process* (New York: Newman Press, 1970), Ch. IV.

[15] See *The Phenomenon of Man* (New York: Harper & Brothers Publ., 1959), p. 264.

[16] *Loc. cit.*

[17] See *The Divine Milieu* (New York: Harper & Row, Publishers, 1960), p. 104.

[18] *Ibid.*, p. 118.

[19] See *The Phenomenon of Man*, pp. 114-115.

[20] *Ibid.*, p. 115.

[21] *Ibid.*, p. 295.

[22] *Ibid.*, pp. 295-96.

[23] *Ibid.*, p. 297.

[24] *Loc. cit.*

[25] See *The Divine Milieu*, pp. 94-95.

[26] See *The Phenomenon of Man*, p. 297.

[27] See the "Decree on the Mission," section 7 in *The Documents of Vatican II*, ed. W. Abbott (New York: America Press, 1966), p. 593.

[28] This point was made by Karl Rahner, "Atheism and Implicit Christianity," *Theology Digest* (Feb., 1968), p. 47.

[29] See *God Within Process*, pp. 69-70.

[30] *Imbid.*, p. 71.

[31] *Ibid.*, pp. 74-75.

[32] See Matthew 25:31-40, in *The Jerualem Bible*.

[33] *Christologie et évolution*, 1933, 13; *Quelques réflexiones sur la conversion du monde*, 1936, *Oeuvres*, ix, 162. Translation into English is taken from Christopher F. Mooney, *Teilhard de Chardin and the Mystery of Christ* (New York: Harper & Row, Publishers, 1964), p. 153—and my article "Process Thinking in Theology" in *Transcendence and Immance—Festschrift in Honour of Joseph Papin* (The Abbey Press, 1972) pp. 21-31.

[34] See *The Phenomenon of Man*, p. 244.

[35] *Loc. cit.*

[36] See Teilhard de Chardin, *The Future of Man*, trans. Norman Denny (New York: Harper & Row, Publishers, 1964), pp. 19, 21.

[37] This is the observation of Reinhold Niebuhr in *Religion and Life* written way back in 1932 but still valid today. The article is reprinted in *Contemporary Moral Issues* ed. Harry K. Girvetz (2nd ed., Wadsworth Publishing Co., Inc., 1968), pp. 450-460.

[38] *Ibid.*, p. 458.

[39] *Ibid.*, p. 459.

[40] *Ibid.*, pp. 458-59.

[41] *The Phenomenon of Man*, pp. 283-85.

Eschaton and Existence: a Phenomenological View

Edward Gannon

PART I. EXISTENCE: MAN IN THE WORLD

CYRANO never uttered a word he had not heard in his heart. "To thine own self be true," is probably Shakespeare's most applauded line. Sincerity has always been ranked as one of the top virtues, and although clichés are sometimes spun out in its name, as witness the young ladies in novels who give themselves generously to needy males, but remain pure withal because they're doing what "comes naturally," to be *genuine* (from the Latin for inborn, native) stands uncontested as a consummation devoutly to be wished. Thus the charm of children and the admirable conquest of the adult who stirs himself, throws off the weight of habit and conformity, of the need to please and keep up, and opts squarely for what *he* values and what *he* wants to do.

The young have only one word more devastating than the word "square." A "square," after all, is innocently "out of it." But be called a "phony" and you've had it. There is no more crushing epithet for turning you back on yourself in confusion and chagrin. The reason is that you know, down deep, that you probably deserve it. Nobody does anything for only one reason, and there are therefore usually elements we distrust in our complex motivation. It is a rare man indeed who can stand up untouched by the accusation. Yet, to admit the truth in the charge is to accept the human condition. The foolish man flings himself into impassioned self-defense. The wise man smiles ruefully. The courageous man refuses to be deterred, despite the truth, because in the context he chooses to find it to be irrelevant.

To be phony is to seem to value or reject what in fact we do not value or reject. It is to lie. The sign does not correspond with the reality. A lie is possible because having an inside and an outside, an interiority and words, we can manoeuvre words, actions, facial expressions to suit our purposes. The do-gooder presumably moved by the needs of others but actually losing himself in activism because he cannot abide himself, the wandering husband who swamps his wife with gifts, the editor whose keen delight in life is to show his superiority to authors, the braggart covering up diffidence—the possibilities are endless.

Our worldly-wise propensity to sniff out phoniness in others is easily come by, because, sensing it in ourselves, we find it slightly unbearable that others be free of it. More tellingly, fallen idols reinforce our suspicions. The psychiatrist Leslie Farber, writing of his days as a student, speaks of his group's

> ... endless and relentless appetite for gossip about our elders in the society. Every new instance of adultery, drunkenness or divorce among our teachers was savored as evidence that they hadn't achieved perfection after all. We simply could not hear often enough of the ways in which they had failed as human beings. When we said to each other, "Well, they're only human," and replied to each other "Of course," we may have been trying to say that perhaps perfection is not a matter of being human, but is beyond the human.

I suggest it could also have been a case of misery loving company. In any case, the faults in their mentors made the fledglings more realistic. Note here that we are dealing with the permissive brotherhood of psychiatry, where wide-eyed admiration of heroes is most unlikely. How much more is the ordinary youngster unhorsed by such revelations. The permanently surprising thing is that the final absolution accorded the erstwhile hero, now dwindling into the everyday, if given at all, takes the form "He's only human." This really says "He's part phony." What he really was slipped out. Much of the rest was façade.

Add to these sobering discoveries of flaws in ourselves and our preceptors the psychologism suffusing modern life, and it is no wonder we are all prone to psychological sleuthing. In merely exchanging technical words like projection, compensation, sublimation, guilt complex, inferiority compex, repression, we say in effect that we all know things are not what they seem. It is an open secret that we are all more or less phony.

AUTHENTICITY (1)

THERE is no more imperious invitation among philosophers of the modern "humanistic" schools (Phenomenologists, Existentialists, Personalists) than the call to be authentic. Their rhetoric in striving to stir readers to start living genuinely separates them from the classical, expository philosophers of the past, and is probably one reason why they are so suspect to the establishment. They don't sound like philosophers. But their sense of mission personalizes all they write, and their Gospel, accusing and challenging, is first and foremost "Be authentic!"

The word appeals. The result has been its quick incorporation into the modern vocabulary, with all sorts of connotations never originally intended—a phenomenon we are all too familiar with when belabored with other honorable words such as liberal, commitment, dialogue, existence!

Whatever, there is a welter of preachment in the name of authenticity.

a) *The Unrelated Self*

ONE very common type of authenticity urges the obliteration of all norms, obligations, restrictions, precepts that encumber and "falsify" the individual except the single stark obligation to dare to be a "self." Acceptance of any imposed rules in inauthentic. The premium is on what I shall call unrelatedness, except to myself. All value is in freedom from outside demands.

Recently, I discovered a paper included in the collection *Démythisation et Morale* (Aubier, 1965, pp. 91-103), called *Les mythes de l'authenticité,* by Alphonse deWaelhens, who traces the curious evolution of the word *authentic.* The Greek *authentikos* meant "that which consists in absolute power" *authentia* meaning absolute power itself. It is in this sense that the law speaks of an "authentic" act. For the jurist, an act is authentic if expressed in an official document, witnessed by a public official. Birth, marriage, death are not authentic in themselves. They become such only if attested to and registered in prescribed forms by a representative of the public power; that is to say, if they are "authenticated." Essential to the meaning then is public witness, public proof. Authenticity thus is a category relevant to others—and not private. It is something related and not sheerly subjective, all of this is sharp contrast to the current meaning that would make it an assertion by the self of the non-public, of the unclassifiable, of the existential rather than of the essential.

It strikes me that this popular modern meaning remains faithful to the root word, which is in the Greek *autos,* the self. The difference is that autonomy in Greece belonged to the group, the public, whereas today we tend to put it in the individual, the self as such.

The evolution of the meaning of authentic followed along with that of another all-important word, *person.* In Roman law, the person was the subject of a right conferred on him according to his capacity, his role (*persona* originally meant a theatrical mask) as spouse, father, citizen, land-owner, all universal categories. Now person means irreducible subjectively, the incommunicable absolute self, the distinctiveness evoked by the word personality. The "true self" is now the person as distinguishable from his public acts. Subjectivity is separable from acts, and true sincerity is the openness of an interiority unaffected by, unrelated to, apart from public demand, approval or disapproval. Hence the truly authentic person has to live up to his uniqueness and reject conduct prescribed by the outside!

It is not unfair to point to Jean-Paul Sartre, whatever his insights, as the wry high-priest of this cult of the self, though in him it is far from exhilarating. For Sartre, knowledge is separation and negation, and love is impossible. Reality is nauseating precisely because "there" and not assimilable, and the self, autonomous in all its acts, stands alone, an unfulfilled and unfulfillable emptiness, *un néant*. In almost ascertical posture against his other existential contemporaries (so much so that Gabriel Marcel has formally renounced the word "existential," shunning guilt by association), Sartre refuses the major advances of modern phenomenologists, who so link the knower and the known, the self and the other, the valuer and the valued that neither component of any relation is intelligible without the other.

Authenticity thus prized becomes a ferocious subjectivism and is, of course, as unviable as all subjectivisms. Reality, which is other people even more than sticks and stones, will simply not leave me unrelated, because I am, willy-nilly, person orientated. A recent newspaper story of a hermit listed his collection of books and recordings. The Fathers of the Desert had their Scriptures and their God. I strongly suspect that in that area in which unrelatedness most seems to be honored, that of the modern art that has banished all subject from the canvas, and expresses subjectivity pure and simple, the artist is fervently trying to say something to the rest of us. Without us, he is nothing. Sartre writes impassioned books for the market, and with all the urgency of an apostle. We all crave a world of relatedness!

b) *Doing What Comes Naturally*

A SECOND kind of preached authenticity is a distant cousin to the first and is closely allied to Romanticism. For want of a better name, I shall dub it Vitalism, but of the Dionysian persuasion. In this philosophy there is the soul of man, which is life, and the mind, which is technical intelligence. True values are "vital." Man is destructive, crushing life. Mind is a metaphysical parasite nesting in the soul and eating it away. If, according to most anthropologists, homo sapiens or homo faber has been by and large progressing, perfecting himself as history unfolds, in this philosophy he has been regressing. Instead of embracing the real, he has been lured by power, and century by century has deserted the real for intellectual constructs and technical mastery. The sense of the cosmic, the pulsing, the physical, is becoming etiolated, especially by the cancer in the intelligence called conscience. Lessing defined man as "that kind of ape who has become more and more of a megalomaniac by the development of his mind." In this thinking, reason is not a spiritual force capable of uniting man with reality, but is, in Schopenhauer's words, "the negation of the will to live."

Intellectual energy, which created states, works of art, science, tools, language, poetry, tears man from his world and from harmony with the vibrating rhythms of the universe. To be authentic demands a return to the all-in-all, the felt, the mood, the pantheistic embrace of the universe. (Spelled out, I imagine this is best experienced in groups; in beer-hall empathy, lynch-mob animosity, grandstand swaying, carnival togetherness, by the shepherd and his nymph in Arcady— or Woodstock!)

This may be Nordic theorizing or Romantic yearning for a lost Paradise. But Tahiti and compliant natives, or any Lotus eater land of fact or fiction awakens longing in many an urban modern, trapped in progress machines, time clocks, taxes, social security, styles, what's "in." I am not referring to the mood the French so felicitously call *la nostalgie de la boue.* I mean that this high call to élan vital, this Nietzschean transvaluation of values seems to offer relief, and the release of dammed vital forces. If conscience makes cowards of us all, this invites to life! And it does demand a kind of relatedness, blurry though the *terminus ad quem* be.

The swinging and unflappable pleasure-seeker appeals to the ordinary consciousness, no matter how we cluck with proper shock. Royal-scale self-indulgence, laughing derring-do, hearty recklessness, even mighty evil are fascinating. James Bond's violence, Zorba's animality, Anthony's destructive passion—the list goes on and on. Milton's Satan upstages his Adam at every turn. Nero and Hitler quicken more interest than Augustus and Frederick the Great. The Marquis de Sade is more assured of immortality here below than the Curé of Ars, Judas than the sons of Thunder. It is a sorry fact that the reckless defier of the code titillates much more unerringly than the faithful greats of mankind.

It is commonplace that the most shocking criminals receive an extraordinary number of proposals of marriage.

The fact is that perversions of every kind interest most normal people. Everybody has some curiosity about them, and most of us experience intense pleasure if they are presented on the screen or on the stage or in a book in a true artistic way. In real life, compulsive killers are guaranteed giant headlines, not because of fear, but because they drew us. As Hollywood would accurately have it, "We thrill with horror."

There is, of course, the attraction of the bizarre, the appeal of the rebel, the "outsider" in all of this. But more deeply we tend to feel

these people are more sincere, less brain-washed. They "think for themselves."

Even psychiatrists admit the appeal of working with schizophrenics,
because there is a kind of rampant honesty and utter indifference to
moral and social opinion in them that attracts, as though this is all
more authentically human.

Let us take one example. One of the new dogmas is that "sex is
the most natural thing in the world and it is insincere to try to control it."

In the opening essay of a famous issue of *Esprit* entirely devoted
to a study of human sexuality, Paul Ricoeur says that the essential
victory of Christianity in destroying the old pagan cosmo-vital pan-
sexualism has been its attempt to establish a new *sacré,* by preaching
that sexuality is a communication between two individuals and not between two forces lost in the flux of generations and regenerations, all
linked to life, death, seasons, food, plants, animals and gods. Marriage
is the precarious institution in which the inter-personal emerges. It is
"our culture's bet on sex." Marriage renders the union human. Rejecting the false antinomy of body and soul, Christianity, says Ricoeur,
tried to recover them, not by a restoration of the old Androgyne myth,
but by the union of two permanently separate and free persons.

He finds the new enemy of this in the present insignificance of sex
and in its function as a kind of revenge on so much of the meaningless-
ness of modern organizational life: if nothing makes any long-range
sense, then immediate pleasure makes sense here and now. He discovers
a third element arising from these two: if sexuality is insignificant
but becomes imperative as revenge on life, it has to be enhanced, built
up. There results a "fatiguing fight against the psychological poverty
of pleasure" and a new eroticism, with refinements, imaginative games,
variations without end. The intense despair of eroticism is in never
compensating for the loss of value and meaning, no matter how many
substitutes it finds for genuine tenderness. Sex then becomes a con-
sumer product, and so forth.

Sex then would be the modern's way of resisting the blandness of
life, and a kind of ready-made specific to inject some meaning, some
feeling of value into the ordinariness of things. Itself not being
enough, it needs flourishes, nuances, piquancy: all the work of imagination. Being so necessary it must be made respectable as an end in
itself. Hence it is "the most natural thing in the world"—and has
going for it the innate desire in all of us.

If Ricoeur's suggestions are valid, and I think they are, the new
authenticity is a new kind of romanticism. If you despise the old
values in the modern mood of disillusionment with reality, you have
to find a metaphysic to justify the demands of sex and a use for it.
If sexuality is insignificant as such because life in general is meaningless, then romanticism must save it. It will always insist on being

saved. That is a foregone conclusion. The new authenticity plays the redeemer.

* * *

If the whole truth were told, most of us resent laws, reminders, fixed norms, checks, because within ourselves we are sure that to respond to the rhythms of life and our desires would be an excellent thing. It should be fundamentally right to let spontaneity rip. We shouldn't be put together so badly. "Love God and do what you please" should be more than a paradox. Love your fellow man and be yourself should be workable. To be yourself, as it occurs to you to be, should be possible. And we wouldn't want to be a Casanova or Billy the Kid anyway. Why can't we let ourselves go? It is because of original sin? It is that we have become sick and are inhibited? What is it?

You may have become impatient with my sympathy for the ideal offered by this vitalistic Gospel of authenticity. I have met it with a kind of honesty, because I think it is *the* ideal. Each of us in tune with nature, with each other, acting spontaneously and freely, unhampered by proscriptions, is a worthy ideal. It is not enough, either, to call all of this a *paradis perdu*. Without something like that, heaven would make no sense.

At the moment, however, reality is against us. It is not that we are flawed. It is that being a man is more a job than a response to the order of nature, more resistant than letting life take its course, and greatly more than an answering embrace. Briefly, our task is not to fit into the marvelous order of the universe; it is to create an order of our own. But our myths, entertainments, escapes, sins, are all proofs that we deeply desire a kind of Oriental blending with the cosmos.

Sadly, even if we tried it, this second kind of authenticity would not work. I can start with a ringing "non serviam." I end up, as all romantics, in isolation. Rejecting any humanly structured (intellectual) real, I am thrown back on myself, as desire. But I alone am not enough. Hence the need for stimulus: drink, narcotics, the dance, the exotic, the violent. Farouk with his erotica is an ugly picture. The fact is that it is only in being released from sheer appetite, only in taking a stance over-against nature, that I can become humanly alive!

c) *Being Frank*

THESE two types of authenticity may seem strong medicine. You may easily dismiss them as so much imaginative talk despite the roster of individuals who have tried to live them. What, then, about the common garden-variety of sincerity so often advocated in lines like "Tell him what you think and have done with it; be honest!" or "It's about time I showed my true colors" or "If you feel like it, do it!" or this faint praise "At least with him you know where you stand. If he doesn't like it you'll know it right away."

Speak your mind, let your feelings show, be sincere! That will clear the air. Frankness evokes frankness, self-exposure elicits reciprocal confidences. Public persons need the long range camera treatment. Once everything is out in the open, things will all work out. Tell it the way it is!

The tangle in this is hard to get through. The sober fact, of course, is that we are rarely good at revealing ourselves. It comes out all wrong. Then there is the question of how much I could reveal is my true self? The revealed is one thing. The authentic is another. When the accusation is made that "you can't get to know him" sometimes he doesn't know himself.

This yen for unguarded and trusting "authenticity" probably comes from a hope that the truth is all that matters, and a sly suspicion that we're all made out of the same cloth. Democracy is invoked to cover up democratism, which says that I am as good as he is, which is another way of saying he's as bad as I am. Yet a little bit of living teaches fast that there is a time and a place for everything, and most particularly for self-revelation.

Let me offer two comments on this exhortation to "Be Yourself!" If I sincerely value another as a person and at the same time have sincerely hostile feelings towards him, to control those feelings, because expressing them would harm him, or me, can be as sincere as telling him off. The question is what matters more, which is to say which would be more sincere. Frankness is the vice of honesty, and letting my less worthy "true self" show can be inauthentic. I suspect there is nothing duller as a matter of fact, than a perpetually "open" man, who is not open in the sense of receptive, but in the sense of visible. Without the hesitation of thought, the seasoning of reflection, the confusion of doubt, the tentativeness of sensibility, there is only stimulus-response.

Second, it is hardly necessary to remark that the tenet which says "Do it, if you feel like it" is, as a general rule of conduct, as irresponsible as Oscar Wilde's dictum that "the only way to get rid of temptation is to yield to it." Surely his silliest epigram.

* * *

In the two formal positions outlined above, there is an inside self that wants to come out, but is blocked by outside forces (in both cases by human constructs). Both, together with the popular cry to "tell in the way it is," recommend liberating this inner self from cramping prohibitions, all of which, it is claimed, obscure the true self. Directives for its action are to come uniquely from within. All three preach unrelatedness in the sense that subjective urges are to determine authenticity.

d) *Spiritualism*

THERE is on other "inner self" theory that is a bit more respectable. It is Platonic. The only true self is the soul residing in mortal flesh as in a prison. This soul is spiritual, the immortal part of me, and all the real matters. Here below is a vale of tears, a time of trial, no lasting home. Withdrawal from this ephemeral world, then, and cultivating the life of the soul is the proper prescription for the good life. Peace and serenity within, wisdom achieved by communion with the absolute, apart from the disturbing and fragmentizing world of the body, is true happiness. In theology, this doctrine is called eschatologism, as opposed to Incarnationalism. In philosophy it is the "host in the machine" theory derided by British positivists. In this scheme of things, *now* matters only inasmuch as now I am in a direct line of flight to the hereafter.

Contempt for the temporal is here evident. To be authentic means to despise *this* set-up and privately to be unsullied by the mundane, the secular. (The young now preach against "materialism.") At its most attractive, this doctrine calls to mind Marcus Aurelius; at its worst it is a kind of solipsism. But it perdures even in Christian believers. Consider the scandal given by Churchmen to other Churchmen when they first marched in civil rights demonstrations, or the caution not to be too concerned about things like the population explosion, hunger, poverty. God will provide! What is important is union with God, who seemed to arrange this world as a hurdle to be leaped, as a maze to be traveled, and basically as an alternative to Himself or as a competitor.

There is only one word for this mentality: blasphemy. We are expected to believe that God created us in order to give us a chance to despise all He made as cheap and illusory, except for our immortal souls. What He made therefore was not, as He thought, good.

We have, then, three theories of authenticity, each locating the true self in something hidden, deeper, harder to find, profoundly inner, and inhibited. In what follows, interiority will again be the locus of the true self: but with the difference that this interiority will be seen to be meaningless except in relation to the already structured and further structurable other-than-me. In a word the interior can exist only if there be an exterior.

e) *Subjectivity and Facticity*

PHENOMENOLOGY has introduced a new dualism into the philosophical dictionary. It is the dualism of facticity and subjectivity.

Briefly, my facticity is the sum total of the past that remains in me, and makes me thus far a given. It is *what* I am as a result of genetics, natural environment, medical history, the culture I live in, the influence of others, my unconscious and my own choices. It is all that I can be classified under. I am, for instance, an American in Colorado who is a ski instructor with a violent temper, powerful arms and legs, a broken nose and a marriage on the rocks. That and much more is already "there." And "even God cannot change the past."

My subjectivity, on the other hand, is myself as potentiality, as an on-going project, as an original and irreducible agent. My realizability differs from that of a thing. A thing can only have things happen to it. My potentiality is realized by me, and, as out-thrust into reality, puts me in advance of myself. I am existence. (At the risk of insulting you, let me spell things out here. Existence is from the Latin ex-sisto. I am out there! Dasein! I am intentionality. I am subject, a meaningless word if there be no object. I am a consciousness . . . of something. Strictly speaking, shells and glaciers and rose bushes and puppydogs do not exist. They are not real intentionality. And are locked in a network of mutual causality. Nor, strictly speaking, does God exist, though He obviously is. God is self-sufficient, without real relationship to other than Himself, though, illuminatingly, God is relational within Himself. Only man exists . . . or, can exist. Many men presumably just are, they do not exist. Existence is an achievement, not a given.)

Facticity and subjectivity work in tandem. I cannot realize myself except in the very matrix of my facticity. That I gave up forestry for ski-instructing was possible because I was a forester, and my brother handled the hiring for the ski resort. But *that* I continue to realize my possibilities is not due to my facticity. Further, each realized possibility creates other possibilities. I now accept the risk of breaking a leg in a jump. If I do, I land in a hospital, with new options. And so forth. As I go on, I write a more and more distinctive personal history. I am always creating my own essence, *what* I am, because I am existence.

This analysis rejects with vigor, therefore, any suggestion that I am nothing but a cross-roads for forces moving through me. I am more than matter that reacts. I am not, in fact, a proper subject at all for physical science to study. Nor am I entirely manipulated by unconscious drives, nor the entirely knowable result of environment. Reading some psychologists leaves the impression that they are patiently awaiting the day when LaPlace's principle can be applied to human nature: once they know *all* the past they will be able to straighten out every troubled man and woman, and arrange a world where there is perfect harmony. In fact for them there is no part of man that cannot be "scientifically" manoeuvred. One wonders when the so-called "social sciences" will acknowledge that they cannot ever be the positive sciences physics or chemistry are. There is an uncontrollable in me because by definition I am an unpredictable subjectivity. Social science studies men!

I abdicate as a true self, and become reified, a thing among things. Marcel wisely insists that to be exclusively occupied on "on-going" into the reality that is horizontal to me, here and now, is to be in proximate danger of turning into a thing and of being tempted to objectify other men, whose presence as selves should rather alert me to the fact that, they being selves as I am, and not being me, there is also a vertical dimension to life. There is Being itself, in which all beings share. "In so far as we are not things, in so far as we refuse to allow ourselves to be reduced to the condition of things, webelongto an entirely different worldly dimension, and it is this dimension which can and must be called supra-temporal." For Marcel man's true motto is not *sum* but *sursum*. Kierkegaard has called the trap of the horizontal the esthetic, and exacts a leap of faith into another dimension. But whatever dimension one insists on, there is not a true self unless the situated interiority that I am is itself light and self-project, and I keep going on, to further and further fulfillment. (Marcel does not like the word "perfection" here, because it suggests something finished, which I cannot be, if I am authentic.)

If my life is all talk, curiosity, ambiguity, says Heidegger, I am inauthentic. Talk (Gerede) means superficial, common, accepted interpretation of reality. Curiosity (Neugier) is not being interested in whatt hings really are, but in what they look like, sound like, are like. It means being distracted by appearances, and hence restless. The light that I am is out of focus. Ambiguity (Zweideutigkeit) means not knowing what I really think about things. The light is not fully bright. Marcel warns of the constant temptation to seek security, to yield to the benefits of technology, to the will of possession, where I pour myself into what I have, and to the comforts of sheer functioning, where I become merely homo faber.

g) *Examples*

LET us bring all of this down to cases. Anyone familiar with the training years for the priesthood in Roman Catholic seminaries is keenly aware that, for the majority of candidates, the final decision to be a priest was not made the day of entry into the seminary. Most thought it was, but as the years turn up their unexpected discoveries about life itself and the candidates himself, most seminarians are faced with a new decision, because new data is at hand. (I would add that possibly the male of the species rarely decides a way of life for once and all. Many a husband will admit that he could at times step out of his marriage without regret, if it were possible, and this not because he no longer loves his wife or children, but merely because he has a new yen for his freedom. I think few males are carried through life on the surge of big decisions. The faithful must often re-choose, which is why loyalty is such a prized virtue.)

In any case, seminarians have to face the choice of staying in the seminary or "going back to the world" much more often than even their families would suspect.

Usually the big moment of choice occurs in the years closer to ordination. If he is in a religious order, the seminarian is then at least over 28 years old. Suppose he sees himself as an essentially haphazard person, unconvinced in many areas, and clearly unsure of himself as a priest. Suppose he spots values in married life which he responds to with spontaneous enthusiasm. Suppose, in other words, that he sees lucidly though painfully that he should get out; in fact, sees in a burst of honesty that this time is the first time in his life he has a chance to make a real decision. He has been carried along so far by applause and support of others, easily repeated formulations of ideals (Gerede), the varieties of courses and subjects studied and the progressive stages of his training (Neugier), never really looking deeper, whether at himself or the priesthood (Zweideutigkeit). Here is the moment of truth. This time it is all up to him and him alone. But he puts off the decision, always drawing nearer to ordination. He knows the ropes, there is no problem in "living the life." Finally, conditioned, he is ordained. The Church is richer by one more inauthentic priest.

I wish to underline the fact that our seminarian did not, simply by not leaving the seminary, actually choose to stay. It is not true that merely by not changing a way of life one re-chooses his present one. Datur tertium. Choosing no way of life, he lets the one he is in shelter him and free him from the need to choose. Lucidity is necessary for choice. Here habit, familiarity, being comfortable, just being "put" all generate so much fog. The tug of the situation wins out. Had ordination occurred after an anguished confrontation of all the hazards and a courageous decision to make it work, the seminarian might have been wrong in his decision (who can say?), but would have really made one.

Another example. This time we have an insurance salesman who had broken all records for sales in his district and often won paid vacations as bonuses, and now has his own company, an expensive home, belongs to the right club, the whole usual story. He understands people enough to talk them into large policies. If you meet him, he is the soul of candor and charm. He is good for big donations to his church. You can fill in the rest.

But he doesn't read, he brings his work home with him, or spends many nights at the office, he cannot relax, and he hasn't really talked to his wife in years. His children have the best of everything, but he doesn't know them. He wasn't always all work. In fact, the very charm he flashes was once a sincere thing that attracted his wife in the first place. He can talk business, which is mainly know-how, but he has given up evaluating practically everything else. He is smart enough, however, to seem to have convictions on many things, and expresses himself well.

Briefly, he is a "dynamo"—the perfect description. He is a function turned on by money, or ambition, or whatever the device that controls him. He is not evil; he is inauthentic. He may some day, like the Prodigal, "come to himself." But until then he is a force in his community, not a person; a performer, not a self. As Marcel would say, he is *homo faber,* tout court.

h) *Conclusion of Part I*

To exist, then, is an achievement of high order and not come by naturally or easily. It is not a matter of shedding relationships and letting the real self loose. It may well be that for most men the moments of authenticity are few and far between, and that the ordinary "mood" of life is inauthenticity. This need not be bad. Just as I can let myself be anesthetized before a serious operation and leave the rest to the surgeon, so often I should be content to be moved along in structured groups (the family, school, job, city, church) with a kind of humility that accepts the human arrangement of things. The horror would be that I never "come to myself." Then I am literally finished.

An aside about routine. In itself it is neither good nor bad. If freely embraced as a means of fulfillment it can be very good indeed. If fallen into as an escape from having to choose, it is bad, even disastrous. I calculate that a mother of four makes 2000 beds a year, butters some 4500 slices of bread for school lunches, peels 2000 potatoes. The job is not the problem. It is the attitude of the worker. Some jobs, however, seem to have inbuilt destructive power: the best argument there is for automation!

A modern hazard in the struggle between being alive or a clod is today's insistence on skill. There must be specialized competence. Competence means training, frequently long training, which in turn means submitting to a time order, rules, routine. These, of their nature, tend to deaden and reduce a young hopeful to a role. The role can replace the man: there is the heart of the problem. The fear of being only a role may be behind the short-range commitment to the Peace Corps, Pavla and the rest, as distinguished from long term commitment to the ministry or social work, or the other professions that serve others. Let us admit that the very repetitiousness of professional work, the role itself, can brutalize and deaden. Toffler suggests that specialization can be a way to escape from future shock. There is the priest who becomes a nodding automatic listener, no longer capable of hearing the frantic plea for help behind the cold recital of sin; the family doctor who has seen it all so often, and unwittingly has become emotionally immunized into a hearty and perpetually cheery professionalism; the teacher who cannot pick up nuances in the question he thinks he has heard a hundred times.

There must be roles. Without them there is disorder, inefficiency, backwardness. But there must also be a self, or I lose my soul.

PART II. EXISTENCE: MAN AT THE WORLD

IN the first part of this paper I tried to spell out the personalistic view of the authentic man as existence, which means that he flies his true colors in trying to be an on-going relation, by intentionality and by being a self-project, with the world.

In the following section I shall address myself to man as being **AT** the world, in the sense that this world is his to make.

Perhaps the arch enemy of this whole idea is rationalism, a consequence of which in the past has been to conceive man more as a responder to a given situation than to encourage him to take over at the world controls. Endeavoring to fit everything together, rationalism has always secretly seconded Galileo's dictum that God made the world mathematical and then made mathematicians to live in it. The new thinking, or the other hand, sees that the world gets its meanings from man, and that it is over against it that man has become increasingly man. The human being is not a finished thing, with built-in stimulus-response, but to-be-made by his going to work on the world. (Here Marx is inspired!)

When years ago I was a student in the classroom Thomistic tradition, the whole emphasis in the treatment of free will was on what was called "absence of psychological necessity." Realistic thinkers in the tradition freely avowed that my moments of freedom may be few and far between; the point was that I had the equipment. So far so good. But my freedom was given to me for a purpose, as became clear in ethics, the crowning science in the whole series, because it dealt with the real man, in action, faced with choices. There we learned about law, natural and eternal, which is the blueprint for human activity enjoined by the Creator and discoverable in His creation. Observing this law was the proof of a moral human. The "come-on" in all of this was that the Law-maker rewarded or punished. Freedom: in order to obey the law; in order to be rewarded. Was the law always clear? Admittedly not, and thus one could gratefully turn to revelation which contained all the rest we needed to know, because it was closed with the death of the last Apostle, and known since the death of that Apostle.

Hence, there are not really new problems. They are new only to us. There have always been answers for each human crisis, found either in the law of nature or the content of divine revelation. Good will and docility will guarantee a meritorious life. There will be mystery and struggle, and suffering; but the law is clear. The attitude of the Christian is *response* to what he is assured he will know to be the will of God. And if "the will of God" is elusive, the subject never goes wrong in obeying his superior, because Providence is the virtue of him who commands and not of him who obeys. Most of us are safe enough.

With all the respect in the world for the mighty effort that has been Thomism and Neo-Thomism, many of us now find ourselves chaffing and restless, even disillusioned with it, at least with the way we learned it. It is not fundamentally false; it simply does not come to terms with life as we live it and discover it. It answers questions we do not ask. I will hazard summing up the new mood as a pulsation of impatience to "renew the face of the earth," in opposition to a former eagerness to explore the will of God. The emphasis in Thomism is to strive to be at home in an intelligible world; the new emphasis is on striving to humanize it. These do not come down to the same thing.

a) *A World to Make*

WHENCE the modern enthusiasm for humanizing the world? First of all, something in religious thinking seems to have at long last righted itself. I am not sure there was every anything official about it, but the Church as a power system, guarding itself from attack in a perfectly understandable human way, did not seem to preach involvement in the here and now as a good in itself. Being of divine origin, it accentuated the divine. The lines in the catechism "God made me to know, to love and to serve Him" seemed to mean that I am made for God, not in order to have a rewarding possession of Him for my sake, but for His. True theological insight always saw that I am given a mind and the job of possessing the earth for myself and other men. God had nothing to gain from creation; in fact, could gain nothing. He was not seeking glory when He flung out the first dawn; that dawn was for me. Creation is an act of love for the creature, and revelations and laws are all so many divine offerings to help me be more human, more of an integrated rich self. I am the absolute from the divine point of view. God is the perfect Humanist in His orientation to men. And God, the absolutely absolute, is at His own behest a means for my perfection. His very supernaturalizing of me in grace is for my sake, not His.

But this great truth was avalanched by brisk warnings about being Temples of the Holy Spirit, or being always under the all-seeing eye of God, or being careful to be respectful to God's representatives. It was all rather that I owed it to God and his representatives, for their sake, to measure up. Things had to be right, so that God be pleased.

I am not, of course, made exclusively for this world. But the self-defensiveness of the Christian mentality very often convinced the believer that his lot in this world didn't matter at all. Only God mattered. Faithfulness was due Him, particularly as He was interpreted

by those who were not living for this world, because He was God,
and not at all because in making me He loved me, and all was for me.
But as André Malraux beautifully pointed out, the success of Christianity in the beginning was not in assuring believers that now they
could avoid hell. "Something was more needful than the promise of
the next world to the beggar, the outcast, the cripple and the slave:
deliverance from life's futility and from the load of sorrows borne in
solitude. Early Christianity won the day in Rome because it told the
slave woman, daughter of a slave, watching her slave child dying in
vain, as it had been born in vain: 'Jesus, the Son of God, died in
agony on Golgotha so that you should not have to face this agony of
yours alone.' "

Somehow, by starting to break out of the old formulas, Christianity
now seems to be finding itself again, with the same emphasis on man
that Christ singled out as the norm for the Last Judgment: "What you
have done to the least of mine . . . " Why this relation to my fellow
man? Because he is why this world exists and he needs me. Hence
all that smells of power, anxious control, propaganda techniques,
ostracizing, separation ,triumphant infallibility, whatever crimes have
been committed in the name of God, are beginning to be called by
their right names. There is no "it" called the Church, no autocrat
called God. The Church is ourselves, and God is Christ. The New
Testament is a document about God-Man's love for men. It is not the
outline of a system. Its premise is the perennial fact that man is to be
made man by men. Its command is that this fashioning should now
be out of love for my fellow man, for him as himself, and not as a
way of pleasing God. God finds him worth it: He came to make him
free; my goal should be the full freedom of my fellow man to enrich
his own life, for his sake, not God's.

Another catalyst breaking down the old mentality is the new religious, cultural, political pluralism. Whatever may be unchangeable
in religion because of divine revelation, there is alarmingly much that
turns out to be of historical human origin though for too long it has
been palmed off as divine. This we know because we are at long
last aware of each other, and have the choice of saying either that
those differing with us are insincere, or that God has been faithful
to those in another religion and they have had true contact with Him,
regardless of what we call error. I vividly remember a young Anglican
priest saying "It is not infallibility that separates us from Rome. I
think we can work that out, because most of us see there has to be
some sense of a divine guarantee in the Church of Christ. But what
we could never take would be having to admit that for four hundred
years we have had a false religion." What photography has done for
the experience of art, by making available to all of us the whole world
of painting in printed collections, publications and meetings and confrontation in the press and open confident exchanges in religious mat-

ters have done to widen vision. God turns out to have been the private preserve of no religion. In fact, there is the danger that heightened anthropological sophistication, especially among the young, prompt more than one person to ask, as did a Peace Corps volunteer after a year in Islamic Iran "Is religion all man-made?"

In other areas, world congresses of physicists, philosophers, mediae-valists are so many occasions to acknowledge that human wisdom is exclusive to no one people, no one continent, and that there are many ways of expressing human values. Democracies have embassies in totalitarian states, socialist states, kingdoms and republics.

Teilhard de Chardin's vision of the increased complexification of the human race, bringing it to a new state of being, turned to itself in a new unity, announces the arrival of the noosphere. This may sound too rosy to many, but nobody dismisses it as deranged. It may be happening after all.

b) *The Will of God*

A N immediate effect of the new mentality about the world-to-make is that we are much more careful in speaking of the will of God than we used to be. God's will is clear in the two great commandments, which come down to one: Love God by loving your fellowman. They say, ringingly, that there is a world to make, jolting though this idea is to the orderly Catholic. The will of God is much more than that we avoid an atomic war; it is that we concern ourselves with making human beings more human. No morality has any true value if it does not show the way for man as an individual and with other men to rise to a finer quality human life—for his and their sake.

In this discussion on the world-to-make, the notion of vocation immediately comes forward. Granted we have been consigned to each other as brothers, neighbors. Are we not so different and variously qualified that the division of work should follow some plan, and isn't that plan evident in vocation, by which each of us is led Providentially to take his special place in the system, so that all work out to the good? Has not God written in us and our history clear signs of the best road for us, which signs we can read if we pray and are open to guidance?

So some like to think, if only because anything like taking full re-sponsibility for our way of life is frightening, and there would be nothing else to carry us along except ourselves. Few men are trail blazers; most won't move unless the highway is marked. And only a tiny minority simply start wandering to see what will turn up; that's too experimental and life is too short. Thus, prodded by their elders, young people at the crossroads look for signs of *where they should go.*

There are, naturally, some signs, but I insist that they are rarely divinely written. St. Paul was blasted by a divine visitation on the road to Damascus, and certain founders of religious orders must have been inspired, as were the Apostles themselves on Pentecost. There have been moments in history when the will of God for this man or this people seems to have been evident. But what of the "vocation" of most of us?

I categorically reject as naive self-deception, or as presumptuous or as spiritual cowardice a widely spread conviction that God has a special plan for each of us, finding which we will be in the "best" life for us. I think it even superstitious. If you insist that this world is manipulated by God and that freedom exists only so that you can leave yourself gratefully in His hands, and thus He can work everything out in detail as He wills it to be, then you must believe in individual vocation, right down to whether or not you should be a butcher or a baker. Or at least in the matter of whether you should be married or single, and, if single, live in consecrated or unconsecrated celibacy. If, on the other hand, you accept the world-to-make idea, this concept of vocation will make you squirm.

It was once my privilege to be a colleague of a gifted man who was not embarrassed to say to a girl "God has certainly picked this man for you." I observed that long as the love affair went swimmingly, no sense of vocation could have been more intense, or more enviably believed in. But there were often, unhappily, smash-ups. This left these alternatives: either this was not our vocation, and we made a simple human mistake, or maybe in a thing like this the idea of vocation is itself erroneous.

A first objection to the "divine vocation" concept is that it is impractical. How do I know God has picked this or that for me? But won't prayer tell me the will of God? I suggest that anybody who has lived under religious obedience knows what it means "to shrivel" if a superior says "I have prayed over this, and I have decided you are to go to India." If the superior merely means he now hopes his motives are good ones, and he has prayed to be surer of this, he deserves congratulations on trying to be "objective." But if he means to motivate his subject into accepting his decision as divinely inspired, he turns off the most willing subject. The subject may gladly go to India, recognizing the divinely-constituted authority of the superior; he will not go because he is now comfortable in the knowledge that God told the Superior to send him. If he cracks up in India and has to come home he may find strength to accept the mistake, because in going in the first place he allowed the consequences of the Superior's choice, and he is "disposible." But in no way was he at the disposition of the superior because he believed God wanted him in India, or as a crack-up. He signed a blank check, as an offering to God. God is pleased with the offering. But there is no sign he had a divine calling to India, or to the crack-up. In fact, it may have been better had he not entered the religious life at all.

The point is that we decide our way of life, and if it is decided with generosity and a minimum nobility of purpose, this is a virtuous decision. It may also be a disastrous decision . There may have been wiser ones to make. We simply cannot know until after the fact, whether what we have chosen is good, bad, better, and never if it was *best* (whatever that means). A serene grandfather, full of years and good works, may just as well have been a Trappist dedicated to silence, celibacy and farming all his life.

I recently asked a religious waiting for an appointment in the Congo if he felt he had a "vocation" there. We were talking French. He said yes, but quickly added that he did not like the English meaning of "vocation"—which is translated as a "call." "When I speak of vocation I merely mean I want to go." As simple as that; he was mature enough to be able to trust his own desire. When I pushed him and asked if he felt God gave him the desire, he smiled and said "I think God approves."

More directly, and secondly, the hazy persuasion that God designs a way of life for each of us is, in my mind, a way of saying that God has a "will" for each of us, which, being a preference, cannot be neglected without unhappy consequences. The conclusion is that most of us have a fifty-fifty chance of being in the wrong boat. The poison this injects into our happiness is incalculable. After all, if God has a preference, we lose if we do not follow it. Yet no teacher of the "divine vocation" idea has ever dared to say it is a sin to reject that vocation. What, then, would be the moral consequences? Or is God's will here a kind of hankering druther on God's part, with no character to it? The Eastern Church for a time revered the rich young man of the Gospels as a saint. He had observed the commandments from his youth. Christ wanted him as an Apostle, and was hurt when he declined. His life from then on did miss something. But he somehow made the hagiography. The last lines about him in Scripture are that "Christ loved him."

I remember the effect of this "secular" idea of a choice of life on a seminarian who was wondering if he should leave the seminary. He put it this way: "If it is up to me, I'll stay." No longer plagued with the obligation to hunt down the will of God, and assured that it was all ultimately up to him, he breathed a sigh of relief, exorcised his own kind of devil and took over his own life.

Thirdly, what kind of a God is it who spreads before me all sorts of possibilities which respond to all sorts of urges in me, and yet has just one in mind for me? The rest are then so many distracting tests of my powers of discernment. This makes the choice of a life a game like "button, button, who has the button!" It doesn't make God such a nice person.

In a word, our liberty is to be a creative liberty. Liberty is not simply finding oneself indifferent before finite objects. Liberty is *initiative.* It *is* to blaze trails. What is the wisest way to choose a way of life? It is ultimately to assess myself and my possibilities, *listen to my desires,* and, being convinced there is no point in being alive except that this world becomes a better place for us, opting among my possibilities and taking full responsibility for the decision. I cannot take refuge in signs, portents, omens. In making me the Spontaneity I am, God had complete respect for me. I am not made to fit into a slot! What father worthy of the name prescribes the lives of his sons? They are to live their own lives, raise their families their own way. So God with me. I am to make my own life. A good father is there to help. So God with me. But he helps me according to my own determinations. He goes along with me.

PART III. EXISTENCE: MAN AS CO-EXISTENCE

a) *The Fear of Freedom*

As a lead-in to the idea of co-existence, let me speak of the strangest of all phenomena, our cantankerous suspicion of freedom, or, better our inborn fear of it. We have often seen the tricks employed to avoid or at least to tame the irrational. Let us here hunt down the reason.

A commonplace in this matter, and a worthy one at that, is Ivan's "poem" of the Grand Inquisitor in the *Brothers Karamazov.* When Christ appears in the 16th century in Seville the day after an auto-da-fe, he is clapped in prison by the old Cardinal, and later blasphemously attacked by him for his lack of love of mankind, by offering men the way of freedom. "The truth will make you free." He had refused to use the forces of miracle, mystery and authority to subdue mankind when tempted by the "wise and dread" spirit in the desert.

> Instead of taking possession of man's freedom, thou didst increase it, and burdened the spiritual kingdom of mankind with its suffering forever. Thou didst desire man's free love, that he should follow thee freely, enticed and made captive by thee. In place of the rigid, ancient law, man must hereafter with free heart decide for himself what is good and what is evil, having only thy image before him as guide. But didst thou not know he would at last reject even thy image and thy truth, if he is weighed down with the fearful burden of free choice? By showing him so much respect thou didst, as it were, cease to love him, for thou didst ask far too much from him, thou who hast loved him more than thyself! Respecting him less, thou wouldst have asked less of him ... We have corrected thy work and have founded it upon miracle, mystery and authority. And men rejoiced that they were again led like sheep, and that the terrible gift that had brought them such suffering was, at last, lifted from their hearts.... We will persuade them that they will only become free when they have renounced

their freedom to us, and submit to us.... The most painful secrets
of their conscience, all, all they will bring to us, and we shall have
an answer for all. And they will be glad to believe our answer,
for it will save them from the great anxiety and terrible agony they
endure at present in making a free decision for themselves.... Tomorrow I shall burn thee. Dixi.

The prisoner had listened intently all the time, looking gently into
(the old man's) face and evidently not wishing to reply.... But he
suddenly approached the old man in silence and softly kissed him
on his bloodless, aged lips. That was all the answer. The old man
shuddered. His lips moved. He went to the door, opened it, and
said to him 'Go, and come no more!... Come not at all, never,
never!' And he let him into the dark alleys of the town. The
prisoner went away.

The Grand Inquisitor is uttering a terrible truth when he says "I
will tell you that man is tormented by no greater anxiety than to find
some one quickly to whom he can hand over the gift of freedom with
which the ill-fated creature is born." And he adds the wise, cynical
line "But only the one who can appease their conscience can take over
their freedom."

Men are thus dependent by nature. When some one comes along
or some religion or some political doctrine or simply some psychological theory that saves them the anguish of decision and still preserves for them the illusion that they are free, thy tend to surrender.
If the offer includes being in the company of others who have made
the same surrender, it is irresistible. "What is essential," says the Grand
Inquisitor, "is that all may be *together* in it."

There is no gainsaying Ivan's insight into human nature. It is only
fact that we want to belong to others, and enjoy depending on authority. A current proof of this is the feeling of betrayal so many Catholics
have because the "new Church" is, in principle, no longer inclined to
issue dogmatic statements, and solve problems from above, for once
and all. The faithful are invited to be adults and find many answers
for themselves. The child is safe: his elders let him know when he
is right and when he is wrong, and take a lot of the responsibility on
their own shoulders. Not so the adult. He must make decisions, and
making them rarely be satisfied that he is completely right. He must
live with the doubts that accompany all choices. As Harry Truman
said of the Presidency, "The buck stops here." No longer are the
faithful assured of some great brain, some one single source of truth
in Rome, which will relieve them of their adulthood. They are given
their freedom, having, as the Grand Inquisitor said, "only thy image"
before them as guide.

I wonder, further, if it is maybe not too much to say that many of
us make only one real choice in life: where to belong, and after that

shore up our defenses, protecting our roof-tree, our little and familiar world. The pain in redeciding "vocation" is proof enough, or moving into a divorce or conversion. There are few who prize their liberty enough to be alert for changes that are vital, or any problems that put everything in doubt. One need not be alert if he is safe behind a Maginot line. If the line is breached, most crumble. Only the special few join the Maquis!

Hence the conformist. He has taken a beating ever since Karl Marx discovered the bourgeoisie. But he has been around from the beginning, so deep inside most of us that we don't even know we fear being free.

b) *The Solitary*

To sum up, I am freedom, but in relation to reality, whose rich possibilities give my freedom its value and alone make it worth my while to activate it. I am freedom *from* reality in order to be freedom *for* reality.

The key reality is other persons. Without them, there is no point in freedom at all. Put Robinson Crusoe on the most salubrious and plentiful island in the world without his man Friday and you have no story. Or, if you do, it could only be written because the derelict kept expecting the joy of reentry, or was deeply religious and thus in personal contact with Another. Or turned into Dr. Doolittle. There is always a story, a life has events, if there are others. Otherwise, there is only Ben Gun.

Contact with others is nonetheless the cause of all problems in life too. Every psychological disorder stems from human encounter, all commandments concern relations with others (God or neighbor), and it would be interesting to know if a dream is possible without other "consciousness" playing roles. (Hostile animals, anthropomorphized, other beings, ordinary humans). Our first and predominant concern is relationships with others, and they are devilishly difficult to get right. Recall Schopenhauer's porcupines. It is winter and they are cold. They try huddling together for warmth. They prick each other. They separate again. They are cold again. They try a more careful huddle. Finally they manage the right closeness for warmth, and the right distance for comfort.

The easiest solution for the problem of contact with others is to withdraw as much as possible and become a solitary. The trouble with this solution is that instead of establishing freedom it creates solitary confinement, which is not freedom at all.

Let us explore the psychology of the solitary.

Finding human reality hostile, for whatever reason, he withdraws for self-protection. Let us admit that we all know the experience of running away. There are certain persons we are simply not up to:

the very lucid or the very successful, the sharply discerning or the cleverly sneering, the deeply suffering. Wounded often enough by un-successful encounters, our solitary finds relief in generalization, and lumping "them" together, opts out from as much personal association with others as possible. If he keeps his distance, he will not get in-volved in their problems. If other people keep their distance, they will not get involved in his. If this works, his own inadequacies will not show. In fact, maybe his own problems will go away, because the more they are his secret, the fewer their social consequences, and hence the less real the problems become. The solitary drinker has always finished his last bottle. He tells himself he is not an alcoholic, because, fancying that nobody knows he is tippling, he is free from the con-sequences of that knowledge, and has no confirmation of his own suspicions.

If I keep my distance from others, then, I can avoid their problems. Listen to Simone de Beauvoir.

> Men are hard on each other, either because of cynical egotism, because their interests clash: Homo homini lupus; or through lack of imagination or dryness or emptiness of heart. That's why wis-dom consists in self-reliance 'One is never better served than by himself.' Life should be arranged so that I need nobody, never having to ask for anything, and in that way I won't be forced to give anything in return. A little goodheartedness (*bonté*) is of course required; after all we are not brutes; but too large a heart is a weakness, a stupidity: a man who is too good gives a bad ex-ample, he is blameworthy, a malefactor. Thus Vincent van Gogh was commissioned to give material help in the Borinage, but was faulted by his superiors and relieved of his duties when he started living on the level of his charges and shared their table. The thing is to mix as little as possible in others' affairs, be discreet, avoid useless responsibilities. Give very little advice; it may be turned against you. Don't do too many favors: you'll get no thanks and in fact may rub people the wrong way.

Simone de Beauvoir is not playing Lady Chesterfield here. She is arguing that her own brand of existentialism is in fact quite reasonable to the ordinary person who has done a little living. The ordinary man will recognize himself in her description and thus will approve when she says "Therefore, life is a cheat." Which is what she has been say-ing all along. It would be wonderful were it not that way. Sharing with others should be so much more rewarding. But it won't work. Leave them alone.

Second, if others keep their distance from me, they will not get their sticky fingers into my life. Better I be unknown. If they know me, they may spot things even I prefer to ignore. (Many of us have more of a fear of being understood than of being misunderstood.) The other (Latin: *alter*) is a threat precisely because if he knows me

I might have to *alter* myself. In conversion, then, let us keep on safe topics, like health or our operations, or travel, or sports. At all costs eschew subjects that call up enthusiasm, strong opinion, resentment. That merely opens the gates, and I am too vulnerable. So, for example, teachers and students pass each other politely, Vice-President A is pleasant with Vice-President B, the college girl talks styles with her roommate, dinner parties go off to the delight of the hostess, because nothing that matters, like politics, or embarrasses, like religion, rears its ugly head, and all the guests depart as they have come, nobody knowing anybody else better. What matters is that the party, the ritual, is run "smoothly."

Finally, escaping real contact with others ,our solitary need not challenge his own ideas on things in general. He may be a great reader, but few books have the urgency of personal meetings. They are "interesting" and leave him largely undisturbed. In fact, to keep his peace of soul, he subscribes only to those magazines that agree with him, and, if a dissenting article slips too often into his favorite journal, he quietly cancels his subscription. It is perhaps one of the surest proofs that we shun change that so many read so much that is congenial, and familiar.

What is salient here is that the fear of dialog is the fear of stepping out of an identity: and we cannot abide the Caliban in us. Somebody has remarked that the reason liberated colonies have evicted the colonizers is that the colonizers wanted to transform the colony without being transformed themselves. Without real communication, hostility festered, and, if lucky, the unchangeable foreigner scrambled home. Those few allowed to stay were useful, or knowable and changeable. The gratifying example of some of our Peace Corps volunteers being protected by the very persons storming U.S. embassies bears this out. They haven't gone native. They merely happen to be open to new attitudes, and don't hide behind their images of themselves.

Thus far, in a general way, the motivation of the solitary. Does he, despite his blinkers, gain a genuine kind of freedom? The answer is that if freedom is only *from* and not *for,* he has the secret! But assuredly freedom consists rather in the indefinite more and more I can enter into. The naked freedom of the transcendental self is a horror. It is a blind giant, a genius in a coma! When Sartre says we are condemned to be free, and this because there is no particular value in any choice except that in the act of choosing, one looks around fruitlessly for examples. Freedom is self-determination before innumerable goods, and there is no power in man that is for nothing, in front of nothing, directed to nothing.

Further, the plant and the animal are by definition successes once they are mature. No bird has to learn how to build a nest, no vine how to climb. What they do, they do well, in their own native way, and, granted a benign environment, they have it made. But they have

vitality, not freedom. They are solitarily confined to one pattern of
action, one kind of perfection. Man, on the other hand, is plastic. He
has myriad possibilities, and without his freedom cannot begin to be
a success. His freedom enables him to choose one pattern out of many,
not in the richness of repeated cycles, proving the weary proverb
"Plus ça change plus c'est la même chose," but in this, that the sky
is the limit, or that there is no limit. He cannot once and for all settle
for the Unlimited, because it can be touched only in the variety of
creation. Those who strive to close the distance between themselves
and God by scorning the here and now, especially their fellows, might
well consider the first case of that. Adam and Eve wanted to "be
like God." The result was the brutal discovery of distance between
each other, and from God.

The solitary, in effect, ends up alienated and thus confined. He
may be a restless traveller, a walking encyclopedia of air routes, the
connoisseur who can tick off the advantages of Maxim's on the Rue
Royale over Maxim's on the Ginza. He may even indulge in autobiography, studded with the beautiful people, although most likely it
would be, as most such ephemera, a mishmash of anecdote and name
dropping, because the beautiful people seem often to be solitaries themselves. Our solitary, the observer and not the participant, the unknown
because the avoider, may thus find his best refuge in the crowd itself.
We have all met the gregarious, easy-going, engaging pipe-pulling
"nice guy," who excels in a group, and is yet an utter loner. Gabriel
Marcel says a real person is "disponsible." Our man is utterly available, but to the group. He functions, but he does not meet persons.

c) Existence Depends on Co-Existence

IF Christianity has so often failed, the reason must be something
deep in our natures. Freedom is a hard saying because freedom
runs up against our basic urge to depend.

Dependence and freedom are the two poles between which each
life is to be lived. If I cannot work out the rights of both, I will live
in permanent crisis. If I yield to either outright, I settle the crisis (at
least periodically), but, if the choice is absolute freedom, it will be
gained at the price of rejection by society. I become an unassimilable
element, to be sloughed off. If, on the other hand, I succumb and
become absolutely dependent, I eviscerate myself.

There is dependence on God and dependence on my fellow man.
The postulatory atheist brands dependence on God as a human flaw,
an original sin. Unable to meet the demands of adulthood and to
measure up to a world-to-make, man, according to the "God is dead"
theologians prefers to be the child, and makes up a God to take care
of things for him. Whereas in other atheisms, the absence of God
has often been considered a misfortune, because so much would make

sense if there were a God, in the new humanism there can be no God precisely because, if there were, human responsibility and liberty would make no sense. Nietzsche wrote "If there were gods, how could I tolerate not being one? Therefore there are no gods!" In a universe created by God, with a plan and a providence, man could simply not be a moral being, a person. If nature and man are under God, the originality of man disappears. Any and every predetermination, pre-destination, pre-emption of the position of judge by an outside agency annihilates man as such. In postulatory atheism the denial of God is the conferral of responsible sovereignty on man. He can have no re-course to a divinity communicating to him what he ought or ought not do, nor to any rewarder or punisher. A man dependent on God can-not be a true man.

Let us honestly admit that we have too readily attributed to the "will of God" human suffering, poverty, death. And have, all of us, often hidden behind a fatalism which encourages us to shrink from rolling up our sleeves and doing something about evil. We admire patience more than intolerance, prudence more than daring. Note also that the new hu-manists are not preaching the arrogant defiance of Nietzsche. In teach-ing the bitter truth that the world is very much up to us, they under-score a difficult morality: love of my fellows. Nietzsche's race of supermen were a singularly ice cold lot; the new breed must be warm to each other. They share with the Christian the conviction that men are to be saved by men!

The need of others is the second everyday, universal ineradicable dependence in all of us. Fear of losing others and standing alone is the root cause of fear of freedom. Paradoxically, however, the quality of this very dependence determines whether or not I will manfully wel-come my freedom.

It is no original fault in my nature that I need others. Even the new atheist sees this. His call to arms to shoulder responsibility for the world is really a call to arms to rally to each other.

Each of us starts life in a state of absolute dependence on others. I am born into a family. If the family is a success with me, it equips me finally to leave it, absolved of need of it, in search of fulfillment, which in turn will give me the courage for another departure, and so forth. But if I need my family when I'm old enough to form one of my own, the family has been a failure. It has occasioned my trading in my liberty, so that I have none to spend on a new way of belong-ing. Freud distinguished being "captive" and being "oblative." The person gripped in a dependence meant to be temporary loses creativity, healthy affectivity is impossible, and he is captive. The oblative per-son, on the other hand, moves from one dependence to richer ones, each more and more of his own choosing.

What determines whether the attitude will be captive or oblative? Whether or not I have the courage to offer myself to new pursuits, to break with the past, to be free? (Every free act is a break with the past.) How is it that some believe in themselves and "walk tall" in life, while others stay put?

The answer is in the kind of acceptance others render. If they take the individual seriously, in himself, and not merely as part of a function, a team, a church, a family, he has a chance of taking himself seriously and exacting performance from himself. James Baldwin has explained why so many Negroes in their ghettos rob, rape, push dope on each other, even slay each other. One would expect that being an oppressed minority they would close ranks against the outsider, the stranger, and achieve a strong unity. Not so. The white man rejects the Negro. The white man is the successful, the important citizen. The Negro, instead of seeing his value reflected in the white man's eyes, finds he has none. He consequently has no self-respect and finds little reason to measure up to values. Hence his predatory aggressiveness against his own!

The writer of the song entitled "You're nobody 'till somebody loves you" has the whole answer about quality dependence in that one line. To be a real self, with a zest for growth and change and freedom, I have to be found important by some other or others. If I am, I have a chance to face up to the job of life. I am a need of others, and the right other gives me a whole world. He bestows my freedom on me.

Being important, in my own right, to some important other(s) (my father or mother or teacher or uncle or the girl next door), I also stand a good chance of relaxing and accepting those elements of my existence that I cannot change, though I would like to with a passion. I lose some of the distaste of myself, and though never thoroughly reconciled to the human condition, can live with less anguish, working out some domestication of my solitude, my separateness, my death, my individuality, my inability to communicate.

If adults understood all of this better, fewer adolescents would be the problem they are to themselves and to others. Fewer young adults would need psychiatrists. The psychiatrists's job, after all, is to restore freedom to the client, and he will succeed to the degree he is client-centered and undefensively for the client, by accepting him. Value judgments, chidings, impatience, condescending encouragement are all ways of rejecting the client, which is another indication that acceptance is the specific for restoring the other to vitality.

The fear of liberty, then, comes from the need of depending. Or the fear of being alone! The truculent delinquent cannot feel he belongs, so his freedom is all at the service of anti-social independence. The coward is afraid to act on his own, being wrongly-dependent. If the quality of his dependence can be improved, he can change. Hundreds of seeming nobodies on college campuses spring into surprising activities and verve due to the love of a girl. Sinners have been turned into saints when finding a liberating dependence on God, long resented because they were sure He rejected them. Many an individual is sparked into a good day's work because of honest encouragement. Nobody can live up to the full stature of manhood unless he matters somewhere, to somebody, as somebody.

In a word, the terror of being free is faced down by self-belief. Self-belief is a gift bestowed by others, or another. The first two requisites for an adjusted life, self-knowledge and self-acceptance, are impossible without a third, acceptance by some other(s). I am not curious to know myself, and have not the courage to accept myself, unless I find I am worth something to start with, and only by discovering that others accept me in my own right can I believe I matter and that there is some point in being a true self. Love of the other has but one purpose, to give him to himself. It has but one test, whether or not my neighbor takes his one life more in hand because I love him. Paradoxically, he will not be free unless somebody gives him the confidence to energize his God-given possibilities. Thus the quality of those he depends on determines the quality of his freedom.

PART IV. THE ESCHATON

OTHERS this week speak with full authority on Eschaton. My only statement about it would be this presumptuous suggestion: that until enough of us *exist*, there will be no eschaton. The Lord, it would seem to me, means to succeed. Teilhard's Omega Point has to start becoming an important element of the new developments of the Christian doctrine, if ours is this world to make, if ours is to prompt each other to exist, if ours is indeed to be in order to love one another. We shall sooner or later bring on the eschaton. God will wait, though being delicately (i.e., not forcefully) in the act every inch of the way. *Leniter et suaviter agit.*

Eschaton and Resurrection: Patristic Insights

Walter J. Burghardt

MY title has something of the weasel in it: it can mean what I want it to mean. In point of fact, it ought to signify something real, a genuine problem. But even granted that, there is still a twin danger, two extremes I must avoid. One extreme is the broad sweep: What is *the* patristic vision of the eschaton? The other extreme is the narrow concentration: What does the *Didache* have to say about the Parousia? I am not denigrating the *Didache*, not forsaking "the Fathers"; I am simply saying that neither approach alone would satisfy the needs of this specific symposium.

What, then, shall I do? Why, steer a middle course, of course! Not just sweeping, not too circumscribed. Generalizations are inevitable, and details dare not be avoided; I must give a vision, and I must give information. But, to keep the general and the particular in fruitful proportion, three stages will mark my presentation. First, a *broad* look at the Christian hope in the first several centuries. Second, *insights* that strike me as theologically exciting, provocative, suggestive, mind-blowing and eye-opening. Third, a *critique:* What have the Fathers to say to us? Are they simply a stage, an early stage, in the Christian's effort to grasp his destiny? Are they worth bothering about, or has the Christian understanding of eschaton grown to such an extent that early Christian theology is valueless? How alive is their resurrection theology?

I

MY first stage, therefore: a broad look at the Christian hope in the first several centuries. On the whole, this material is not a Burghardt find; it is the common possession of scholars. And so I may be forgiven for giving it quickly, succinctly, with sparse detail

and little documentation. What I have in mind for this first stage is
a broad picture into which I can fit the specifics of my second stage,
with a view to the critique in my third stage. To recapture this broad
vision is to set before you a limited number of critical developments
in patristic eschatology.[1]

First on the patristic scene is a basic, uncomplicated vision of the
Christian's destiny. It is affirmation rather than argument, faith rather
than theology, and it bursts confidently from the Apostolic Fathers,
from the last years of the first century and the first half of the second.
J. N. D. Kelly has phrased it pithily:

> Four chief moments dominate the eschatological expectation of
> early Christian theology—the return of Christ, known as the
> Parousia, the resurrection, the judgment, and the catastrophic end-
> ing of the present world-order. In the primitive period they were
> held together in a naïve, unreflective fashion, with little or no
> attempt to work out their implications or solve the problems they
> raise.[2]

In this early understanding of Christian hope, (1) the Lord will
return in these our "last times." The hour is uncertain ("near" and
"far" are not datable adverbs for a Hermas), but it will dawn when
the Church has reached completion and the Antichrist has shown his
face. (2) This Parousia is power and majesty will be preceded by
(or at least linked with) the resurrection of the dead: resurrection
of the good and the bad, resurrection in the same flesh we carry now,
resurrection whose prototype is the Saviour's own rising. (3) What
links Parousia and resurrection is judgment: the God who sent His
Son as Saviour will send Him again as Judge. Not that individual
judgment immediately after death is unknown to these writers; rather
that, on the whole, judgment is seen as universal and in the future.
The Judge will separate the good from the bad: the bad will perish
eternally, the good will reap endless life in joy with the angels. (4)
Heaven and earth as we know them will disappear—by blood and/or
fire. "The cosmic order as we know it must be transformed, and so
made fit for God's elect."[3]

This primitive eschatology moves into a somewhat new phase about
the middle of the second century. The same four themes are still
dominant: Christ's return and man's resurrection, divine judgment
and cosmic transmutation. But time has passed and new situations
have arisen; apostolic witness has been complexified by apologetic
argument; sheer assertion makes room for sophisticated speculation.
It could hardly be otherwise; for Jew and pagan and Gnostic were
forcing on the Church a process that would never end: the need for
continual reflection, deepening self-identification. Doctrine begins to
"develop."

In this second stage—roughly from the Apologists to Nicaea—how

Admittedly, my facticity situates me, puts me here as this modified and classifiable history, and by its intimacy is always a threat to my subjectivity. But, as Heidegger says, I am "concern" (Sorge), "the only being which, in being is concerned about its own Being." When I awaken to a new day, it is *my* day. I look out at my world, center and gather it around myself in reference to myself. Viktor Frankl, the Jewish psychiatrist who writes of his experiences in a Nazi concentration camp in "Man's Search for Meaning," recalls that though he was stripped, bathed in Lysol, had his head shaved and was thrown prison dress to put on and given a number, he still had a decision all his own which his jailors could not control, namely the attitude he was going to adopt to the depersonalization they were working him into. He decided, as a scientist, that he would study the effect of this mass depersonalization on himself and his fellow prisoners. The result is his new and healthy Logotherapy.

There is then in me the already given, but I am not a clock. There is also the undetermined, though I am not a Superman. I am situated *and* autonomous. It is this dualism that is meant when phenomenologists define man as "consciousness-in-the-world."

f) AUTHENTICITY (2)

WITH situated consciousness in mind, some modern philosophers discuss authenticity. What they say comes down to this: to the degree my facticity takes over, and shrinks my openness to the world, I am that far tending to inauthenticity. To the degree that I am my orientation to the world, I am authentic. I can either be responsible and the cause of my own acts, or, because I am always in the world, let it anchor me. Authenticity and inauthenticity are always my permanent possibilities. If I resist inauthenticity, I am the true article (authentic), in the sense of the words "Be a man." We never say to a dog, "Come on, be a dog!"

Authenticity consists in more than self-project, however. There is a kind of passion and energy in thought as well, which should not be merely receptive activity. The essence of thought is, as Marcel says, in "lighting," not in being lit. (This realization has been in the public domain since Aristotle's *intellectus agens*.) Instead of being reflected in me as in a mirror, the world is itself unveiled by me, as by a light that swings across it. Or again, I am the questioner, and according to my question is the world's answer.

The authentic self is thus an on-goingness, due to itself. If I get stuck in things, routine, prohibitions, even ideals that block out the periphery of vision, in what Heidegger calls "everydayness," which is the life of the "one like many" (signified by the German *Man* and the French *On* as distinguished from the primary "Who" that I am) and am had by that very world without which I would have no place to go,

do the four dominant motifs develop? (1) Increasingly attractive to
theologians, increasingly popular among the people, is the persuasion
that when Christ returns, He will reign on earth with His saved for a
thousand years in idyllic felicity. Not all Christians share this conviction, but Justin Martyr is not alone when he appeals to Isaiah and
Zechariah and the Apocalypse; and millenarianism "clearly counts in
his eyes as an unquestioned article of orthodoxy."[4]

2) The resurrection is not only preached as indisputably Christian; it is argued as eminently reasonable: from man's body-soul
make-up, from his creation in God's image, from the necessity of adequate sanctions, from human teleology. The Gnostic thesis that flesh,
intrinsically evil as all matter must be, cannot share in salvation, is
furiously assailed. For Irenaeus, salvation must touch the whole man;
the body that co-operated with the soul in doing good should share
the soul's reward; above all, the Word of God who took human flesh
as His very own must have done so to save it. Similarly, Tertullian
tells the Gnostics that God cannot abandon what His own Son took to
Himself. In a word: God *can* raise the flesh to life; justice demands
that He *should;* revelation and reason assure us that He *will.*

3) There is heightened theological interest in the fate of the soul
as it waits for the resurrection of the flesh and ultimate judgment.
The Gnostics are in error: save for martyrs, souls do not pass to heaven
immediately after death; they remain in an underworld, somewhat
after the fashion of our Lord's own descent, to sojourn there till the
earth is destroyed, when they will rejoin their risen bodies and the
whole man will come to the sight of God. In this anticipatory state,
the souls of the saints are consoled with expectation of resurrection,
the souls of sinners taste something of their future condemnation.

4) The resurrectional life is man's definitive participation in God's
own life, in His immortality, His incorruptibility. This is the consummation of man's imaging: man, fashioned to God's image in the
beginning, defaced and debased through sin, restored to resemblance
in Christ, progressively divinized through history and mystery, is forever and profoundly "like" God.

5) At this period of development the eschatologist par excellence
was Origen. Three problems especially anguished him. First, he had
to defend bodily resurrection "against (a) the crude literalism which
pictured the body as being reconstituted, with all its physical functions,
at the last day, and (b) the perverse spiritualism of the Gnostics and
Manichees, who proposed to exclude the body from salvation."[5] He
found his solution in the *logos supermatikos* "inherent in each body
which enables it to be resuscitated, although with a different set of
qualities, exactly as the seed buried in the earth, as the Apostle showed,
survives death and decomposition and is restored as a blade of wheat."[6]

Origen's second problem was God's righteous judgment: How hold
fast to the traditional dogma and reinterpret it for the intelligent be-

liever? As he saw it, the sequence of eschatological events would go like this: *(a)* death, *(b)* provisional separation among souls, *(c)* probationary period in preparation for eternal destiny, *(d)* judgment at world's end, with definitive separation between good and bad. Reluctant to destroy traditional imaginings of an enthroned Christ separating sheep from goats, yet aware that the popular Parousia involved serious difficulties, he explained the Gospel imagery as symbolism.

> The real meaning of the Parousia, we are told, is the manifestation of Christ and His divinity to all mankind, good and bad, which will result in the disclosure of their true character. The Saviour will not appear in any given place, but will make Himself known everywhere; and men will present themselves before His throne in the sense that they will render homage to His authority. They will see themselves as they are, and in the light of that knowledge the good and the bad will be finally differentiated.[7]

Origen's third problem: the nature and duration of damnation. For him, the kingdom the righteous inherit is the contemplation of divine truth (no millennial meat and drink and sex). The sufferings of the damned, therefore, are similarly spiritual: not material fire, but intense realization that they are severed from God, who ought to be their happiness and their supreme good. Moreover, all punishment, even hell, will have an end. Successive cycles of worlds will lead to the moment when all reality (the devil included) is brought into subjection to God: at the end, as in the beginning, He will be all in all.

A third stage is most in evidence after Nicaea and has to do with resurrection, Parousia, and judgment. In this stage the resurrection remains, for the Greek and the Latin Fathers, an unquestioned article of the faith: all will rise, and the body in which they rise will be in an authentic sense the body they have now. Most of the writers do not speculate, do not philosophize; they affirm, they defend.

> On the other hand, there were two groups of theologians in this period whose thought about the resurrection merits attention—(I) those who led a revolt against Origen's rational analysis of it, claiming that his theories amounted to a virtual denial of any real resurrection; and (II) those constructive thinkers who strove, some of them along cautiously Origenistic lines but omitting what was most characteristic of Origen's teaching, to understand the mystery at a deeper level than the crude popular faith allowed.[8]

First, the revolt against Origen. In the East, perhaps the most articulate of the reactors are Eustathius of Antioch (d. before 337) and Epiphanius of Salamis (d. 402). "In fact, however, both these teachers were indebted for the bulk of their arguments to the classic onslaught delivered against Origen by Methodius of Olympius († c. 311) several decades earlier."[9] If, argues Methodius, the body that rises is not the material substratum *(to hylikon hypokeimenon)*, which is in constant flux, but the distinctive form *(to charaktērizon eidos)*, which abides unchanging, then there is no real resurrection: what is raised is not the body. As with Christ, so with us: one same body for Him on the cross and with doubting Thomas, one same body for us here and hereafter. Heightened in quality indeed, impassible, glorified, but still *materially* identical with the body before death.

In the West, the archfoe of Origen was his former admirer Jerome. Till 394 his resurrection theology was sheer Origenism: the natural body disappears, and at the resurrection the elect are transformed into purely spiritual beings. After 394 he would be crassly realistic: the risen body is physically identical with the earthly body. It is to this stream of patristic thought, in the period from Methodius to Jerome, that you can trace the familiar conviction within much of traditional Christianity: the risen body has to be, in some genuine sense, identical with the body of earth, not with some distinctive form of the body.

Second, the effort to probe more deeply, to understand more than superficially. In the East, Cyril of Jerusalem expressed a cautious theory when he saw this very body raised *(touto)* but somehow spiritualized *(ou toiouto)*—Paul's "pneumatic body" (1 Cor 15:44). As Didymus was to develop it, resurrection life will not destroy our earthly body, but will absorb it, impart to it superior qualities. Gregory of Nyssa, like his beloved Origen, distinguished between the existential body's ever-changing material elements and the bodily form *(eidos)* that is changeless, characteristic, individual. Sheer quantity of matter will not matter at the resurrection; the soul, which knows the physical elements that belong to the *eidos,* will be able to draw to itself such of those elements as it requires. And this risen body will no longer share death's consequences: illness and age, deformity and death. It is human nature indeed, but restored to the primitive state lost through Adam's sin.

In the West, Hilary of Poitiers, like Cyril of Jerusalem, saw God reconstituting the body's matter just as it once was, but altered in quality to suit its new state. So too for Ambrose: "resurrection" implies the identical body, but spiritualized. To Augustine, resurrection is dogma, and it means that "this identical flesh will be raised which is buried, which dies, which is seen and touched, which must eat and drink if it is to go on existing, which is sick and subject to pain."[10] But this same body will be clothed in incorruptibility—the elect and the damned alike. An omnipotent God can restore even what has been totally devoured or destroyed; but not every segment of flesh must be recaptured as it once was. The risen body will be perfect and entire, with no admixture of the ugly or deformed; and St. Paul's "spiritual body" is not a new substance but complete subjection of flesh to spirit.

In this same period (I mean the fourth and fifth centuries) the Second Coming is uncommonly prominent as object of theology and homiletics. On the one hand, OT and NT imagery are accepted realistically; on the other, visions of a millennium are all but gone: even Augustine, so attracted to millenarianism in earlier days, could not ultimately abide the materialism of it all:

> he changed his attitude and favoured an allegorical interpretation of the seer of Patmos. The first resurrection, according to this, is our restoration from the death of sin and our summons to the Christian life, while the reign of Christ and His saints is to be understood as the Church carrying out its apostolate here on earth. The thousand years are to be explained either as the final millennium preceding the judgment or, preferably, as the total duration of the earthly Church.[11]

In this same post-Nicene period, judgment is just as much in evidence as Parousia, at times even more imaginative. Some Eastern authors, from Athanasius to Chrysostom, take the biblical descriptions quite literally: God notes our conduct in a book; we render an account of our deeds; rewards and punishments are distributed; each man's life and God's justice stand revealed. Other Eastern theologians interiorize judgment: my conscience is what accuses me; the Judge's countenance is God's light illumining my guilty heart; our only accusers will be our own remembered sins; judgment is the weight on my conscience; my own sins will condemn me.

Kelly finds Latin thought "on the whole closely aligned with Greek," but "its general flavour tends to be more archaic."[12] Peculiarly Western (e.g., Hilary, Zeno, Ambrose, Ambrosiaster) is this thesis: indeed, all men will stand before Christ on the last day, but "only those wayward Christians whose lives have been a mixture of good and evil will in the strict sense be judged. Of the other two groupings into which men fall, the righteous need no judgment, and the wicked have been judged already."[13] Influenced by Greek thought, Ambrose sees judgment taking place in the sinner's own conscience; God knows man's heart; the thrones of the Judge and apostles are a metaphor; the sentence simply signifies ratification in eternity of a man's actual merits. And as so often, Augustine is splendidly balanced: judgment day is when God's wisdom and righteousness, permanent features of history, become obvious to all; the judgment indeed belongs to a Christ-come-in-triumph, but the book that is opened is the conscience of each man.

What of the soul's lot immediately after death? Here the Greek Fathers are not at peace (their friends would say they are uncertain, their enemies would say confused). The parable of Dives and Lazarus compels or compounds the confusion: Are these gentlemen already judged and requited, or does the parable prefigure the last day, or are there two moments of divine retribution? The Latins are more definite. Hilary rests the righteous in Abraham's bosom, has the wicked beginning torment now, to be ratified on the ultimate *dies irae*. Am-

brose has "storehouses" that are at once foretastes of doom and waiting rooms for final judgment. Jerome is the first to clearly describe
the immediate allocation of rewards and punishments as a judgment.
Augustine sees the intermediate period (between death and last day)
as involving the soul's joy or torture: it seems a consequence of God's
judgment, but he reserves the term "day of judgment" for the ultimate,
universal assembling.

Is damnation eternal? In the East, yes—certainly by the fifth century. But Basil has intriguing news for us in the fourth century: most
ordinary Christians expected a time limit, Scripture notwithstanding;
and these lay minds must have found solace in the hesitations of Gregory of Nazianzus and in Gregory of Nyssa's final restoration, à la
Origen, of all things (devil too) in Christ. Western thought was
more nuanced. Hell is eternal enough in older writers such as Hilary.
But Ambrosiaster and Ambrose and Jerome distinguish classes of
sinners. Augustine is open to proportionate punishments within the
real, material, inextinguishable fire; he allows for a purification of
"earthly loves" in purgatorial flame; but on the whole he can only go
along with Scripture, where he sees "the everlasting death of the
damned, i.e., their alienation from the life of God,"[14] without term,
without hope. And still, in Augustine's time

> a wide variety of opinions were in vogue, some holding that the
> pains of hell would be temporary for all men without distinction,
> others that the intercession of the saints would secure their salva-
> tion, others that salvation was guaranteed for those, even heretics,
> who had been baptized and had partaken of the Lord's body or
> at any rate had received these sacraments within the Catholic
> Church, others that all who had remained Catholics, even if they
> had lived disgracefully, must be saved, others that only those
> sinners who had neglected to practise almsgiving when alive were
> destined to eternal chastisement.[15]

Finally, for the Fathers, what is life everlasting? Different writers
stress different facets. For Origen, the blessedness of the saints is a
gradual progress in understanding until, loving God so utterly as to
outlaw sin forever, they have "only one occupation . . . the contemplation of God, so that, being formed in the knowledge of the Father,
they may all become in the strict sense Son, just as now it is the Son
alone who knows the Father."[16] In Cyril of Jerusalem's grasp on the
Creed, "eternal life," the purpose of Christian existence, means being
forever with the Lord. For Basil, the risen enjoy one another and God
as friends, contemplate God with rapturous awareness of His person
and presence. For Gregory of Nazianzus, heaven is festival unending,
joyous gazing on the Trinity, deification. This deification finds extraordinary stress in Gregory of Nyssa, for whom to know God is to be
like God, and to be like God is to share in all His perfections. Similar-

ly, for Cyril of Alexandria, redemption is deification, and deification will reach its climax when oneness between man and God will be indissoluble, when partial knowledge will give way to "a more blinding gnosis," when our risen bodies, no longer enslaved by corruption, will share Christ's life and glory. Chrysostom sees the saints' most intense delight in clear and perfect knowledge of God, though His essence remains incomprehensible. And Theodore of Mopsuestia points to the "many mansions" in the Father's house: felicity is graded in proportion to merit. To know God, to be like God, to live God's life, and all this intensely and rapturously, ceaselessly and consummately—this is heaven for the Greek Fathers.

Latin thought is not basically different. If any one aspect is more strongly emphasized than in the East, it is heaven as communion of saints. Not only is blessedness an incredible oneness with God; love binds the saints to one another.

> The prospect of meeting and conversing with the saints in heaven played a great part in Western ideas about the future life at this epoch. It was characteristic of Ambrose, and Jerome dwelt on it with eager eloquence, pointing out that in heaven he would meet the Blessed Virgin, and St. Anne and other blessed ones whom he had never known on earth. While brought to its fulness after death, this intimacy between the saints and their ardent lovers on earth has its beginnings even now. Hence Niceta was able to promise his catechumens that in the Church they would attain, among other privileges, to 'the communion of saints,' and a mention of this supernatural blessedness soon found a place in the Western Creed.[17]

It is in Augustine that patristic insights into eternal life find their summation and climax. Only God can satisfy man, and so ultimate happiness lies in knowing and loving the triune God. It is indescribable here below; but somehow in the body we shall see God everywhere present in the new heaven and the new earth. God will be our joy: contemplation without ceasing, love without cloying, praise without wearying. Degrees of blessedness, but no envy; free will, but freed from delight in sinning; the fulfilment of the Psalmist's "Be still, and know that I am God."

II

WHAT, then, was the Christian hope in the patristic era? The Lord will come again; the dead will rise in the flesh they bore on earth; the wicked will be sentenced to eternal anguish, the good welcomed to endless joy; the cosmic order will be transformed, to be made fit for God's elect. Problems arose in plenty when these four motifs were analyzed and dissected. Several of the problems reached solution: e.g., millenarianism rose quickly, only to fade slowly.

Most of the profound issues that challenged the early theologians were not satisfactorily resolved—and understandably so: What, if anything, does the soul do between death and resurrection? When does judgment take place, and what does it mean to be judged? What is "life with God" like? What does it mean to be damned, and is damnation really forever? Come the resurrection, what sort of bodies will we bear?

The second stage in my presentation: insights that strike me as theologically exciting, provocative, suggestive, mind-blowing and eye-opening. I shall develop three: (1) death as a remedy for sin; (2) God's glory—man alive; (3) Jesus Christ as the Eschaton (capital E).

DEATH AS A REMEDY FOR SIN

TOWARDS the close of the third century a bishop named Methodius, one of the early adversaries of Origen, composed a treatise *On the Resurrection.* A theme that pervades much of his first book is the thesis that God "invented death" as a remedy for sin. The problem he presents is clear enough: as long as the body lives, sin lives within it, even in the baptized, though sin's roots are concealed, its power inhibited, its sprouts checked. The solution? Perhaps the most intriguing passage in this connection is the following:

> Take, for comparison, a consummate craftsman who recasts a statue. The statue as originally fashioned, from gold or some other material, was a lovely thing, every part of the body beautifully proportioned. All of a sudden the craftsman finds it mutilated— damaged by an evil man too envious to endure its loveliness. . . . If he does not recast or refashion it but simply treats and repairs it, the fire and the forge will inevitably change it from what it was originally. If, therefore, the craftsman would have his masterpiece utterly fair and unblemished, he must crush it to pieces and cast it once more, in this way to destroy the deformities and alterations that treachery and envy have laid on the statue, and restore it undamaged and unalloyed to its original shape, as like itself as possible. It is impossible, you see, for a work of art to be lost under the hands of the original artist, even if it be melted down again; it can be restored.
>
> Such, I would say, was God's dispensation in our regard. Seeing man, the fairest work of His art, marred by envy's malicious treachery, God, lover of man that He was, was not content to leave him in this condition, lest man, with the flaw in him immortal, bear the blame to eternity. He dissolved man into his primeval matter, in order that, by a process of remodeling, everything blameworthy in him might melt away and disappear completely. For the melting down of the statue in the example above corresponds to the death and dissolution of the body, while the refashioning and restoration of the original material finds its parallel in the resurrection. . . .
>
> For I call your attention to this. As I said, after man transgressed, the mighty Hand was not content to abandon as a trophy of victory

its own work adulterated by the Evil One..., but melting it, He reduced it afresh to clay, like a potter who refashions a vessel so
that, through the process of refashioning, all the deformities and
bruises may vanish and the whole become faultlessly pleasing again.
...Does not God have power, by a refashioning and a restoring
from the selfsame primeval matter of each man, to raise each man
separately either to our honor and glory or to dishonor and condemnation?...It is not in our power to destroy the root of evil
completely, but it is in our power not to allow it to expand and
bear fruit. For its utter, universal destruction at the very roots God
effects by the dissolution of the body, as I have said, while the
partial destruction is ours, so that it does not put forth shoots.[18]

This idea of death as a divine remedy for sin is not confined to
Methodius' treatise on the resurrection; it shows up, if more briefly,
in his better-known *Symposium,* which is actually a manual of Christian doctrine, of philosophy and theology, unified under the concept
of chastity. Methodius writes:

Then will all our tabernacles be established, when our bodies rise
again, their bones once more fixed and compacted with flesh. Then
shall we celebrate to the Lord the day of joy in a pure manner, re-
ceiving now eternal tabernacles, never more to die or to be dissolved into the earth of the grave. For our tabernacle of old had
been firmly made; but it tottered and fell by the Fall. And God
put an end to sin by man's death, lest man become a sinner for all
eternity, and, since sin would be living in him, be under eternal
condemnation. And this is the reason why man, though he was not
made mortal and corruptible, dies and his soul is separated from
his body, in order that his transgression might be destroyed by
death, being unable to live after he was dead. Thus with sin dead
and destroyed, I can rise again in immortality and sing a hymn of
praise to God who saves His children from death by means of
death....[19]

The thesis that death is God's remedy for sin, so congenial to Methodius, has a more impressive patristic history than theologians have
realized. It may be that Methodius discovered it in Theophilus of
Antioch or Irenaeus of Lyons, both of whom wrote about the year
180.[20] Theophilus, having spoken of man's ejection from Paradise,
of his sufferings, and of death, continues in the following vein:

God did man a great service (*energesian*) in that man did not live
on forever in a state of sin. Rather, God cast him from Paradise
in something like an exile. His purpose was that when man had
atoned for his sin through punishment for a fixed time and had been
chastised, he might afterwards be recalled. That is why, when man
was first formed in this world, the mystery-laden words of Genesis
suggest that man was set in Paradise twice (cf. Gn 2:8; 2:15):

once when he was placed there [in the beginning], the second to be actualized after the resurrection and judgment. Not simply that. Take some sort of vessel that is discovered to have a particular defect after its completion. It is recast and refashioned, so that it becomes new and perfect. A similar thing happens to man through death: he is, if I may put it that way, broken in pieces, that he may be found whole and sound at the resurrection—I mean spotless, just, and immortal.[21]

St. Irenaeus, perhaps indebted to Theophilus in this area,[22] has a parallel passage on the providential function of death:

For this reason God "cast [man] from Paradise" and removed him far from "the tree of life" (Gn 3:23-24)—not that God envied him the tree of life, as some presume to say, but rather from compassion. He did not want man to continue a sinner forever, did not want the sin that enveloped him to be immortal, the evil to be interminable and incurable. He set a bound to man's sinning, by interposing death and so causing sin to cease. He put an end to sin by dissolving the flesh—which should take place in the earth —in order that man might one day cease living to sin, might die to sin and begin living to God (cf. Rom 6:2).[23]

After Methodius, the tradition seems to strengthen; and I find it significant that the thesis turns up in influential Fathers like Gregory of Nazianzus, Gregory of Nyssa, John Chrysostom, Cyril of Alexandria, and Procopius of Gaza.

In the garments of skin with which God clothed man after the Fall, Gregory of Nazianzus finds, as a plausible interpretation, "a grosser, mortal, stubborn flesh. . . . Here indeed man derives some profit: death and sin's cessation, that evil might not be immortal. And man's punishment by God is turned into God's love for man *(kai ginetai philanthrōpia hē timōria)*. This, I am confident, this is the way God inflicts punishment."[24]

In an interesting passage from the *Oratio catechetica magna,* Gregory of Nyssa asserts that after being "transformed to wickedness" in Adam, "man, like some earthen vessel, is again resolved into earth, in order that he may part with the sordidness in which he is now involved and be refashioned through the resurrection to his original appearance."[25] But far more significant, because highly pastoral, is the funeral oration which Gregory of Nyssa delivered in 385 for the six-year-old princess Pulcheria, the only child of Theodosius the Great. The sermon ends with a final effort at consolation, and the effort runs along the lines we are tracing: death is *agathon,* a good thing; it is a singular way to our original state:

Death, for men, is nothing else but purification from wickedness. For in the beginning our nature was constructed by the God of the universe like some vessel fit to receive what is good; but when the enemy of our souls through treachery poured into us what is evil, no room remained for the good. For this reason, in order that the inborn (implanted ?) wickedness might not be eternal in us, a surpassing providence opportunely dissolves the vessel by death, so that when the wickedness has flown forth [melted away, disappeared: *ekryeisēs*], the human being might be refashioned and might be restored, unmixed with evil, to its original life. For this is the resurrection, the regeneration of our nature, after dissolution, to its primordial state. . . .[26]

Chrysostom, preaching at Antioch in 388 on Genesis, speaks in the same vein as the Gregorys, though he is of the Antiochene school and therefore by predilection an exponent of the literal sense. Dealing with Gn 3:22-23 (God exiled man from Paradise, to keep him from eating of the tree of life and living forever), he says:

... death was a dispensation of the Lord to man's advantage. [God exiled man from Paradise for one reason:] His love for man (*dia tēn philanthrōpian tēn peri auton*). [The danger was that within Paradise man's sinning might be deathless; exile was preferable.] Consequently, man's banishment from Paradise was rather an act of solicitude than of anger. This is the way our Master acts: He reveals His solicitude for us no less when He punishes (*timōroumenos*) than when He grants favors; He inflicts this punishment (*tēn timōrian*) for an admonition. If He had known that we would not become worse by sinning with impunity (*atimōrēti*), He would not have punished (*ouk an oude etimōrēsato*); but in checking in advance our continued deterioration and cutting off sin's onward march, His punishment is an expression of His love (*tēn oikeian philanthrōpian mimoumenos timōreitai*). This is what He has done in this instance; for the exile He ordered from Paradise reveals His concern for the man He had fashioned first.[27]

Cyril of Alexandria seems to suggest the same basic idea: "The death of the flesh was invented for man's advantage. It did not consign this living being to utter destruction. Rather, it preserved him for renewal and, if I may phrase it so, for remolding (*anaskeuēn:* remodeling, refashioning) at the right time, like some vessel that has been crushed."[28] In Cyril, the remedy for sin does not come through with clarity.

Finally, Procopius of Gaza, who often copies out passages from Methodius and sometimes cites him explicitly, has a pertinent passage on Gen 3:22:

Some interpret [Gn 3:22] thus: God does not speak from envy; He was showing the care He had for the vessel whose perfection had been marred through its own fault, that it might not remain permanently imperfect, but like an excellent potter who returns a damaged vessel back to its own (original) mixture, earth, at the resurrection He will refashion the just in glory immortal, capable of enjoying the kingdom, the unjust capable of enduring the punishment to which it is condemned.[29]

In the theology of the Greek Fathers, death is a benefit. Not simply for the reasons that have been diligently culled from their writings: not simply because death is a spur to virtuous living; not simply because it forces frail men into community; not simply because it makes for salutary fear; not simply because it is preferable to a life of anguish; not simply because it is a release of the soul from the prison of the body; not simply because it solves a demographic problem. Death is a benefit because it enters intimately into God's design for redemption.

Timōria is turned into *philanthrōpia*. It is not that the Greek Fathers are unaware that death is punishment—a sentence for sin. This they know, if only because they take Genesis seriously: "Because you have disobeyed, you shall die" (cf. Gn 2:17; 3:17-19). An inherited sentence for another's sin. Cyril of Alexandria is sufficiently typical of Greek patristic thought in this area. His most thorough and penetrating treatment of death's transmission is contained in the following passage:

> We must inquire how it is that our first father Adam transmitted to us the punishment laid on him for his transgression. He heard the words, "Earth you are, and into earth shall you return" (Gn 3:19), and the incorruptible became corruptible and bound with the chains of death. But because he begot children after falling to death's estate, we his progeny have become corruptible, since we are born of a corruptible father. So it is that we too are heirs of the curse in Adam; for surely we have not been visited with punishment (*tetimōrēmetha*) as though we disobeyed with him the divine command which he received, but because ... become mortal he transmitted the curse to the seed he fathered. We are mortal because mortal-sprung.[30]

Yes, for the Greek Fathers death is a punishment, an inheritance from Adam's sin. But it is more: death is not only punitive, it is providential; it is not merely vindictive, it is corrective. Death is not simply a punishment for sin, it is a remedy for sin.

The underlying idea would seem to be this. Ever since the first sin, man is a mutilated thing. He is a "sin-ful" creature. Not that he is incapable of love; not that his every action is vitiated by vice. Rather that in his very make-up, in his inmost being, are the seeds of sin. Even after he has laid hold on Christ, even after his total self-giving to his Saviour, he remains a paradox; his situation is ambivalent. Even when Father and Son have made their home in him, a legacy from Adam's sin abides in him—what the Church so vividly

calls the "touchwood," the "tinder," of sin. It is the native attraction
which evil has for fallen nature, even after Christ has possessed that
nature. Before I can say yes or no, my flesh is inflamed by forbidden
fruit, my mind is invaded by pride or envy, by doubt or rebellion,
by thoughts that scandalize me.[31] It is Augustine confessing, ten years
after his baptism, that he is still wrestling with the lust of the flesh,
the lust of the eyes, and the pride of life: with the memory of illicit
love, the allurement of beauty sundered from Loveliness supreme,
"the desire to be feared and loved by men for no other reason than
the joy I get from it."[32]

In the analogy of Methodius, as long as the divine Craftsman simply
treats and repairs His product, the work of His hands, it remains imperfect. If it is to be utterly fair and unblemished, if the deformities
and alterations that sin has laid on it are to be destroyed, the work
of art must be melted down, recast, remodeled.

This, in God's design, is the function of death. If the flaw in man
is not to be immortal, man must dies; soul must be severed from body,
and body dissolved into its elements, so that God can once again cast
man as he once was.

Death, then, reveals not only wrath but love. Death is not simply
a chronological end to sin; death destroys sin by a divine dispensation.
Risen man is not the old man simply earth-bound no longer; risen
man is a new man, dissolved and recast. Death is part not simply of
the Fall but of redemption as well.

Kai ginetai philanthrōpia hē timōria. Punishment is turned into
love—man's punishment into God's love.

GOD'S GLORY: MAN ALIVE

A SECOND patristic insight into eschaton that strikes me as theologically exciting stems from early Eastern understanding of
God's image in man. Obviously, in a single paper focusing not on
image but on eschaton, it is impossible to sum up in a handy package
the image doctrine of the Fathers; the problems are complex, the
literature is enormous.[33] I shall concentrate on one facet of image
theology: I mean incorruptibility and/or immortality; and I shall
limit myself to the Alexandrian tradition and its intellectual and
spiritual background.

Aphtharsia plays an important part in the anthropology of the sec-
ond-century Apologists. And all of them intimate what Theophilus of
Antioch enunciates: participation in the immortality and incorruptibility that is proper to God implies an assimilation to God, a divinization.[34] But, as so often, it is Irenaeus who spells out what is inchoative, halting, tentative in his predecessors and contemporaries. For
the Bishop of Lyons, the successive stages of man's journey to God,
his progressive resemblance to the divine, can be traced on the lines

of incorruptibility. At the close of a careful lexical and theological study of *aphtharsia* and *athanasia* in Irenaeus,[35] Michel Aubineau has summed up his position splendidly:

> On the level of the body, incorruptibility appears as emancipation from the biological process which sweeps it to its destruction. But this liberation is the expression of a more radical transformation. The incorruptibility which penetrates the whole man, body and soul, is a participation in the incorruptibility of God, in His perfect, uncreated, immortal nature—not that which the philosophers of antiquity dreamed for the soul, but that which the Father bestows on His adopted sons.
>
> Man reaches incorruptibility by stages; for God's pedagogy respects man's freedom and the law of progress written in his nature. Adam received a fragile incorruptibility, without deep roots, proportioned to his imperfection as a child. He lost it, Irenaeus says, more through carelessness and surprise than through malice. If sin disturbs God's plan, it does not alter its essential lines. Christ, in His coming, brings humanity a firm, stable incorruptibility, which is disseminated in the Church, through the sacraments [baptism and the Eucharist], under the breath of the Spirit. Received by Christians in harmony with the whole scale of participations, incorruptibility ascends like sap in each of them, to make them produce and mature the fruits of immortality. It is in vision, finally, that perfect incorruptibility finds its full bloom. There is no break in the continuity of this movement. In each stage of his growth man possesses, in his soul and in his body, one same homogeneous principle which makes him kin to God—not a divine fragment that has escaped from the pleroma, but incorruptible life communicated gratuitously.[36]

Here, I am convinced, is the profound meaning of Irenaeus' famous *Gloria Dei—vivens homo:* "God's glory—man alive!"[37]

For Clement of Alexandria, to become like God *(kath' homoiōsin)* is equivalent to divinization *(ektheousthai);* and this takes place primarily through participation in God's *aphtharsia,* the incorruptibility in which antiquity recognized God's proper reality and glory in contrast to mortal man. The stages in human divinization are three: (1) life, (2) good life, (3) eternal life.[37a]

It is in this area of incorruptibility that Louis Bouyer discovers a striking illustration of Athanasius' originality.[38] For Athanasius, there are two, and only two, modes of existence which are radically distinct. One is God's, and it implies *aphtharsia;* the other is the creature's, and it implies *phthora. Aphtharsia* is not merely the fact of not dying; it is the property of a life which has in itself no reason for ever ceasing to be. As such, it is strictly proper to God. *Phthora* is man's natural condition, sin or no sin; he is ephemeral as well as dependent. It is only in consequence of incredible generosity, it is only by God's

self-communication, that creatures can *become* incorruptible. How is
this achieved? Through knowledge—the knowledge whereby the purified soul contemplates the eternal God in the image which the Word
impresses on it. By the indwelling of the Word, man contemplates
God in the mirror of his soul. Contemplating the incorruptible God
as He is, man participates in God's incorruptibility. It is here that
the two primary aspects of the Athanasian image make contact. As
long as man is *logikos*, i.e., as long as he participates in God's Word,
he is *aphthartos*, i.e., he shares in God's life—unending life. This is
the realization of the biblical declaration "You are gods" (Ps 81:6).[39]

As for the restoration of the image in Christ, the fundamental principle of Athanasian soteriology is that the Word took on Himself our
phthora in order to consume it by His *aphtharsia*. As Bouyer puts it,
"the life which emerges triumphant from the tomb on Easter morning,
and which is to become our life, is no longer the life subject to the
phthora of sheerly human beings—which we had become by sin; it is
divine life, *aphtharsia* in us."[40]

Gregory of Nyssa likewise sees an aspect of the divine image in
man's immortality *(to athanaton, to aïdion)*.[41] But Gregory is absorbed
not by the immortality which concerns Socrates in the *Phaedo*, not by
the incorruptibility of the *Enneads*. His perspective is totally theological; he is engrossed in the immortality *(athanasia)* which transforms us, by God's free giving, to the image of the Immortal,[41a] the
incorruptibility which is a participation in the God who "is Incorruptibility" *(aphtharsia)*.[42] Daniélou has recaptured Gregory's preoccupation:

> [For Gregory] there is not a natural state of the incorruptible spirit,
> to which the divine life would come to be added. There is only the
> real, true state, that of divinized man, who is *aphthartos*, and the
> state of fall, *phthartos*, the state where he is not physically cor-
> ruptible but immersed in corruptible realities. And it is this positive
> corruption which is significant. The term *athanasia*, which we find
> beside *aphtharsia* to designate the state of "image" . . . calls for
> the same remarks. The opposition is not between existence and
> nothingness; for we are on the human level, where the spirit is
> endowed with a radical immortality. The opposition is between
> the state of mortality, that is to say, the condition of man separated
> from God—which is the real, true death—and consequently in-
> vested with an animal nature subject to mortality, and the state of
> *athanasia*, which is at once life of the soul united to God and libera-
> tion from biological mortality.[43]

It is in Cyril of Alexandria, however, that the two basic Alexandrian
insights on incorruptibility reach their peak.[44] I mean (1) that *aphtharsia* may well be the most significant facet of the divine image in
man; and (2) that *aphtharsia* is only secondarily biological (=life);
it is primarily theological (=God's life).

In his *Commentary on John,* Cyril recalls that man was made in the beginning "to the image of the Creator" (Col 3:10), but that "the idea of the image is a varied one; for there is not just one way of being an image; there are many. Nevertheless, the part of the likeness *(emphereias)* to God the Creator which is most remarkable [most conspicuous? *diaphanestaton*] is incorruptibility and imperishability *(to aphtharton kai anōlethron)."*[54]

This incorruptibility, this share in a divine prerogative, in God's own nature, what is it? For Cyril, man is a fascinating blend of the mortal and immortal, the corruptible and incorruptible. (1) If we regard man as a human being and nothing more, his body will necessarily be abandoned by the soul and will dissolve; for dissolution is innate in flesh. Man, the composite, is mortal and corruptible. Human life must end. (2) The soul's status is paradoxical. In one sense it is naturally impermanent: since it is a creature, whatever permanence it has is a free gift of God. In another sense it is naturally permanent: God has freely elected to root permanence in the soul's constitution, in its very texture. The soul's life cannot end. (3) The transitory life of the flesh and the endless life of the soul are each the consequence of a participation in God's nature, specifically in the Word who is Life. Since this participation does not lift man above the level of the human, it can be denominated natural. (4) In an excess of graciousness God gave to Adam, and through Christ has given to us, a richer participation in His life, in His incorruptibility, a sharing in the Spirit of life which constitutes a divinization of the human. What precisely is this *athanasia,* this *aphtharsia?*

First, the image of God which Cyril finds in *aphtharsia* stresses the body's incorruptibility rather than the soul's. As he understands the methodology of the Incarnation, "that in us which was especially in danger [because of the curse consequent on the first sin] had to be rescued the sooner, and by being intertwined with Life-by-nature be recalled to incorruptibility." That is why the body which had fallen was united to the life-giving Word, and flesh partook of immortality.[46]

Second, this *aphtharsia* Cyril sees as the body's continuation in existence for eternity, its immunity from death and dissolution. In this sense of the word, Cyril maintains that the entire human race, no man excepted, was refashioned in Christ to *aphtharsia,* just as in Adam's transgression the whole race was condemned to *phthora.*[47] But two important distinctions must be remembered. The first is the distinction between hope and realization, between promise and fulfilment, between first fruits and final harvest. Incorruptibility has indeed been communicated to redeemed humanity; in fact, it was communicated to human nature as a whole in the Incarnation; in His resurrection Christ raised human nature with Him; and incorruptibility is achieved in the Eucharist too, where we are restored to our primeval state.[48] But the flowering of the seed, the full realization of our hope, the fulfilment of the promise—this is reserved for the consummation of the world. There is an aspect of our resemblance to divinity whose actualization has been temporarily withheld. We *shall* be like Christ in incorruptibility and in superiority to death, as evidenced by Col 3:3-4 and Phil 3:21.[49]

The second distinction has been tersely phrased by Cyril: all the dead will rise in *aphtharsia,* but not all will rise in *doxa.*[50] The universal resurrection has for its basis a physical relationship, a physical oneness, with the Incarnate Word, who in His own resurrection raised all men with Him; the glorious resurrection is grounded in a mystical relationship, a mystical oneness, with Christ, because some have "become conformed to the image of [God's] Son" (Rom 8:29).[50a]

Third, therefore, Cyril has a richer, fuller concept of incorruptibility for which the notion of mere duration in existence is little more than an indispensable foundation. For him, the more profound significance of *aphtharsia* and *phthora* lies in their moral implications. *Phthora* is not simply subjection to physical death and subsequent dissolution. It is that, and more. *Phthora* is the condition of a rational creature who is deprived of precisely that life which is divine and eternal. And if God's life has gone from man, human life itself is doomed to death and decay; it has no finality. Life left Adam's body because life had fled from his soul.[51] Similarly, *aphtharsia* is a concept paradoxically simple and complex. It means that man, the whole man, is alive. Not with a double life, natural and supernatural, human and divine. Man, this composite creature of soul and body, has been divinized; *he* is alive with *God's* life. It is this incorruptibility that must be "the most remarkable part of the likeness."[52]

It remains true, however, that Cyril's preoccupation is with "that in us which was especially in danger," the naturally corruptible flesh. If we must say in brief what corporal *aphtharsia* meant for him, it is this: the body will know neither physical nor moral imperfection, neither physical weakness nor fleshly concupiscence.[53] The process was initiated when the Son of God quickened corruptible flesh with His incarnation; it is individualized and heightened through Christian living; it will be consummated when our bodies participate definitively in Christ's life and glory.[54]

It cannot be sufficiently stressed, however, that, despite certain emphases, Cyril's outlook is holistic. It is sinful man, and not simply the body, that is *phthartos,* because it is man who is dominated by concupiscence and is a rebel against God; and it is sanctified man, and not simply the body, that is *aphthartos* (inchoately now, consummately later), because it is man who is lord of his passions and one with his God. It is here that the image which is *aphtharsia* joins hands with the image that is *hagiasmos;* for humanity has "sprung back to incorruptibility through sanctification in the Spirit."[55]

It is my conviction that Alexandrian image theology, at its best, is a ceaseless play on Irenaeus' theme "God's glory—man alive!" And to be alive is, in Athanasius' terse phrase, *to kata theon zēn;* God communicates His own divine life—now and eternally.[56]

JESUS CHRIST AS THE ESCHATON

IN 1950 the Protestant theologian Jean-Louis Leuba charged that the Council of Chalcedon with its substantialist and static approach to Christ, had immobilized Him outside time, had fashioned an ahistorical Christology antithetic to the New Testament "movement" of salvation, and so had limited or repressed the relation between Christology and eschatology.[57]

It is true, as Daniélou remarked in his response to Leuba, that the eschatological issues, e.g., millenarianism, which preoccupied the Church from Irenaeus to Augustine, had receded into the background in the fifth century; and indeed Chalcedon was more anxious to define the constitutive principles of Christology than its significance in the history of salvation.[58] But—and here Daniélou is strong[59]—this does not mean that eschatology is of no interest to the fifth century; quite the contrary.

> If, at the time of Chalcedon, attention focuses on the person of Christ in its constitutive elements, the reason is that here ultimately lay the decisive question for eschatology itself. It is, in point of fact, the union of the two natures which enables us to show how Christ is the coming-to-a-head of the Old Testament, how He is the end, the *telos,* of salvation's whole plan, how at the end the return of Christ will bring this plan to consummation. It is the dogma of Chalcedon, then, that allows for a genuine theology of history. Without it, a theology of history is in constant peril either of losing itself in some sheer becoming or of dissolving into an atemporal ideal....[60]

First, Christ and the Old Testament. The basic New Testament message is that two lines that are absolutely distinct in the Old Testament converge in Jesus: the coming of Yahweh at the end of time to judge the world and the coming of the Messiah to free Israel from its enemies. In interpreting the New Testament witness, patristic theologies ran two large risks. On the one hand, there was the Antiochene approach that led to Nestorius: the danger of so stressing the distinction of "natures" in Christ as to see in Him only a man in whom God dwells. On the other hand, there was the Alexandrian approach: the danger of so stressing the unity of "natures" in Christ as to minimize His authentic humanity and "the importance of His human genealogy, thanks to which, in Him, it is the race of Abraham that is really recaptured so as to attain its end."[61]

It is here [says Daniélou] that the Chalcedonian dogma strikes us as the response to the problem with which eschatology confronts Christology. Because He is at once perfect God and perfect man, Christ realizes in His person the prophecies concerning the eschatological coming of Yahweh just as much as the prophecies that relate to the coming of the Messiah. And it is the unity of the two natures in His person that lets us see how these two lines are reconciled. So it is in the mystery of the hypostatic union that eschatology finds its final explanation. Only if you resolve Christology can you grasp the genuine meaning of eschatology. Chalcedon's relation to eschatology is not, therefore, a secondary aspect of the dogma. It is the union of the two natures in the person of Christ that is properly the realization of eschatology. Eschatology is not merely knowledge of the *eschaton,* the last times, but knowledge of the *eschatos* who constitutes these last times.[62]

Second, Christ as the end, the *telos,* of salvation's whole plan. The point is, the eschaton is not only a chronological conclusion; it is an absolute term, the completion of God's plan. The paradox is this: although time continues to unfold and we are still awaiting an eschaton to come, the ultimate reality is already present in the person of the Incarnate Word.[63] This definitive, once-for-all, eternal character of the Incarnation, so vividly sounded in the Epistle to the Hebrews (9:12-26; 10:14), finds expression in a number of Church Fathers.[64]

But what does it mean to say that the Incarnation is the *telos,* that beyond it there is nothing? Chalcedon responds: the union of human and divine in Christ is *telos* because it is *teleiōsis,* not only end but perfection. By this union human nature realizes perfectly the end to which it is destined. The grace of the hypostatic union, proper to the person of the Incarnate Word, is the principle of divinization for all those united to Him; He is St. Paul's "first fruits" of divinized humanity. Here Gregory of Nyssa develops splendidly the patristic theme so constant in the fourth and fifth centuries:

> In the last times the Word, uniting Himself in lowliness to our nature, was made flesh for love of man, and uniting Himself to man, took in Himself our whole nature, in order that, by its mingling (*anakrasis*) with the divine, human nature might be divinized with Him (*synapotheōthē*) the whole dough being sanctified by this firstling.[65]

Here is the thesis so dear to the Cappadocians, so much a part of the Greek tradition: what was not assumed cannot be divinized. If human nature is to be raised to participation in divinity, the Word of God had to take that nature to Himself in its totality. And here lies the eschatological nature of the Incarnation: the integrally divine and the integrally human, once united in Christ, can never be severed. Christ is the *telos* of humanity, because He is humanity's *teleiōsis;* beyond His humanity there is no humanity. Even risen and transfigured,

His humanity (insists Chalcedon against Eutyches) is not absorbed in divinity. He—not His divinity but He—is the Eschatos, and He abides forever as the perfection of humanity.

Third, the return of Christ as consummation of God's plan. Christ is indeed already the *telos* of history, but these "last times" are still an era of expectation, until the perfection that is Christ finds its full echo in humanity as a whole. He is not only *telos,* end of the original creation; He is *archē,* beginning of the new creation.[66] In a sense, the *novissima* (the "last" things and the "newest") are already accomplished in Christ: Parousia, judgment, resurrection. He who "is to come" (Mt 11:3) has come; "now," says John, "is the judgment of this world" (Jn 12:31); He is "the resurrection and the life" (Jn 11:25). And yet, He remains the One who is to come; the Prince of this world retains much of His pre-Incarnation power; and the Easter victory of Christ has still to flame in the bodies of His elect.

But how conceive this period of expectation, this "time of the Church"? Is it to be seen as genuine development, a forward movement—of Church, of secular history, of man, of civilization, even of "the mystery of iniquity"—until a peak is reached that calls for Parousia and resurrection and judgment? Or is Christ's return unconditioned, an action simply of God's sovereign freedom, while man waits and the Church preaches penance?[67]

The New Testament witnesses in some measure to both of these approaches, and each orientation evokes a responsive chord in the Fathers. For some, the second coming of Christ, like His first, follows upon a maturing of man, a progressive "education," an evolution of history, even a high pitch of evil; recall, e.g., Hippolytus and Eusebius.[68] For others, e.g., Origen, there is a radical separation between temporal history and eschatological expectation.

I suggest that the two approaches are best seen as complementary rather than contradictory. And such, Daniélou claims, is precisely what comes out of Chalcedon's definition.[69] Not only does the hypostatic union project its light into the past and reconcile the two Old Testament lines mentioned above; it projects its light into the future and shows us how to interpret the history of humanity as it awaits the Parousia. On the one hand, this history is indeed the story of God's activity continuing in the Church through sacramental actions that prefigure and prepare for the ultimate eschatological events; and "this history has no law save God's sovereign wisdom and freedom."[70] On the other hand, this history is the prolongation of the Incarnation. And the Word inserted Himself into the continuity of a race wherein by His grace the entire universe yearns for freedom and adoption (cf. Rom 8:19-23), where in a genuine sense human persons make history (including their own) to be what it is, where salvation is effected in man but not without man. In the words of 2 Peter 3:12, we not only "wait for," we "hasten," the coming of God's day.

Such complementarity is alone compatible with Chalcedon. The history of man is not simply God's activity superimposed on a world in waiting, nor is it simply the effect of human progress evolving in God-less freedom or under natural determinism. It is a wedding of divine and human that leaves each intact and integral, that preserves in history and mystery God's sovereignty and man's freedom. "It is simultaneously true that Christ will return at the end of time and that the end of time will be constituted by the return of Christ."[71]

III

MY third stage is a rather brief critique. What have the Fathers to say to *us?* Are they simply a stage, an early stage, in the Christian's effort to grasp his destiny? Are they worth bothering about, or has the Christian understanding of eschaton grown to such an extent that early Christian theology is valueless? How alive is their resurrection theology?

These are questions so vast and profound that they can only be adequately answered in the context of all the theology that has followed after the Fathers down to our own day. I must content myself here with certain assertions which (1) will reveal my own convictions and (2) may stimulate intelligent discussion.

First, two eschatological affirmations of the Fathers are so constant, so unwavering, so dogmatic that they must be seen as basic to the patristic vision of Christianity. (1) When history ceases, when time is no more, when the world as we know it is somehow transformed, every human being will initiate a real life that involves in some authentic fashion the body he bore in this life. (2) This perfection of humanity redeemed finds its origin and its end, its cause and its model, its *raison d'être* and its endless joy, in Him who is the Eschatos: Jesus Christ, perfect God and perfect man. On these two issues, patristic eschatology seems so consonant with the inspired word which inspires it and with the traditional belief which continues it that I personally am compelled to conclude: here the Christian stands, and he can do no other.

Second, the patristic effort to get beneath the surface of the eschaton, to fathom Christ's coming and man's rising, is dissatisfying on the whole. It could hardly be otherwise. (1) The mysteries of which they speak are so profound, so far removed from earth-bound experience, that no one, from St. Paul through the medieval mystics to Karl Rahner, can do more than stammer in abstractions or paint vivid imaginings. Who (or what) is God? What does it mean to see God as He is, to live God's life, to love as He loves? And how can time-bound man explain eternity? (2) The philosophies that permeate patristic speculation—Stoicism, Neoplatonism, Aristotelianism, and versions or perversions thereof—are inadequate to the task in hand.

Not that any given philosophy will ever be adequate; but postpatristic philosophers from Aquinas to Heidegger have so immeasurably expanded our grasp on God and man that any simplistic "return to the Fathers" for systematic or speculative insight runs the risk of antiquarianism. I am thinking, for example, of Whitehead, and how exciting, how enriched, our eschatologies might become if we incorporated into our search his width of human experience:

> Nothing can be omitted, experience drunk and experience sober, experience sleeping and experience waking, experience drowsy and experience wide-awake, experience self-conscious and experience self-forgetful, experience intellectual and experience physical, experience religious and experience sceptical, experience anxious expereince care-free, experience anticipatory and experience retrospective, experience happy and experience grieving, experience dominated by emotion and experience under self-restraint, experience in the light and experience in the dark, experience normal and experience abnormal.[72]

And despite my ignorance I dare to suggest that process thinkers have much to say to Christian eschatologists, if our traditional metaphysical conception of God as *Ipsum Esse Subsistens* is to prove compatible with a God who really cares.[73]

Third, I submit that within patristic thought there are insights worth recapturing today, even though (or especially because) we are in a position to carry them further than any Father could have suspected. I have mentioned only three: (1) death is really punishment transmuted into love; (2) the most significant facet of man's resemblance to God: God's glory is man alive; (3) only a Christology which does justice to the integrally human and the integrally divine in the risen Jesus can do justice to the eschaton, can give Christian meaning to our Christian hope. There is more, much more, within the wealth of those early centuries. I regret particularly that I have not taken advantage of the literature in languages other than Latin and Greek: I mean the Coptic and Ethiopic, the Georgian and Armenian, perhaps especially the Syriac.[74] Here, I surmise, is supplementary material that will bring to our Western mentalities the contemplative and mystical perspectives we so often miss and for which a new generation is beginning to yearn. But one patristic scholar can do only so much (or so little) on the eschaton, and the moment comes when he must write his own eschata.

NOTES

[1] Here I should confess my deep indebtedness to J. N. D. Kelly's *Early Christian Doctrines* (2nd ed.; London: Black, 1960) pp. 459-89. My first section is little more than a rapid summary of his tight summation, with occasional personal insertions from my own reading of the evidence.

2 *Ibid.*, p. 462.
3 *Ibid.*, p. 464.
4 *Ibid.*, p. 466.
5 *Ibid.*, p. 471.
6 *Ibid.*, p. 472.
7 *Ibid.*, p. 473.
8 *Ibid.*, p. 475.
9 *Ibid.*
10 Augustine, *Serm.* 264, 6.
11 Kelly, *op. cit.*, p. 480.
12 *Ibid.*, p. 481.
13 *Ibid.*
14 Augustine, *Enchiridion* 112 f.
15 Kelly, *op. cit.*, p. 484.
16 Augustine, *In Ioan.* 1, 16.
17 Kelly, *op. cit.*, p. 488.
18 Methodius, *De resurrectione* 1, 43, 2—1, 44, 4. (*GCS* 27, 289-94);
translation mine. Note a different approach in *2 Clem ad Cor.* 8 (*LCL,
The Apostolic Fathers* 1 [Cambridge, Mass., 1945] 140) and Origen,
Hom. in Jer. 18 (*PG* 13, 464): As long as we are in this life, the
vessel can be repaired; once death comes, once the vessel has been
"put into the fiery oven"*(Clem.)*, once it has been fired either by God's
flame or the Evil One's darts (Origen), there is no possibility of
mending, of re-formation.
19 Methodius, *Symposium* 9, 2 (*GCS* 27, 116; *Sources chrétiennes*
95, 270); tr. H. Musurillo, *ACW* 27 (Westminster, Md., 1958) 134-35.
20 For the influence of Theophilus on Methodius, cf. N. Bonwetsch,
Die Theologie des Methodius von Olympus (Göttingen, 1903) pp. 163 f.
According to J. A. Fischer, *Studien zum Todesgedanken in der alten
Kirche: Die Beurteilung des natürlichen Todes in der kirchlichen
Literatur der ersten drei Jahrhunderte* 1 (Munich, 1954) 116, Methodius follows Theophilus "am spürbarsten."
21 Theophilus of Antioch, *Ad Autolycum* 2, 26 (*Sources chrétiennes*
20, 162-64).
22 So careful a scholar as Karl Müller spoke of Theophilus as an
apologist "whom Irenaeus did not know" (*Kirchengeschichte* 1 [2nd ed.,
1924] 219). Harnack was very dubious about any possible use of the
Ad Autolycum by Irenaeus, because of the short interval of time. On
the other hand, Friedrich Loofs, *Theophilus von Antiochien adversus
Marcionem und die anderen theologischen Quellen bei Irenaeus* (*TU*
46/2; Leipzig, 1930), has for special object to show that Irenaeus
incorporated, more or less verbally, in his *Adversus haereses*, without
acknowledgment, the lost work of Theophilus against Marcion, and to
reconstruct that work (cf. esp. pp. 45-46, 62, 70 ff., 79, 407 ff.). "Most
student," says Robert M. Grant, "have rejected his [Loofs's] arguments without explaining the striking resemblances between the two
authors" ("Theophilus of Antioch to Autolycus," *Harvard Theological
Review* 40 [1947] 227). "We may conclude that Irenaeus might well
have known the first two books Ad Autolycum, but that they are not
likely to have formed the core of his own work" (*ibid.*, p. 228). 8, 9-
33 (exegesis of Gn) "contain the passages of Theophilus most frequently cited by later writers, and they reveal him as the forerunner of
the later Antiochene school of scriptural interpretation. In them . . .
there is a strong note of literalism and a clear reliance on Jewish
exegesis" (*ibid.*, p. 235). The most detailed critique of Loofs stems
from F. R. Montgomery Hitchcock, "Loofs' Theory of Theophilus of

Antioch as a Source of Irenaeus," *Journal of Theological Studies* 38
(1937) 130-39, 255-66. Hitchcock argues, with Müller, that Irenaeus
did not know Theophilus. Strangely, Hitchcock does not take up the
related ideas in *Ad Autolycum* 2, 26 and *Adversus haereses* 3, 23, 6,
even where (p. 264) he brings in the former passage.

23 Irenaeus, *Adversus haereses* 3, 23, 6 (*PG* 7, 964).

24 Gregory of Nazianzus, *Orat.* 38, 12 (*PG* 36, 324).

25 Gregory of Nyssa, *Oratio catechetica magna* 8 (*PG* 45, 33).

26 Gregory of Nyssa, *In Pulcheriam* (*Gregorii Nysseni opera* [Jaeger] 9, 472).

27 John Chrysostom, *Hom. 18 in Gen.* 3 (*PG* 53, 151-52).

28 Cyril of Alexandria, *Glaph. in Gen.* 1 (*PG* 69, 24).

29 Procopius of Gaza, *Comm. in Gen.* 3:22 (*PG* 87a, 224-25).

30 Cyril of Alexandria, *De dogmatum solutione* 6 (Pusey, *In Ioan.* 3, 560).

31 Cf. Methodius, *De resurrectione* 2, 6, 4-6 (*GCS* 27, 340).

32 Augustine, *Conf.* 10, 36; tr. Sheed, p. 249.

33 Cf., e.g., my *The Image of God in Man according to Cyril of
Alexandria* (Washington, D.C., 1957), with the select bibliography on
pp. xiii-xv; J. E. Sullivan, *The Image of God: The Doctrine of St.
Augustine and Its Influence* (Dubuque, 1963); the patristic treatments in *Dictionnaire de spiritualité* 6 (1967) 812-22 (Greek Fathers,
by J. Kirchmeyer), 7/2 (1971) 1406-25 (Latin Fathers, by A. Solignac), both with fine bibliographies.

34 Cf. J. Gross, *La divinisation du chrétien d'après les Pères grecs*
(Paris, 1938) pp. 133-43; for Theophilus cf. *Ad Autolycum* 2, 27
(*Sources chrétiennes* 20, 164-66).

35 M. Aubineau, "Incorruptibilité et divinisation selon saint Irénée,"
Recherches de science religieuse 44 (1956) 25-52.

36 *Ibid.*, p. 52. Whether Irenaeus regarded the human soul as naturally immortal is debated. Some scholars conclude that, for Irenaeus,
the soul's physical subsistence for eternity depends on its conduct in
time; so J. Quasten, *Patrology* 1 (Westminster, Md., 1950) 310; J.
Lawson, *The Biblical Theology of Saint Irenaeus* (London, 1948) p.
208. Others prefer to distinguish. In one sense the soul is naturally
immortal: God has endowed it with immortality. In another sense it
is not immortal by nature: it does not have of itself the power to continue in existence. The elect will have immortality not only of being
but of blessedness as well; the damned will have the former alone.
So F. Vernet, "Irénée, Saint," *Dictionnaire de théologie catholique* 7,
2498-99.

37 Irenaeus, *Adversus haereses* 4, 20, 7 (*PG* 7, 1037).

37a Cf. A. Mayer, *Das Gottesbild im Menschen nach Clemens von
Alexandrien* (Rome, 1942) pp. 11-12, 88-89. Cf. *ibid.*, p. 89, n. 47:
"According to Clement, all men belong to the perishable realities *(ta
thnēta)* in so far as in virtue of their nature they are merely 'to the
image' of God; imperishability *(aphtharsia, athanasia)* is a free gift
of God's grace *(charis)*, and it is allotted to those who fashion themselves in God's likeness, as far as this is possible for created nature."
Gross is of the opinion that immortality plays a secondary role in
Clement—"not astonishing in a disciple of Plato who recognizes in
the soul a natural incorruptibility and sees in the gnosis which is vision
the last end of man" (*op. cit.*, p. 174).

38 Cf. L. Bouyer, *L'Incarnation et l'Eglise-Corps du Christ dans la
théologie de saint Athanase* (Paris, 1943) pp. 36-45.

39 Cf. Athanasius, *De incarnatione Verbi* 4 (*PG* 25, 104; Thomson

ed. 142-44); *Contra gentes* (*PG* 25, 5-8; Thomson ed. 4-8). This is the life which the angels live, blessed life, a life of familiarity with God, here and now.

40 Bouyer, *op. cit.*, p. 43.

41 Cf. Gregory of Nyssa, *Oratio catechetica magna* 5 (*PG* 45, 21-24).

41a Cf. Gregory of Nyssa, *Hom. 12 in Canticum canticorum* (*PG* 44, 1020-24; Jaeger ed. 6, 346-54).

42 Cf. Gregory of Nyssa, *Adversus Apollinarem* 55 (*PG* 45, 1257; Jaeger ed. 3/1, 224-26).

43 J. Daniélou, *Platonisme et théologie mystique: Essai sur la doctrine spirituelle de saint Grégoire de Nysse* (Paris, 1944) pp. 55-56.

44 Cf. Burghardt, *op. cit.*, pp. 84-104 and "Jewish-Christian Dialogue: Early Church versus Contemporary Christianity," in *The Dynamic in Christian Thought*, vol. 1, ed. Joseph Papin (Villanova, 1970). pp. 186-207.

45 Cyril of Alexandria, *In Ioannem* 9, 1 (Pusey 2, 484).

46 *Ibid.*, 1, 9 (Pusey 1, 138-39).

47 Cf. *ibid.* 6, 1 (Pusey 2, 220-21); also *Homiliae paschales* 27, 4 (*PG* 77, 940-41).

48 Incarnation: cf. *Homiliae paschales* 17, 4 (*PG* 77, 785-88); *In Ioannem* 10, 2 (Pusey 2, 618). Resurrection: cf. *In Ioannem* 6, 1 (Pusey 2, 233, 220). Eucharist: cf. *In Ioannem* 3, 6 (Pusey 1, 479); also the long passage *ibid.* 4, 2 (Pusey 1, 529-32); *Adversus Nestorii blasphemias* 4, 5 (*ACO* 1, 1, 6, 87; *PG* 76, 197). For Cyril's conception of the vivifying power of the Eucharist, see H. du Manoir, *Dogme et spiritualité chez saint Cyrille d'Alexandrie* (Paris, 1944); E. Weigl, *Die Heilslehre des hl. Cyrill von Alexandrien* (Mainz, 1905) pp. 203-20.

49 Cf. *De dogmatum solutione* 3 (Pusey, *In Ioan.* 3, 555-57); also the other references in Burghardt, *op. cit.*, p. 93, n. 39.

50 Cf. *In ep. 1 ad Cor.* 7 (Pusey, *In Ioan.* 3, 309).

50a Cf. *ibid.* (Pusey, *In Ioan.* 3, 316-17).

51 Cf. *De dogmatum solutione* 7 (Pusey, *In Ioan.* 3, 563).

52 *In Ioannem* 9, 1 (Pusey 2, 484).

53 Cf. *In ep. 1 ad Cor.* 7 (Pusey, *In Ioan.* 3, 310-12); *In ep. 2 ad* frag. (*PG* 72, 471-72).

54 Cf. *In ep. 1ad Cor.* 3 (Pusey, *In Ioan.* 3, 266); also *In ep. 2 ad Cor.* 3, 1 (Pusey, *In Ioan.* 3, 347). A restricted but useful study of Cyril's conception of incorruptibility is G. Langevin, "Le thème de l'incorruptibilité dans le commentaire de saint Cyrille d'Alexandrie sur l'Evangile selon saint Jean," *Sciences ecclésiastiques* 8 (1956) 295-316.

55 *De sancta et consubstantiali trinitate* dial. 3 (*PG* 75, 853); cf. the same idea in *De recta fide, ad augustas* 5 (*ACO* 1, 1, 5, 28; *PG* 76, 1341): Christ has become "the head, that is, the principle, of those who are reformed through Him to Him unto incorruptibility by sanctification in the Spirit."

56 Cf. Athanasius, *De incarnatione Verbi* 5 (*PG* 25, 104; Thomson ed. 145).

57 Cf. J.-L. Leuba, *L'Institution et l'événement: Les deux modes de l'oeuvre de Dieu selon le Nouveau Testament* (Neuchâtel, 1960) p. 49.

58 Cf. J. Daniélou, "Christologie et eschatologie," in A. Grillmeier and H. Bacht, *Das Konzil von Chalkedon: Geschichte und Gegenwart* 3 (Würzburg, 1954) 269-70.

59 *Ibid.*, p. 270.

60 *Ibid.*

61 *Ibid.*, p. 273.

62 *Ibid.*, pp. 273-74.

[63] *Ibid.*, p. 275.

[64] Cf. *ibid.*, pp. 276-78.

[65] Gregory of Nyssa, *Adversus Apollinarem* 15 (*PG* 45, 1152; Jaeger ed. 3/1, 151).

[66] Cf. Daniélou, *art. cit.*, p. 280.

[67] Cf. *ibid.*, p. 281 .

[68] Cf. *ibid.*, pp. 282-83.

[69] *Ibid.*, p. 284.

[70] *Ibid.*, p. 285.

[71] *Ibid.*

[72] A. N. Whitehead, *Adventures of Ideas* (New York, 1967) p. 226.

[73] Cf. N. Pittenger, "Trinity and Process: Some Comments in Reply," *Theological Studies* 32 (1971) 290-96, esp. 294-96.

[74] Cf. *Die Religion in Geschichte und Gegenwart* (3rd ed.): 1, 142-44 (Ethopic); 1, 611-12 (Armenian); 2, 1399-1400 (Georgian); 4, 8-11 (Coptic); 6, 581-83 (Syriac).

Biographical Notes

CONTRIBUTORS

*†Baltazar, Eulalio R.

*†Burghardt, Walter J.

Crowe, Frederick E., Prof., Regis College, Willowdale, (Toronto); (Federated member of the Toronto School of Theology); Pres., 1969 ; Editor, *Spirit as Inquiry: Studies in Honor of Bernard Lonergan, S.J.*, Lonergan's shorter writings, *Collection*.

*†Dulles, Avery

Gannon, Edward, Prof., St. Joseph's College, 1947-1955 Wheeling College, 1955-1962; St. Joseph's College, 1962-1964; University of Scranton, 1964-

*†Papin, Joseph

*†Stendahl, Krister

EDITOR

Joseph Papin†

ASSOCIATE EDITORS

James J. Cleary†
Francis A. Eigo†
Donald R. Schultz††
    Instr., 1969-1973, Asst. Professor, 1973- , Villanova University

*Biographical information taken from the *Directory of American Scholars*, 1969.
†See Volume I.
††Biographical information taken from the Villanova University Bulletin.

Index of Names

Large Roman numerals refer to volumes; small, to pages.

Daly, Michael
  IV, 20
Daniel
  IV, 158
Daniel, Iulii M.
  II, 90
Dániel, Joseph
  V, 51
Daniélou, Jean
  I, 11, 62, 80, 88, 204, 206; II, v,
  21; IV, v, 20, 164, 167; V, v, 1,
  218, 221, 223, 228, 229
Dansette, Andrien
  IV, 166
Dante, Alighieri
  I, 122; III, 281; IV, 33; V, 40
D'Arcy, M. C .
  I, 11; V, v
Darda
  III, 222
Daube, D.
  IV, 166
David
  I, 118, 123, 160; III, 221; V, 165
Davidoff, N.
  V, 51
Davies, W. D.
  II, 21
da Vinci, Leonardo
  III, 281
Davis, Charles
  I, 257, 262
Davis, Edward
  II, 6
Dawson, Christopher
  III, 246, 250, 258
de Albornoz, A. F. Carillo
  IV, 108
de Beavoir, Simone
  V, 196
de Boland, Louis
  V, 3
Deborah
  I, 181
de Foucault, Michel
  IV, 68
de Gaulle, Charles
  IV, 146, 164
Deissler, A.
  I, 184
de Jong, Johannes
  II, 147
Delhaye, P.
  IV, 109
Dellaseta
  V, 51
Delitzsch, Franz
  I, 179
de Lubac, Henri
  IV, v, 20, 165; V, v
Demianovich, Charles S.
  IV, 18
Democritus
  I, 111

Denier, I.
  V, 51
Denissoff, E.
  V, 49
Denny, Norman
  V, 172
Denzinger, H.
  I, 222; II, 143; III, 258; V, 100
de Régnon, Theodore
  IV, 165
Descartes, René
  III, 274, 276; IV, 48; V, 3
de Waele, Ferdinand J.
  IV, v, 20; V, v
de Waelhens, Alphonse
  V, 175
Dewart, Leslie
  I, 42, 49, 81, 182, 247; IV, 27
Dewey, John
  I, 16, 18, 19, 24, 25, 26, 27, 28,
  29, 31, 35, 38, 40, 41, 42
d'Herbigny, M.
  IV, 12, 17; V, 48, 51
Dickens, Charles
  III, 281
Didymus Arius
  I, 89, 111, 113; V, 207
Diekmann, Godfrey L.
  I, v; II, v, 23; III, 291; IV,
  v, 16; V, v, 232
Dieska, Jan
  V, 11, 12
Dillenberger, John
  IV, 109
Dilthey, Wilhelm
  IV, 48
Diognetus
  IV, 21
Dionysius
  I, 122; IV, 13; V, 15, 25
Dobbin Edmund J.
  V, 56
Dobzhansky, T.
  III, 261, 263, 288, 289
Dodd, C. H.
  IV, 166; V, 2
Doherty, Edward C.
  II, 6
Döllinger, Johann
  IV, 104
Domb, Yerachmeil
  III, 259
Dominic
  IV, 35
Doms, Herbert
  I, 218, 222
Donceel, Joseph
  I, 251, 252; III, 267, 288, 289;
  IV, 142
Donne, John
  III, 287
Dostoyevsky, Feodor M.
  I, 13; II, 87, 88; III, 274; V,
  2, 13

84, 88, 102
Papin, Joseph
I, v, 1, 9, 10, 12, 40, 253, 280;
II, v, 1, 5, 6; III, 292, 293; IV,
v vii, 1, 11, 16, 17, 18, 19, 20,
109, 165, 169, 170; V, v, 1, 48,
49, 50, 53, 56, 67, 102, 171, 172,
228, 231, 232, 233
Parkes, James
III, 195, 218
Parsons, Talcott
III, 258
Pascal, Blaise
II, ix, 8, 16; IV, 8, 65; V, 4, 131
Pasternak, Boris L.
II, 90
Patterson, Lloyd G.
IV, 141
Patulo, Jane
IV, 20
Paul
I, 46, 48, 63, 64, 65, 66, 68, 74,
79, 83, 91, 121, 133, 137, 199,
200, 202, 204, 216, 249, 250, 256,
275; II, 7, 8, 9, 10, 11, 12, 13,
14, 15, 16, 17, 18, 19, 20, 21, 28,
32, 73, 80, 119, 137, 141; III,
233, 240; IV, 56, 57, 60, 100,
102, 103, 110, 118, 142, 149, 150,
164; V, 14, 18, 25, 62, 64, 65,
66, 67, 68, 71, 72, 94, 96, 116,
125, 126, 127, 131, 134, 148, 161,
163, 168, 171, 190, 207, 222, 224
Paul V
III, 250
Paul VI
I, 8, 9, 238, 240, 274; II, 4, 33;
III, 163, 254, 260; IV, 16, 20,
41, 42, 138, 142, 154; V, 17
Pearlman, Moshe
III, 218
Pearson, Birger
I, 51
Pelagius
V, 159
Pelikan, Jaroslav
I, 10, 13, 81, 280; II, v; IV, 16;
V, 232
Penfield, W.
III, 290
Perry, Ralph
IV, 141
Peter
I, 83, 132, 133, 256, 263; III,
185, 258; IV, 2, 3, 13, 16, 100,
118, 149; V, 15, 63, 70, 127, 223
Peter ,Carl J.
II, v; IV, v, 16, 20; V, v
Peter the Great
II, 86
Petrouski, A.
V, 53
Petrus, Cantor
V, 100

Pettazzoni, R.
I, 171
Peyton, Patrick
IV, 41
Pfleger, Karl
V, 50
Pharaoh
III, 212
Phidias
IV, 33
Philip
IV, 126
Philip the Fair
IV, 121
Philo
I, 86, 88, 98, 119
Phineas
I, 206
Picardi, Rose
II, 6
Pickar, Charles H.
I, 9, 14
Pieper, Josef
IV, v, 20; V v,
Pierce, Charles Sanders
I, 18, 26
Pierling, Paul
V, 5
Pilate, Pontius
I, 87, 99, 190, 191, 206; II, 71,
130
Pire, Fr.
I, 6, 9
Pisarev, Dimitri I
V, 2
Pittinger, Norman
II, 121, 142; V, 229
Pius V
I, 213, 220
Pius IX
III, 246; IV, 104
Pius X
IV, 110; V, 17
Pius XI
IV, 110, 144, 154; V, 16
Pius XII
I, 55, 218, 222, 238, 253; II,
126; III, 158, 199, 200; V, 17
Plato
I, 24, 98, 99, 100, 105, 109, 110,
226, 227, 228; II 49; III, 196;
V, 3, 39, 87, 102, 153, 227
Pleger, Karl
IV, 18
Pliny
I, 94
Plummer A.
IV, 2
Plunkett, Joseph M.
II, 15
Pogodin, A. L.
V, 53
Pohle, Joseph
I, 253

THE DYNAMIC IN CHRISTIAN THOUGHT

Edited by Joseph Papin

Volume I

Contents

CHRISTIAN ACTION
AND
OPENNESS TO THE WORLD

Edited by Joseph Papin

Volumes II-III

Contents

THE PILGRIM PEOPLE:

A VISION WITH HOPE

Edited by Joseph Papin

Volume IV

Contents

THE CHURCH AND HUMAN SOCIETY AT

THE THRESHOLD OF THE THIRD MOLLENNIUM

Edited by Joseph Papin

Volume VI

Contents